EASILY ENTICED

PART II
VANTAGE POINT

Shanelle Sara'Nita

SHANELLE SARA'NITA ENTERPRISE LTD. CO

Easily Enticed Part II: Vantage Point

Shanelle Sara'Nita Enterprise LTD. Co
www.shanellesaranita.com
A Light of Rae Production LLC

This novel is a work of fiction. Any names, characters, places, and incidents are the products of the author's imagination or are used fictitiously. Any similarity to real persons, living or dead, is coincidental and not intended by the author.

ISBN 978-0-578-79480-8

Printed in the USA

Acknowledgments

It took six years for me actually to sit down and write this book. Let me be honest. I did a lot of procrastinating. I filled myself with a lot of fear as well. So many transitions happened in my life during those six years. I moved to Georgia, had a new baby, got married, moved around a little, and lost a few close family members; the list goes on. Life happened; I mean, really happened. In the midst of it all, I subconsciously forgot my mission. It was there, but the fire dimmed a little. I forgot about why I moved to Georgia in the first place, which was to start fresh and hit the ground running in my career. I had a plan that I failed to stick to. But I am still grateful, and I am still standing. I thank God. My light dimmed a little, but it never went out. I have dealt with experiences over the years that have built my character, resilience, and writing. I still have the support of my family and the friends that are still here. Although I believe I am often overlooked, it no longer bothers me. I believe God has kept me hidden, and when he is ready; all that should manifest will. With that, I say thank you to all of you who have supported me throughout the years. Thank you for the great feedback and constructive criticism. Thank you for the kind words of encouragement. Thank you for never giving up on me and this story. All of the emails and posts, asking, "What happened to Porter?" I pray that I've served you well and that you enjoy the last part of this precious piece, my baby, "Easily Enticed."

I would also like to send a special thank you to my mother, Wendy Williams. She moved all the way to Georgia to better her life and to help me with mine. She is a precious rare jewel. God chose a rare soul for this world to experience, and I am grateful to have gotten a front-row seat. I love you.

My daughters Chloe'Rae and Harley… You two are quite amazing. I could write all day, and I still would not have the words to express how much you mean to me. I love you always, always. Chloe'Rae, you have grown to be a bright, beautiful young woman filled with wisdom. Within the last nine years of your life, you have taught me so much, and I cherish your beautiful soul. Harley, you came in and turned our world around. You've brought me so much love and laughter. The peace and beauty you possess in your soul surpass what the world could ever offer you. You both have so much to offer. Sprinkle beauty into this world and light it up with that fire that burns so deep inside of you.

To my husband, Anthony, I thank you for seeing my vision and being a part of my creativity. You have pushed me to keep going, coming up with ideas for me, even when you have your own stuff going on. I appreciate your dedication to that part of me. I love you.

So many other people have been there during this journey. You know who you are. Thank you so much.

God has been so amazing in my life, and he continues to bless me every day. I am so grateful for the vision and the perseverance to see it through. It was all YOU!

This is the last novel, but just the beginning for Easily Enticed. Thank you, and enjoy!

Prologue

It's crazy how life unfolds. The past few years have been filled with ups and downs, but I didn't see this one coming once again. The night I gave birth to PJ was an emotional roller coaster. The birth of my son was a glorifying experience, and it instantly filled me with joy. I finally felt love. Not the "I love you, but-" kind of love that I was used to. It's the "I will lay down my life, climb many mountains, my heart is bursting because it's so full," kind of love. The moment he looked up at me, my heart shattered into little butterflies. I felt an overwhelming bliss. Those big, bold brown eyes... I couldn't stop staring at them.

At that same moment of me gazing into PJ's eyes, Carter's doctor scurried into the room to give me some great news. Carter finally opened his eyes! Life was looking up, like all of the tragedy and drama was now a cold dark memory that I no longer wanted to hold on to. Finally, we can all be together. We can all be happy.

Then... the top story of the night broke. There was a hit and run accident that caused severe life-threatening injuries to one of the drivers. Before making my way to see Carter, Trish, Eric, Torin, and I raced to the Intensive Care Unit where Porter was admitted. To our disbelief, he was the hit and run victim with life-threatening injuries. As we entered the room, Trish instantly broke down. She screamed and shouted as we watched him lying on the bed, damn near lifeless. I could barely move. I stood there, frozen in my thoughts and my movement, wondering how this could have happened. We just brought a baby into this world, and Carter is finally awake. This is supposed to be the most gratifying time in our lives.

Why can't we be happy? Why can't I have joy? All I feel is anger and devastation. I don't understand how this moment could have flipped into a disaster so quickly. As I stand there and grieve, I watch as Trish gives Porter a tender kiss on his forehead as the tears run down her face. Porter has gashes and bruises across his skin, and pieces of shattered glass pierced into his cheekbones. I stepped out of the wheelchair and walked up to the bed. I can feel the weakness in my legs as I collapse to the ground. My heart couldn't stand to be broken again. Eric helped me up off the floor. I quietly wept as I made my way to his bed.

"Porter… Porter… wake up… He's here… Porter, he's here! Our son is here! Porter, please… We need you! We need you here! Porter, wake up!" I cry frantically. I lost total control of my emotions.

The meter on his heart rate monitor begins to rise as I cried out to him. The doctor rushed in and asked us to step out of the room for a moment. The sound of my voice made him excited, and his heart rate shot up instantly.

"Okay, everyone, you all will have to exit out for a moment. We do not want his heart rate to get too high." Carter's doctor walked in to escort us out of the room.

"Hi, Dr. Hill," I said with despair.

"Hello, Ms. Bryant. Stay back for a moment. I would like to speak with you," he says as he softly grabs me by the arm.

Everyone, including Trish, went into the hallway. "It saddens me to say congratulations, and I am sorry in the same breath," he says as he pierces my eyes with his.

"It has already been established that Mr. Garrett will need surgery. He has had severe injuries to numerous parts of his body, especially his head. He was hit by a truck on the driver's side. The officer on site said that the truck was going at a very high speed by the look of it. Porter could possibly suffer brain damage." At that moment, I felt like I took my last breath. My stomach folded up in knots, and my heart felt tight enough to rip through my chest.

Dr. Hill's lips were still moving, but all I could hear was a silent noise beep through my eardrums. I tuned out everything as I glanced over at Porter lying on the bed, barely breathing and covered in blood and bruises. It felt like it was just he and I in the room. Everyone else disappeared, and I heard him say, "Bre, it's okay."

"We have scheduled his surgery to take place in the morning," said Dr. Hill.

"Does he have that long? That's hours from now," Torin inquires.

"At the moment, our goal is to stop the bleeding in his brain. That is what we are doing. I cannot guarantee, but we will do all we can to save Porter."

"That isn't good enough!" yelled Eric as he barged back into the room.

I had to interrupt, "Eric, Torin, it's okay. Dr. Hill, I trust you and your judgment. Please do all that you can to save him."

Before Dr. Hill exited the room, he walked up to me and hugged me.

"Remember what I told you," he whispers.

From everything that he told me, all I can remember is, "God doesn't make mistakes." Porter was only allowed to have one person to stay with him. Trish stayed as I went to check on Carter. When I walked in, all of his tubes were removed, and he was sitting there with his eyes open. Trying not to cry, I made my way to the bed.

"Carter," I whispered. "I'm so sorry…" I wept as I rubbed my fingers down the side of his face.

Not being able to speak loudly, he looked up at me and whispered, "What's going on?" I looked up at the doctor as he shook his head, signaling me not to explain yet.

I looked Carter in his eyes and kissed him on the lips. " I will explain in the morning; get some rest."

This day changed my life forever.

Chapter 1
A Change of Heart

The Day of Porters Accident

Porter

I can feel the vibration from my phone, signaling me to wake up. I don't know what I was thinking of setting my alarm clock for 5 am. But I figure I should prepare myself for the new baby. I'm freezing my ass off; I can't push myself to come from under the covers. Aubrey's got the whole house feeling like an igloo. Lately, Trish has been sleeping so close to her side of the bed. I haven't felt her body heat in weeks. I turn over to kiss her on the cheek right before I get out of bed. This situation we got going on is nothing short of untraditional. I never thought I would be sleeping in the guest room, with my girlfriend, in a house I once called home with my ex. Aubrey is due any day now, I really don't want to move back into the other house and leave her alone, but I know it would be selfish to leave Trish and Colby.

After I throw on my robe, I race to the thermometer and turn on the heat. Aubrey is going to kill me. She has hot flashes all day. Lights are on all through the house, and cookie crumbs lead to Colby's room. I'm going to hide all of the snacks from her tonight. When I open up her door,

I lean on the doorway and watch her sleep. She must be having a good dream because she's squeezing her teddy bear while her dimples pop out of her cheeks. I kiss her on the forehead and pull her blanket further up on her shoulders.

On my way to the bathroom, I hear Aubrey's television blasting. I don't know how she sleeps like that. Reruns of her favorite show, "Martin" is on. It's the episode when bruh man stole Martin's cd player, and Martin made everybody dress up like that scene from "New Jack City." I go in and turn it off. She has her blanket pushed off of the bed. She looks miserable with her legs stretched wide across the bed while she sleeps sitting up. I can't believe she has gained so much weight. I would NEVER tell her that shit, but she's huge! We have to hide ice cream from her because she will eat the whole tub by herself. Even though I think Trish still gives it to her when I'm not around. I toss the blanket back up on the bed, but she throws it back on the floor without even opening her eyes. I go into the bathroom and quietly shut the door. Bath toys are everywhere.

I can feel the stress leave my body as the hot water drops on the crown of my head and roll down my back. I just want everybody to be happy. For the first time in my life, I am ready for change. So much has happened in the last year, I don't have too many choices but to grow up. Before, it was Aubrey and me. Then me, Trish and Colby. Now it's me, Aubrey, Trish, Colby, and the new baby. One big unorthodox, somewhat dysfunctional, untraditional ass family. I'm under so much pressure, but I can't bitch up now.

After my shower, I get dressed and put on my jogging suit. From the look of the weather app on my phone, it's a good day to go for a run.

****

So many people are out running this morning. I guess they all got the weather memo. Before I start my run, I go to the top of Federal Hill and stretch a little bit. The lights from the buildings shine over the water. I feel like I see this view with a new set of eyes. I run down to Key Highway towards the condominiums that sit on the water.

Flashback

In 2006, Porter and Aubrey walk through the new townhouse developments on the water. Aubrey is amazed and excited as if she already owns the place, "Let's go to the top floor!" says Aubrey. Aubrey and Porter run to the top floor of the townhouse and step out on to the deck. They overlook a view of the Harbor all the way to the Chesapeake Bay Bridge. "Oh my God!" she says. "Look at this view!" Aubrey screams. "One day, we are going to own this place," Porter says as he indulges in the beauty of the scenery.

Damn, I guess I let all of my plans get into the way of our plans. This last hour of jogging around the pier has brought back a lot of memories. Our favorite restaurants, our drunk nights in Federal Hill. We would sit on the bench at the edge of the water and watch the sun come up while we recite the lyrics to Mary J and Method Man's "You're All I Need." We would forget we were in Baltimore City. It was like an escape from real life. All of that shit was stressful. I was so sick of being "the basketball superstar." Too much pressure, too much bullshit. I went after a dream that I never really wanted in the first place. Aubrey was my escape. She saw past my arrogance and all of the hype. She saw who I wanted to be. She was patient with me and tried to show me another side of myself. I took advantage of something good. Yeah, Trish and I are good, but if I would be honest with myself, Aubrey will always be the one.

The sun rises as I get closer to the pier. My favorite breakfast spot should be opening soon. I can smell the biscuits a block away from the restaurant.

"Hey, Porter! We haven't seen you in a while!" says Teddy. He is the manager of Sugar, Honey, Iced T Breakfast and Brunch. He is as sweet as they come, but I can respect that. He's not "down-low," and he doesn't throw no shit my way.

"Aye, Teddy! What's up, man?" I reply with a dap.

"Nothing much just trying to keep this place running, you know bills gotta get paid." He guides me towards a booth by the window. I always sit at the booth. I like to look out of the window at the water.

"I hear you!" I say, following his lead.

"Speaking of bills… You know they are selling the place," he whispers as I take my seat.

"Damn, for real?"

"Yup, I know you got your spot, but you might want to look into it." He drops the menu on the table.

"I'm going to do that." I love this spot, but I would love it even more if I owned it. I pull up the commercial real estate app on my phone and put in the address.

"Twenty thousand dollars in back taxes! That's it! This can't be real!" I say to myself.

"Teddy!" Teddy rushes over to the table as I wave him down.

"What's up?" he asked.

"Do you think you can get all of the owner's information to me before I leave?"

"Yeah, that's not a problem at all." He waves it off as if it's not a big deal.

"Cool, thanks, man." The waitress walks over, a young Hispanic woman. She's Jennifer Lopez, fine.

"Good morning! How are you today?" she says with a bright smile.

"I'm doing great, and yourself?" I reply.

"I'm great, thanks for asking!" You would think it's the middle of the day. Instead, it's six-thirty in the morning, and she is bright-eyed and bushy-tailed.

"What can I get for you?" she asked, as she takes her pin out of her apron.

"Can I have a French vanilla coffee with hazelnut and French vanilla crème and sugar? The butter pecan pancakes, scrambled eggs with cheese, four slices of turkey bacon, a small plate of honey biscuits, and a glass of orange juice," I smile, knowing that I've ordered a shit load of food.

"Sounds good. It will be out shortly." She prances off.

They fixed this place up nicely. I remember when it was the identical twin of IHOP. The food has always been better, though. It has a home-cooked meal feel. But the décor was plain and kind of run down. Now it feels like a breakfast spot in the middle of Paris. It has a homestyle yet warm, classy touch to it. Soft jazz music playing, chandelier's falling from the ceiling with warm dimmed lights reflecting off the gold-painted walls covered with paintings of pancakes, biscuits, and other breakfast favorites. I wouldn't change a thing.

Aubrey would die if she knew I was here. I will just get a large order of food to take back home to everybody. She has tasted everything on the menu at least three times. We used to cut school and come here before third period at least once a week. One time my car broke down, and my mother had to come to pick us up. She screamed at us all the way back to school, but she never told my dad, and she never told Aubrey's parents. She knew her mom couldn't stand me.

After I ate every bit of that delicious meal, I wait for the to-go order and Teddy to bring the owner's information. I see him walking from the back with my order and a torn piece of white paper in his hand.

"Here is the information you asked for, and here is your food. I added a few extra things in the bag."

"Thanks, Teddy, I appreciate it."

"I hear that they own the place outright, but they are really behind on taxes. I guess the renovations in the place messed up the money. I wish I could afford to buy it, but not on this salary."

"Well, when I get it, I will make you general manager and give you a raise," I say as I take the bags out of his hand.

"Damn, Porter for real?" He looks surprised.

"Yeah, man, why not? You run the hell out of this place. I've been coming here since I was in high school. You've been here for at least ten years. You deserve to have a raise and be top dog."

"Aw, man, thank you! Well, look, you jump on that as soon as possible then, because honey, I need an upgrade! And tell Aubrey I said hello!" he says as he stands back behind the desk.

"I will do that." Instead of walking all the way back to my car, I take an Uber to it. The food would be cold and nasty by the time I got to the car.

I look at my phone, and it's eight-thirty. It's a Saturday, so everybody is probably still asleep, except Colby. She wakes up early and steals her mother's phone to watch a bunch of videos online of kids playing with their toys. That's the dumbest shit ever. Just play with your toys! On my way home, I take the city instead of the highway. It's been a long time since I've come this way. I drive through my old neighborhood, Poplar Grove, and Winchester. As a kid, I knew I lived in the hood, but I didn't realize how rough it was until my folks moved us out. I pass the first house I could remember me and my parents living in. It's still holding up, but the houses around it are boarded up and falling in. One day I'm going to buy this block and fix it up. On the corner, near the liquor store my father used to go to, I see one of his old buddies sitting on a broken chair. He looks like he's about to fall out of it. I pull over.

"Aye, Mr. Chuck!" He looks up with a smile. He reeks of alcohol.

"Aye! Man, how are you doing?" I know he doesn't remember me.

"Do you remember me? I'm Sam's son, do you remember Sam?" He tries to think.

"Sam? Sam?… Oh! Sam! Sam and Darlene, right there on Poplar Grove and Winchester! Yeah, my man, Sam!" He gets excited as if he is reminiscing on the good old days.

"Yeah, that's him. You used to give me money to buy candy from the store all of the time. How are you doing, man? I haven't seen you in a while," I ask as he goes off into a daze.

"Man, I'm doing good, I'm doing good. After you were born, I went off to the war… when I got back, ya momma gave you to Sam. Shit, I knew I wasn't ready to be no daddy-" He starts rambling like an old drunk, but what is he saying? My heart dropped to my knees. Maybe he doesn't know who I am- maybe he's drunk and just talking. Naw… he doesn't know what he's saying.

"What? Naw Mr. Chuck, I'm," I reply, barely letting go of my breath.

"Porter, ain't it. Yeah, man, baby Porter. My granddaddy said, 'name that baby after me.' I can't believe she kept the name, being though I left and all." My heart stopped, and everything around me was spinning except Mr. Chuck and me.

I struggled to my car with weak knees. I get to the door and open it.

"Aye! You think I could borrow a couple of dollars?" he yelled.

I go into my pocket and pull out three hundred-dollar bills. I walk it back over to him without saying a word and hand it to him.

"Damn, thank you, man, 'preciate it." I get into my car and drive off as fast as I can.

****

Quietly, I open the door, sit the food on the kitchen counter, and run upstairs. I check myself in the mirror in the hallway. I don't want any questions asked about why I look so angry. I walk past Colby's room and can hear her on her tablet watching those stupid videos. It looks like Trish is still sleeping. I grab some clothes and shoes and go into the bathroom to take a shower. As the steam rises up in the bathroom, so does my anger. How could they not tell me this man was my father? All of these years, I've taken shit from a man who's not even my blood! He looked me dead in my eyes and told me that, "A man should not lie. Take responsibility for your shit." He looked down on me when I failed! And my mother sat there and let it happen. She let him treat me that way. How could she not tell me? She let me live a lie. My father is a drunk! A fucking drunk, and it's probably all because of them! Tears fall from my eyes as I fall back and trickle down to the bottom of the tub. I can't hold back my cries. There is a knock at the door, and a little voice speaks.

"Daddy?" Colby says in her most innocent voice.

I straighten up and wipe my face before I answer. "Yes."

"Are you okay?" she asks.

"Yeah, Colb, I'm okay."

"Okay…"

I stand up and turn off the shower. Three more knocks at the door.

Knock, knock, knock. "Daddy?" she says again.

"Yes, Colb."

"I love you." A warm feeling came over my body.

"I love you too, baby." I step out of the shower, dry off, and get dressed for the day.

I walk into Colby's room to give her a kiss. She is sitting on the floor, playing with her dollhouse, dressed in a sequence tutu.

"Where are you going?" she asks.

"I'm going to visit some people that I haven't seen in a long time."

"Can I go?" I pause for a second and think it through.

"Yeah, you can go, but you have to change your little tutu get up." She laughs.

"This is not a get-up, daddy. I'm a dancing star princess."

"Well, can you just be my Colby Bear Princess?"

"Yes, if you want me to." I go into the closet and pull something out for her to wear.

"What about this?" I say as I pull out an outfit.

"Are we going to a funeral?" she replies with speculation. I look at it again.

"No," I answer.

"Then, we should try this again." She is so damn witty and quick with words.

I pull out three more outfits, and she finally agrees. We sit on the bed, and I brush her EXTRA long thick hair into a ponytail and put a headband on it. If I knew getting her dressed would be all of this work, I would've awakened Trish for the job. Colby grabs a purse and her favorite doll. She runs downstairs to the door. I leave a note next to Trish to let her know that I have Colby with me. I would text her, but she will see the note before she looks at her phone. I have a better chance of not getting cursed out for no reason. I grab some food out of the bag on the counter. We get to the car, and Colby hops in the back seat and buckles up.

"Here, baby girl, I got you some food." Usually, I wouldn't let her eat in my car, but I guess I've got to get used to a little mess every once in a while.

"Thank you." She grabs the bag and opens it up.

"Where are we going, daddy?" I look through the rearview mirror, and her face is covered with honey, and her mouth is stuffed with biscuits.

"I want to introduce you to some people."

"Who are these people?"

"My parents- you're grandparents."

With surprise, she responds, "I have grandparents!"

"Yes, you do. I'm sorry that I didn't introduce you to them earlier."

"It's okay, you didn't introduce yourself earlier either," she says with a naïve forgiving tone while she still stuffs her face with biscuits, fruit, and eggs. I look through the rearview and smile gently at her, not believing that she just said that.

It takes us an hour in a half to get to my parent's house. They live in Chesapeake City, Maryland. After I graduated college, they sold their home in Woodlawn, Maryland, to a developer who wanted to build new houses on all of the extra lands they owned behind it. They packed up, moved to Chesapeake City, and opened a bed and breakfast that has become pretty popular. I haven't seen them in a few years. Two maybe... I speak to my mother a few times a month, but not my dad, or whoever he is. We only talk during the holidays. He never invites me out and has basically held a grudge against me since college. The only thing he ever cared about was me making it to the NBA. That didn't happen, and neither did our relationship. I guess now I know why.

Finally, we pull up to the big white cottage styled house that sits on the water. Honestly, it looks like it belonged to somebody's master many years ago. I won't say that out loud to my mom, though. My mother always dreamed of having a porch wrapped around the house with flower beds leading you up the pathway to the stairs. There's a rocking chair and a red and black seating area on the front porch. I knock on the door.

"Who is it!" I can hear her yell as she walked towards the door. She opens the door, and her face lights up with joy!

"Oh my!" She jumps up into my arms. "Porter! Oh, my goodness! Look at you!" She rubs her hands gently across my chest. This is a touch that I have missed.

"Hey, Ma… How are you doing?" All of my anger magically dwindles away. I feel like a little boy being picked up from daycare, anxiously waiting to see my mother.

"Oh, I am doing fine. Come in this house! Don't stand there like a house guest!" We walk in, and Colby follows behind me quietly with her hand in mines. She holds on tight. Her face is buried in her doll's hair. For the first time, she is shy.

Mommy leads us to the kitchen. "And who is this beauty?" Mommy walks up to Colby and lifts her face out of her doll's hair. She stares deeply into Colby's eyes. "My goodness, you have fallen from heaven." Mom smiles, and so does Colby.

"Porter?" she continues to gaze into Colby's eyes.

"Is this your way of telling me I have a grandbaby?" She looks up at me, and the sassy Darlene from Poplar Grove and Winchester shows up.

"I guess it is. I'm sorry it took so long." She ignores my comment and reaches out for Colby's hand.

"Baby, are you hungry?" She smiles gently with her eyes as she gazed into Colby's.

"No, ma'am. I ate already." Mom smiles as she leads her to the tea room.

"Well, you must love tea time! Every princess loves tea time. Let's have some tea and biscuits while we get to know each other!" she says.

"Oh, goodie! Yes, please! Can we?" Colby jumps up and down with joy.

"Of course, we can! Let's leave daddy here to think about his actions."

Mom looks at me and licks her tongue as they walk away.

"Bye, daddy! You will figure it out," she shouted. Mom laughs, and I wave back at her. I sit down on the stool, and my phone rings. "No ID?" I answer the phone, but all I hear is silence.

"Hello! Hello!" Nobody answers so I hang up.

I walk around this big house and admire how my mother's decorating skills have come along. There are pictures of them everywhere and a few of me from infant to adult. They spend most of their free time traveling around the world. I take my time to work up the nerve to confront her. I thought I would be upset and too angry to look her in the eyes. But for the first time in a very long time, I feel like I am home, at least until my father gets here.

I walk into my mother's lounge area, where they are on a small pink sofa, eating cookies and drinking tea. My mother grabbed some old church hats and pearls out of her closet for them to wear as costumes. I stand in the doorway as they laugh and carry on as if I'm not here. Finally, I get enough nerve to speak.

"Ma, can I talk to you for a minute?"

"Yeah, baby, come in." She moves over to make room for me.

"Colby, daddy, and grandma are going to go into the kitchen to talk. Stay right here and play with your doll. We will be back shortly."

"Okay, daddy," she answers with a smile. My mother follows me out of the room into the kitchen.

"What's going on baby, why do you look so drained all of a sudden?"

"Ma, I'm going to ask you a serious question, and please don't lie to me."

She takes a seat on the stool at the counter. Confusion is all over her face.

"Okay... Well, what is it?" she urges me to spit it out.

"Who's my father?" I ask with fear of the answer.

"What?" As if she didn't hear me the first time.

"Ma, who is my father?"

She lowers her head and looks away while she carefully searches for her next words. "Who told you?" she asks regrettably.

"Why does it matter? You didn't! How could you do this to me? My real father was a block away from me, and you never said a word." I find it hard to control my emotions. The words start running out like water.

"Porter, let me explain-" She tries to calm me down.

"Explain what? How he went off to serve his country, and you gave his baby to another man?"

"Porter, if you would calm down, I can explain!" The base in her voice urged me to take a seat and listen.

She takes her time as she paces the floor.

"Yes, Chuck gave you life, but Sam is your father. When I got pregnant with you, Chuck didn't want any parts of being a father. Everything he said to me up to the day I told him I was pregnant was a bold-faced lie! He said he was going to marry me, and we would have kids. He asked me to name his first born after his granddad if it was a boy. There was a life I dreamed of, but things happened a little differently. I got pregnant first. One day he came over to my house, and I told him we were going to have a baby. I thought he would be just as excited as I was. He wasn't; in fact, he was disappointed. He said that he had enrolled in the army and didn't have any plans on becoming a father right now. That day he left my house and never came back. I figured I would give him a few days to get his mind right, but when I went past his house, his mom said he shipped out and was placed in Hawaii for four years. I never told her I was pregnant. Months went by, and I heard nothing from him. Not even a letter. I remember how much I cried. I cried for days at a time. I was so depressed I couldn't eat. Sam lived a few blocks up from us. I had known him for a few years, but we never dated.

He saw me walking down the street one day after I had given birth to you. I had you in one arm and grocery bags in another. I was struggling. I never thought I would make it home. Sam walked up to me with that charming smile of his and insisted that he get me home. He offered to give me a ride, but with me being strong and stubborn, I wanted to walk. So, he walked. And every day after that for almost a year, he walked. Finally, I gave in. He would pick me up from work and drop you off at your grandma's house every day before he went to work. He never asked me for a dime, and he never came on to me. Our conversations would get so deep that I could look past that smile and see his soul. It was deeper than any ocean. He taught me things that I never knew."

I sit so still, I can barely blink as I listen to my mother tell me my tragedy, but her love story.

"The day after your first birthday, Sam came over with a gift for you, but I had no idea he had a gift for me too. He walked into the house, stood in the center of my living room, and confessed his love for you and me. He said he had spent the entire year with nothing or no one on his mind but us. We had never slept together or gone out on a date, but he said he knew I was the right one. He got down on one knee and asked me to marry him. Of course, I accepted.

Three years went by, and word on the street was that Chuck got thrown out of the army for disorderly conduct. One day, he saw you and me at the corner store. He rushed up to me as if we had just spoken yesterday. So much time had gone by. We had a new life, and I was in love with your father. I couldn't jeopardize that for a man who left my baby and me. Sam didn't know who your father was. I told him he left me, and that was that. I told him that he better not ever bring trouble to my family. He was a part of my past that had died. He could not be a part of your life. At the time, I thought I was doing the right thing for you. I still believe I did the right thing because he left you! He left us! And he never looked back, so why should we! I would see him giving you money for the store, and I wouldn't keep him from doing that as long as he kept our secret safe."

Tears fall from both of our eyes. I feel like I'm in an old soap opera. As if there hasn't been enough drama in my life, here is more. I'm sure God is laughing his ass off at me right now. I want to stay mad at her, but I can't. I can't! She is the reason I am here. I don't know who I would be if the neighborhood drunk raised me.

"Ma, I would be lying to you if I said I wasn't upset. For my entire life, I thought a man was my father, who's not."

"I am your father. I raised you, didn't I? I put food in your belly and clothes on your back. I got you out of that raggedy-ass neighborhood, didn't I?" I hear my father's voice moving closer towards the kitchen. Finally, he appears and drops his fishing bucket and case next to the door entrance.

My father reminded me of James Earl Jones when he played Leroy from the stage play Fences. He was hard and didn't take no shit. Sometimes he was too hard, but he did make sure I had what I needed. Like I said… Years went by, and we grew further apart.

"C'mon, boy, let me talk to you." My mother stands there, staring at me with a pitiful expression. I glance over at her and nod my head in forgiveness. I can't stay mad at her forever. She was trying to protect me. And she did what she felt was right. Now my father is a different fish to fry. We have other issues. I follow him out to the shore. He stands next to me, boldly, with no expression on his face. There is a silence between us. All you can hear is the waves from the water and the seagulls.

"How have you been, son?"

"I've been good, Pop. Working hard, raising a family."

"How is Aubrey?"

"Aubrey is good. She is due any day now."

"And who is the pretty little girl in your mother's sitting room?"

"That's your granddaughter Colby." His face lit up like a Christmas tree, but he still stayed silent.

"I guess we've got a lot of catching up to do, huh, son?"

"Yes, we do," I followed.

"Let's start with the elephant in the room," he says. He turns and looks me square in the eye, man to man.

"I am not your blood, you were not produced through me, but I am your father. I raised you, loved you, taught you how to walk, gave you your first baseball glove, and guided you through life. I may not have been perfect, but I did everything my father didn't do for me. Was it wrong for us to keep this secret for so many years? Yes, I agree that it was, but it would have never changed anything."

"It changes things for me. I spent my whole life trying to please you and do what you wanted me to do. The moment I decided for myself, you turned your back on me. Maybe, my real father would have understood. Perhaps he would have taken me under his wing and kept guiding me, maybe-"

"Your real father left you! I wonder where you would've been if I would have turned my back on you too! You are the same ungrateful little brat that you have always been. I busted my ass to take care of you! Do you know I couldn't give your mother babies? I couldn't have kids of my own. So, I raised the hell out of you! And look at you standing in my face whining. I didn't turn my back on you. You turned your back on you. You gave up on your dreams because they were too hard. Nobody could go to the gym and make those jump shots for you. You had to do it yourself. You had to wake up early enough to be great. To be better! You gave up on your dreams and took your trust fund money to open a business. I'm proud of what you are doing. I'm proud of what you did. But my question to you is, if you had to work for every dime, would you have the restaurant?"

I can't form a word to speak… He's right. For years I have been holding this grudge against him. I was feeling like I failed him as a son. I've walked around with a chip on my shoulder filled with arrogance because I wanted to prove to him that I am better than the man he wanted me to be.

"Daddy!" Colby comes running out of the house and jumps into my arms. Mom is behind her. "Daddy, can I stay with grandma? Please, daddy!" she yells with big puppy eyes and a pouted lip.

"Colb, let me run it by your mom. But first I would like you to meet someone. Colby, this is your grandpa Sam."

"Like Sam, I Am?" Dad burst out laughing as his eyes light up like a Christmas tree again, and tears well up in his eyes. I've never seen him cry before.

"Yes, Like Sam, I Am. It is a pleasure to meet you, Colby," he says as he reaches out for a hug, but instead, she jumps right into his arms and gives him a big hug.

"It is a pleasure to meet you too, Grandpa Sam I Am." She squeezes him tight around his neck, and he squeezes back.

"Wow, what a day this is!" my mom says.

A thousand pounds of weight has been lifted off of my shoulders. I thought it would take me more time to get over all that has happened today, but I guess it had to happen for us to finally mend. My mom and I watch as dad carries Colby closer to the water while she tells him everything she knows about the ocean.

"Mom, I'm going to call Trish?"

"Who is Trish?"

"Colby's mother."

"You've kept me completely out of this little loop you've created."

"Never again, Ma, and I'm sorry for everything. I shouldn't have stayed away this long."

I walk away to call Trish, but before I call her, my phone rings. It's that unknown caller again. I answer the phone.

"Hello? HELLO? Look, stop playin' on my goddamn phone!" I hang up and call Trish.

"Hello," she sounds like she's out.

"Hey babe, what's going on?"

"Nothing much. Are ya'll having a good time?"

"Yeah, we are. It's been a long day."

"It's only 1 pm."

"Yeah, but so much has happened. I will tell you about it later."

"Where is Colby?"

"She is at the water-"

"The water?!" she yells.

"Not in the water Trish, at the water with my dad."

"Oh, okay, well, tell her I love her."

"Will do. Look, I'm calling because Colby would like to stay with my parents. Not overnight, just until tonight. I will come back to get her. It seems that they are having a good time with their long-lost granddaughter."

"If you are comfortable with it, I trust your judgment."

"Okay, cool, it's done then. Thanks. I love you…"

I know she is still on the phone, but she hasn't said it back. "Hello?"

"Oh, yeah… Ditto…"

"Ditto?"

"Hey, I'm in the middle of something. I will see you when you get back to the house."

She quickly hangs up the phone without responding. I don't know what's going on with her. But I'm going to find out today.

"Ma, I'm about to get out of here. I will be back to get Colby later on tonight."

"Okay, son, let me get you something to eat before you go. You still like salmon and rice?"

"Yes, I do." She bops towards the house like she can't wait to get lunch cooking. I walk towards dad and Colby as they walk back towards me.

"Pop, I'm happy we had this conversation. I'm sorry, man. I held a grudge against you for years. I've been working on myself, and I want this relationship to be a part of my growth. You know?"

"It's okay, son. I'm happy we had this conversation too." He stares into my eyes with a peaceful smile.

"So daddy, can I stay?" Colby interrupts the moment.

"Only if you give me a bunch of hugs and kisses..." She jumps in my arms, squeezes my face really tight, and fills me with kisses.

"Alright, alright! You can stay!" She jumps out of my arms and back into dad's arms.

"Yaaaayyyyy," she yells. He squeezed her head close to his face, and they walk back to the water.

****

If I knew traffic would be this bad on the Chesapeake Bay Bridge, I would've chilled with my family. Parris, the restaurant manager, has been texting me about inventory all morning. I pick up the phone to call and check on Aubrey.

"Hello, yeah," she answers like she's focused and in a rush.

"Bre, what are you doing?" I ask.

"I'm watching that new show by Lena Waithe. I've been waiting for Trish to get back with ice cream since forever."

"Ice cream, Bre, your doctor said you've got to stop eating all of that dairy. It's making you gassy."

"First of all, Mr. Garrett, what does my gas have to do with you?" She's too damn smart.

"Everything, when I have to be around your funky ass!" we both laugh.

"Well, when the baby comes, there is going to be a whole lot more funky asses around here," she responds. I smile from ear to ear.

"I can't wait, Bre."

"Yeah, me either." The phone gets silent.

I wonder if she is thinking what I am thinking. I want to be able to give my kids what they deserve. That includes a strong foundation at home with a mother and a father in the household. How am I going to do that?

"Okay, well, you are ruining my show. So, I will talk to you when you get here."

"Alright, cool, and don't eat that whole tub of ice cream."

"Bye, Porter!" she hangs up in my ear.

Finally! I made it to the end of the bridge.

I finally get to La'Rose, and it looks like everything is running smoothly. During the day, we get a lot of professionals that come in for lunch. One, in particular, is my lawyer, who I see sitting at a booth with a colleague. I'm surprised to make it back to my office without anyone stopping me. My manager is usually on my back about something. She must be tied up in the kitchen.

When I get to my office, it looks like the cleaning lady has been in here because my desk is completely cleaned of all of the papers and receipts that were covering it—everything except a yellow envelope. I start to open it and then...

"Porter, where have you been all day? We have to go over this inventory and the private event for the mayor next week. We haven't discussed the decrease in numbers from last week or the work order that has been put in a thousand times for the freezer. All of the food is going to spoil if we don't do something about it..."

She is going to go on forever. Parris is the best manager that has worked for me, but she is always in panic mode.

"Parris, relax. Get the company on the phone for the freezer. Let them know if no one is here by the end of the business day; I will call my lawyer and have our contract voided. I've already looked at the decrease in the numbers. However, we can't cry over spilled milk. Strategize on what we can do to move forward, and let's do that." She watches my every move as she takes in everything that I say. "Let's work on the mayor's event tomorrow morning. And I keep telling you that inventory is your thing unless something is missing or rotten, I'm good."

She looks disappointed. "Porter, this isn't like you. Usually, you are on top of everything."

"Well, I'm doing things differently now. I can't do my job and yours. That's why I hired you."

There is a knock at the door.

"Who is it?"

"It's Lily. Your attorney Ms. Karen Welch is here to see you," Lily responds in a delicate tone.

"Come on in," I say.

Lily walks in with Ms. Welch following.

"Thank you, Lily."

Karen walks in dressed in a two-piece maroon suit. She has got to be the sexiest woman I've ever met in their fifties.

"Parris, we will finish this conversation later. Get to work. Thank you."

Parris grabs all of her papers off of my desk and walks out with an attitude as always.

"Hey Karen, how is everything going?"

"Everything is great, Porter. I just thought I would stop by to say hey. And to see how Aubrey and the babies were doing."

"Everything is great. She is due any day now, but listen, now that you are here, I would like to discuss some changes with you. I would like to make some changes to my will and talk about a few new investments. Do you have time?"

She pulls out her iPad and sits her purse on my desk.

"Yes, I do. In the meantime, let's go over everything, and I will have all of the official paperwork faxed over for you to sign."

"Okay first thing first. I am buying Suga, Honey, Iced Tea. They are back on their taxes, and I want to make the transaction today. It's twenty stacks, but I want to include an extra twenty for the owners to pocket. This place is going to belong to Aubrey. She loves that place, and I think if anybody should own it, it should be us."

"Are you sure about that? You guys aren't married. You're not even together."

"No, but she is the mother of my child and one of my best friends. She helped me to build this place from the ground up. This whole place has her touch on it. I think she deserves a place of her own." She nods her head in agreement.

"Okay, then I am on it. Anything else?"

"Yes, if anything happens to me, I want Trish and Aubrey to become co-owners of this place. Those two together would be a force to be reckoned with. When the kids turn eighteen, I want them to become co-owners as well. As a matter of fact, let's do this today. As of today, I want all of them to have shares of the lounge and any other business I open."

"Porter, I love where you are going with this, but I don't think it's the best idea."

"Why, they are all I got. I have to set them up."

"Well, for starters, you don't know who your children will be in a few years and what if Trish or Aubrey turn on you at some point."

"What? That doesn't matter, I have forsaken them enough for all of us, and they all forgave me."

Karen doesn't say anything else. She finishes typing on her iPad.

"Lastly, I would like to invest in a few more stocks and property. I think it's time for me to build equity. I want to take my family and me to the next level. Please look into what will be the best tech companies to purchase. That industry is about to explode."

"I will get your accountant on the phone right away, and we will get this squared away."

"Thank you."

Karen gets up and grabs her purse.

"Porter, I think that what you are doing is proof that people can change. You are an honorable man. Forgive me for going against your plans. That was just my fear from my own experiences," Karen adds as she prepares to leave.

"Thank you, Karen. Damn... I appreciate that. And it's cool. I understand."

"I'm going to get on this as soon as I get back to the office," she says.

"Perfect, have a good one."

"You too," she walks out. I sit back in my chair with another weight being lifted off of my shoulders. It feels good to do something for somebody else. It took a lot of time for me to get here. I feel like I see the world a lot differently."

I call Lily on the phone at the front desk.

"Hey, Lily, could you send a bouquet of lilies to Trish and orchards to Aubrey? Send them to Aubrey's house. Thanks."

"No problem, pimp, I mean Porter."

"Ha Ha, so funny," she laughs and hangs up the phone.

****

"Yo, yo, yo!" says Ryan in a loud raspy tone. He reminds me of the rapper Beanie Segal when he talks.

"What's up bro," I hook my phone up to my Bluetooth so that I can drive.

"Aye, man, I'm down by Presidents Street, and I see Trish in the sushi spot with some guy."

"Some guy. What guy?"

"I don't know. I've never seen him before."

I knew something was going on. "Aight, man, I'm sure it's just a client. You know she's doing real estate now, so…"

"Man, get your sister-wife in check, bruh!" I swear he has the shittiest jokes.

"Man, get off my phone. You and your loud ass mouth meet me at the court in the morning So I can rat-a-tat-tat that ass," I boast a little. He knows that my three-pointers are ruthless, but he will never admit it.

"Yeah, aight, homie. I'll be there!" he shouts and hangs up.

****

"How is he doing today?"

"Oh, hey, Porter. He is doing just fine. I just finished bathing him."

"Carter? Your brother is here," the nurse whispers to Carter as she checks his vitals. He is still in a coma.

"He is improving every day. He is strong. I think he will be coming around soon. I'm not a doctor, of course, but I got a strong feeling," she smiles at me warmly as she exits the room. I had to tell them that Carter is my brother, so they would let me come in. So, I thought, but after I realized it didn't matter, I had already started the lie.

I wonder what he's thinking. He is probably wondering why I'm here to see him every week. After what he did for Aubrey, it's only right for me to come and check on him every now and then. Aubrey comes in and changes his flowers once a week. I stand over his bed and stare down at him. It kills me to know that he is in love with Aubrey, but the truth is, he deserves her. She deserves somebody who is going to love her the way she should be loved.

My phone rings.

"Hey, Bre, what's up?" I whisper.

"Hey, Porter. Thank you for the flowers!" I signal the nurse sitting at the desk outside the room that I am leaving.

"No problem, how are you doing?" I ask.

"I'm doing okay, a lot of kicking today. I guess she is ready to come up out of there."

"She? How do you know it's not a he?"

"Well, if you would have let me look at the gender, we would not be going through all of this."

"It's nothing like a surprise," I laugh. I can hear the aggravation in her voice.

"Have you spoken with Trish?" she asks.

"No, I haven't. She hasn't been answering my calls."

"I spoke to her a few times. She has called to check on me, but I haven't received my damn butter pecan yet."

"Well, good, because you don't need it anyway."

"The conversation was going well until you got disrespectful... I hope she is okay with all of this. She's been a little distant lately. If she's not, I completely understand."

"You understand what?"

"Come on, Porter, this, us... This situation is as unorthodox as it comes. Your pregnant ex-girlfriend, new girlfriend who happens to be the mother of your first born, which might I add you cheated and made a baby with, then went back to her after all of this, living in the same house. Honestly, homie, you got it made," she laughs as she munches on something loudly in my ears.

"Yeah, it sounds like it, huh?" I reply, but I feel the total opposite. I'm just trying to make it work.

My phone rings again.

"Hey baby, we were all wondering if Colby could stay the night?" My mother puts on the sweetest, most pitiful voice. And then I hear my dad and Colby in the background.

"Please, daddy!" they both yell loudly.

"I'm not sure about that. I have to ask Trish if it is okay. If she says yes, then I don't have any problem with it."

"Well, how about I call and ask her myself?"

"Ah, well… okay. Call her. The number is-"

"Just text it to me, boy. I don't feel like searching for pen and paper." She is so demanding.

"Okay, Ma."

"Oh, and don't worry about clothes. We are on our way to the outlet mall to do a little shopping." I can hear the smile through the phone. My mother loves to shop, and so does Colby.

"Okay, Ma, don't spoil her too much."

"Oh, yes, we will! For every year we missed! Talk to you later, baby." She hangs up the phone without a response.

****

On my way back to La'Rose, my phone rings again. But there is no answer. I can't block the number because there isn't a number showing up on the screen. I walk into the place, and business is going well as usual. Happy hour is over, but it's clear that these people have been here for some time now. When I get into my office, I see the inventory list and the numbers from last week on my desk. I guess Parris decided that what I say doesn't matter.

Lily walks into my office.

"Hey Porter, Trish is out here. She wants to talk to you. Oh, and these faxes came while you were gone."

"Okay, send Trish in. And I'm going to sign these papers. Please send them back to my attorney."

I look over the paperwork and begin to sign them one by one, barely reading over any of them. Trish walks in and stands in front of my desk. Tears fall from her face. She looks as nervous as a criminal waiting for a sentence. I put down the pen, walk from around my desk, and stand directly in front of her.

"Trish, what's wrong?"

"I- can't- do this…" she can barely catch her breath.

"Do what?"

"I can't be with you."

I feel like I just jumped off a cliff with no rope. My heart is beating out of my chest. Her eyes are red, and her fingers are trembling.

"What? What in the hell are you talking about?"

"Porter, this is all for convenience. This is all for Colby, and I can't stay in a relationship with you and pretend to love you when I know that you are still in love with Aubrey."

"Trish- I'm not-"

"Porter, please don't lie to me. I am a big girl, and I know love when I see it. And what we have isn't love. We have a child together, and we make it work for her. You still love Aubrey, and that is okay. She loves you too. It's okay if we are not together; that doesn't change our friendship, and it doesn't change how much you love Colby. You are a great dad; she couldn't ask for a greater dad."

I'm embarrassed to say there is another sense of relief for me. I do love Trish, but I am still in love with Aubrey.

"That is not all. Over the past month, I have been seeing Grant, my ex-fiancé. He has been here from Chicago working on the new mall that they are building in Owings Mills."

"Fiancé?"

"Yes, he proposed to me a few months before I left Chicago, but I was too afraid to say yes. He wanted to live a life that I wasn't ready for. He saw the world with optimism. All I saw was constant disappointment. I didn't know how to enjoy my life. Colby, work, and home were all I had." All I heard was fiancé.

"So that is why you haven't answered the phone? That's who you were with today downtown at the sushi bar? That is what this is all about, isn't it?"

"What? You've been spying on me?"

"No, but I have friends everywhere. Why are you just telling me?"

"I didn't know how to tell you. I didn't think that old feelings would brew."

"That's bullshit, and you know it! You walk up in my office with this well put together performance about how I am in love with Aubrey. This isn't about Aubrey and me. This is about your lame ass confession."

"First of all, you will not talk to me using that language, and secondly, what's 'Bullshit' is you dragging me on when you know there is nothing there for us. This isn't real, and you know it! This is some fantasized 'Modern Family' shit that you've put together—thinking that it's making everyone happy when really, I am looking like a damn fool. I love Aubrey, but I don't want to look like an idiot knowing that you two still love each other. She deserves to be happy, so do you. And… so do I. I have another chance at love, and this time I'm going to take it." She stands firm in front of me on her decision. Her head is held high with more confidence than I've ever seen in her, like some grown woman shit.

"Trish, you can't take my baby back to Chicago with you," I stand firm too.

"Porter, I don't plan to. We are all still a family. He says he likes Baltimore. I'm sure he would consider moving here if it came down to it."

"So, what now?" I ask as we lean up against my desk.

"Well, first, I have to take care of something, then go back to the house. I have lasagna baking."

"What about Colby? How are we supposed to break all of this shit down to her?" I ask while we scramble our brains.

"Porter, I don't know, but I do know that I don't want to spend my life hating you because I didn't speak up. Let's give it a little time. I will go back to stay at the house until after the baby is born, as we planned. Colby will be with me and stay with you too."

"You don't sound too sure."

"Because I'm not! Porter… Okay? I'm not sure. I'm not sure about any of my actions lately! It's a lot going on! We will figure it out. Whatever is supposed to happen will happen. It's as simple as that." I think she is trying to convince herself.

Trish leans up off of the table. I sit there in silence.

"Porter, I have something else to tell you… Somebody."

There is a knock at his office door.

"Not right now!" I'm sure the look in my eyes said enough. I had enough conversation with her for one day.

"That's, that's okay… We will talk about it later." She walks towards the door.

"Oh, and I spoke with your mother. It's okay that Colby stays. I'm happy that you finally made up with your parents. Life is too short to hold a grudge forever."

I glance up at her in silence and take a seat back at my desk as she walks out of the door. I take my time with handling anything else on my to-do list. I sit back in my chair and try to take in that whole conversation with Trish.

I notice the envelope that has been sitting on my desk. I pull out a long sheet of paper that reads, "YOU SHOUD'VE CHOSE ME." In big, bold letters. I put the letter back in the envelope and in the drawer where the other letter from Lana is. I grab my cell phone off of my desk and call my boy Charles. He is a detective for Baltimore City and a longtime customer of La' Rose.

"Charles! What's going on, man?"

"Nothing much P. What's up?"

"Look, man, I got a situation. You know about what happened with Lana, right?"

"Yeah, that's the crazy chick who's doing time for trying to shoot Aubrey, right?"

"Yeah, man, she's sending me all types of letters. And I think she's calling my phone or she got somebody calling my phone."

"All from jail?"

"All from jail… I think she even has somebody following me. She isn't supposed to contact me at all."

"Damn Porter, so what do you need me to do?"

"What can you do?"

"How about this let me look into-"

The phone line beeps.

"One-second."

"Yeah."

"Porter! I'm in labor. Meet us at the hospital."

"I'm on my way!" I start to panic as I click back over.

"Charles, let me get with you about all of this later. Aubrey is in labor."

"Awww, man, that's great! Okay, get at me later." I hang up the phone and grab my keys and the documents on the desk. I walk past Lily and hand the papers to her.

"Lily, please send all of the papers back to my attorney. They are all signed and ready to go."

"Sure thing. See ya later."

I storm out of the building and hop into my car. It's raining so hard I can barely see out of my front windshield. I try not to get anxious, but I can't believe it's happening.

My phone rings. I've been receiving blocked calls all day!

"Hello? Hello? Stop playing on my phone! I yell through the phone."

"Poooooorrrrrrrrttttteeeeerrr-"

In the rearview mirror, I see the same car following me from earlier. My phone rings again. I pressed the button on my car to answer it.

"Hello!"

"Hey Porter, it's Karen."

"Hey, Karen, did you get the documents?"

"Yes, I did, and I took care of everything. I also spoke with the owners of the restaurant, and they were delighted to get a generous offer from you. It looks like you and Aubrey are the new owners! We will go in and sign papers on Monday."

"Sounds great, Aubrey is in labor, so this is the next best news I've gotten all day."

"Great! Well, congratulations Porter; today is your day!"

"Yeah, I guess it is. Okay, let me get off the phone. This rain is vicious."

"Alrighty, be careful. And Porter?"

"Yeah."

"You are finally becoming the man you've talked about."

She hangs up before I had the chance to say thank you. The rain is coming down as hard as a hurricane in Florida. The car that was behind turned its lights off and pulled up beside me. I reach in the glove compartment to get my gun and before I knew it...

BAM!

Chapter 2
Breathe Deep

One Day Before Porters Accident

Trish

He always set the mood just right. I haven't had this kind of treatment in a long time. Candles lit all over the hotel suite. We have been going at it for hours. My body is covered with massage oil, with Boyz 2 Men playing from his playlist. His strong hands stroke every part of my body. He kisses me from the back of my neck down to my inner thigh. Finally, his lips meet my deep sea, and he goes for a dive. I inhale and hold my breath, trying to avoid a loud moan. This man has always known the right spots on my body to make me scream. I've missed him.

"I needed that," I say as I turn over and look him in his deep brown eyes. He grips my back and pulls me closer to him.

"I've missed you. I've missed you so much." I hop on top of him and kiss him on the shoulders of his chocolate skin.

"You wanna go again?" I whisper.

"No, I just want to hold you." With him, I know that I am wanted. I know that it's not for convenience. I know that he is still in love with me.

We lay there in the bed covered under the comforter. We gaze into each other's eyes.

"I don't want to share you," he says softly. I can't bare to hurt him again. I am getting another chance at love, except this time, I'm not running from anything or anyone.

"Grant, things are complicated right now."

"Wait, you're talking to me like I'm some kind of fling. You left me and my ring on the kitchen counter. You took Colby away from me without giving me a chance to say goodbye. Why are you making it so hard for me, Trish? Damn… I love you! I guess you forgot what that means, huh? It feels so good, it hurts. You took love from me, and I still came for you."

He gets out of the bed and puts on his pants.

"Where are you going?"

"I'm leaving Trish, what does it look like? You don't want me. I'm going to stop wasting my time," he exclaims.

"Grant, please just give me some time," I plead with him, anything to keep him here.

"Some time to do what LaTrisha? I gave you time. You moved all the way back to Baltimore. I didn't call you; you called me."

"Look, Grant, when I saw you come across my timeline, I felt an urgency. I had no idea you would be here. I've missed you so much," I cry out.

"Really? But now it's complicated, right?" he snarls while he buttons up his shirt.

"Grant, please don't leave. Just give me a chance to talk to Porter, please."

I walk up to him and unbutton his shirt. We have a vibration that feels electric when we touch. I have never felt this with any other man.

"You need permission to love me? Trish, I can't keep doing this to myself. We have been sneaking around long enough. You have to make a decision." He pushes me off of him.

"I love you, but I can't share you. You have to make a decision, Trish, period."

He grabs his trench coat and leaves out the door. While I sit here in the center of the bed, wrapped in bedsheets… alone.

Grant was my night and shining armor. He was the man that every woman dreams of marrying. Great career, a family man, who puts God first.

He treated me like a queen. There were days when I couldn't find the beauty within myself. I didn't know my worth or if anyone truly loved me. Grant showed me what love looks like. He put a mirror in my face, showed me every nook and cranny of my body, and made me feel beautiful.

We met at a poetry reading in downtown Chicago one Sunday night. My girlfriend told me to go out to get some fresh air, and she would watch Colby for me, so I did. I sat in the back of the café and sipped on a cup of tea that my coworker spiked with a little vodka. Poetry wasn't my "thing" until that night. Grant was sitting in the audience with a friend, a female friend. She was a beautiful woman with milk chocolate skin. She reminded me of Tika Sumpter, definitely wife material, from where I was standing. I watched him as he watched me, but I was turned off by the fact that he was watching me with his woman sitting next to him. Finally, he got up and came over to my table.

"Are you enjoying yourself?" His smile could light up a room. He reminds me of the singer Mario. A very cool and calm spirit with a lot of swag.

"Yes. As a matter of fact, I am enjoying myself. Does your girlfriend allow you to approach random women?" I ask as I sip on my tea.

"If my woman allowed me to do such a thing, she would not be my woman," he says arrogantly. For a few seconds, I fell into a trance as we gaze into one another's eyes. I could tell that he was good with wordplay.

"You have beautiful eyelashes."

"Eyelashes? Is that the best you can do?" I laugh flirtatiously.

"No, I could've said I love the olive tone in your skin or the effortless messy bun on your head or the way you bite your lip when you are really into what the poet is saying... but then I would sound like a creep," he laughs. His smile was contagious.

I felt like a sixth-grader with a crush. My smile was way too big to hide. Grant is the type of man that brings peace into a room but demands attention at the same time. He speaks with boldness and confidence. His strut is one of a King, and he carries himself as such. He is very aware of who he is and who he is becoming. Not arrogant at all, just a confident man. I love that about him.

I felt like I was making love to him with my eyes.

"No, not creepy at all," I replied. The woman he was sitting with walked over to the table.

"Hey Grant, I'm going to head out before my two years old drives my husband crazy."

"Okay, cool, see you at the office tomorrow. Oh, Gia, this is…"

"Trish, it's nice to meet you." I reach out to shake her hand, and she does the same.

"Yes, nice to meet you as well. You two have a great time. I will see you later. Oh, and kill it tonight."

"Already done," he answers. He turns back to me and gives me his undivided attention.

"So, Grant, what are you going to kill tonight?"

I was thinking my backbone, but…

Before he could answer, the host gets up on the stage and introduces him.

"Coming to the stage is one of my favorites. He is as smooth as a bottle of cognac. Welcome to the stage, my guy Grant."

"I will be right back." He walks up on the stage, and the applause comes to a halt.

My, my, my
Thirty seconds with you has changed my life
Forgive me for being forward
Are you looking for a husband
I believe in love at first sight
And surely, I have met my wife
Forgive me, forgive me, I just like what I see
Your vibration cover's the room on a high frequency
I need all of that energy
Fill me up Love
Give me what I've been yearning for
Let's create something real
I can make you feel alright
So, let me love you, let me feel you, let me see you
Your soul, that is, spread it open
Let me discover you
Let me make waves over you

If you don't mind
Let me bless you with what you've prayed for
Let me heal your wounds
Let me sing you a tune
Let me fine-tune that thang
Fix your broken wangs
I want you to become the best part of me
Come into my universe.
Let's see what this can be.

I could not take my eyes off of him, and he never took his eyes off of me. I could feel him from the stage. It felt like electricity was pulling us closer together. No one else was in that club, but he and I. That night was the start of something. He was different. He wanted a different part of me. A part of me that I haven't even met. He made plans for us. I remember the day he told me he was saving himself for his wife. Months went by almost a full year before we had made love. He gave in after a night at a Tyrese concert. We had way too many drinks and could not keep our hands off of each other. Every touch gave me fever. It was well worth the wait. He took complete control of my body as if it wasn't his first time touching me. He knew my body and took me on a natural high every time.

My heart feels as empty as this hotel room. I can't live like this. I have to do something before Grant is done with me forever. Finally, I get dressed and leave the hotel. Porter has called me at least six times, and Aubrey has texted me three times about her ice cream. I get off the elevator in the parking garage and walk to my car. I get to my car, and I hear a voice that I haven't heard in years.

"Tink, or is it LaTrisha? I always wondered why you were so mysterious. You are a sneaky little bitch, aren't you?"

"Doc? What- What are you doing here?" I thought I saw a ghost. My heart is beating out of my chest, and I cannot control my nerves. I may not make it out of this garage.

"Why are you acting so jibber, Tink? I guess you should be a little afraid right? Beings though you took all of my money and let me rot in jail." He circled my body and got close enough to me that I could feel the heat from his breath hit my face; it made me sick to my stomach.

"Doc, please don't hurt me. I- I didn't mean for things to happen like that. I didn't know what to do," I cry like I am begging for my life.

"How about what the fuck I told you to do? Bury my money in the park next to the oak tree. Those were clear fucking directions. Clear!" He gets closer to my face and stares deep into my eyes.

"Doc, I tried! I really did. I tried… But when I got there, I saw that they were doing construction. They were building a bathroom in the middle of the park," I reply.

"Yeah, I saw that, but where were you? You stopped answering my phone calls. Moved out of town… Dyed your hair. That's a nice color, by the way. I like the blonde better though- So, where the fuck is my money Tink?" Reluctant to answer, I froze. I knew that the next words that came out of my mouth could cost me my life.

"I spent it…" I murmur.

"You did what?" he replies.

"I spent the money," I speak firmly.

"Oh, you said that with power, like you had a right or some shit. You're telling me that you spent sixty-eight thousand dollars."

"Yes, I did. I'm sorry. Times got pretty hard, and I didn't know what to do. I thought I would have enough time to get it back. I didn't expect you to be out so soon!"

"You know, Tink, I thought we were better than this. When you moved to Chicago, I let you into my operation. Put money in your pocket. Had you move merchandise here and there. I kept your hands clean. We even had our little situation going on for a second. And you turn around and completely fuck me. It took a lot of time to find you. I remember the last thing I saw you in was a Morgan sweatshirt, so I took my shot. The internet is a motherfucker. Now here we are! Check this out I'm giving you twenty-four hours to come up with my money. If you don't, I'm going to start laying bodies down." I tremble in fear as he walks away.

"Oh, and I love your little family situation. It's weird as fuck, but whatever floats your boat. Porter seems to have it going on in Baltimore, so I'm sure you will come up with some way to get my money. Get creative." He walks away and gets into a black Malibu.

I held my breath until he pulled off.

"Shit, shit, shit, shit!" I scurry back and forth across the parking lot, trying to come up with a plan. I look down at my phone and saw a missed call from Porter. I got myself together before I called him back.

"Hey Porter, you called?" I say as I get into my car to pull off.

"Hey, where have you been? I've been calling you," he questions.

"I've been at the office all day looking over contracts. I have a few closings next week." I hate lying. I just don't know how to tell him the truth.

"Okay, well, I am still at the lounge. I will be home in about an hour. I was thinking that we can have a surf and turf dinner night. I got the cook to whip up all of our favorite seafoods with chicken, steak, and a few sides."

"That sounds good," I murmur.

"What's wrong? You sound like something is wrong." I felt like I was being cross-examined.

"I'm fine, Porter, just a little tired. I will see you when I get home."

I have to find a way to tell him about all of this. And keep Doc tamed. I met Doc when I first moved to Chicago. Colby was still a baby, so he never came in contact with her. I didn't have a good job at the time, and I wasn't making much money, so I had to find a way to take care of us. Doc ran a few businesses, but none of them were legal. He ran an illegitimate insurance company that I helped him with. He collected insurance premiums from falsely insured people with health insurance, home insurance, and car insurance. Money laundering was a part of my job as well. I would help clean the money, bringing in salons, lounges, and places like that. When he got busted, I was home in my bed. He told me to move the money. I moved it and got him a lawyer with some of the money. Instead of going to court, he took a plea of ten years. I don't know much about the court system or prison, but I know he didn't do ten years. How did he find me? I never told him where I was from. I made up names for his businesses to keep myself disguised. Even if he looked me up on social media, he would have never found me by my name.

I pull up to Aubrey's house, and before I get out, I sit in the car and gather my emotions. I don't want them to rub off on Colby and Aubrey. As I sit here,

I notice that the blinds are open in the front window. Aubrey and Colby are dancing and prancing around wildly. Colby loves her some Aubrey. Aubrey always says that Porter had the best-kept secret.

I walk through the door, and the room smells like warm vanilla. The music was blasting with Colby's favorite Kids Bounce on the speakers. She runs up to me as soon as I open the door.

"Mommy!" She screams with excitement.

****

The dining room table is covered with seafood. There were crab cakes, snow crabs, scallops, shrimp, blue crabs, enough food for the entire week. I sit there in silence while Aubrey eats like there is no tomorrow, and Colby irritates Porter with opening her crabs.

"Girl, what is wrong with you? You look like you lost your best friend," says Aubrey as she passed the bowl of butter to Porter. He looked over at me, awaiting an answer.

"Nothing, I'm fine. Just a little exhausted from work. I think I'm going to go to bed."

"Okay, well, good night. I will save you some crabs."

"Thanks," I answer as I drag up the stairs.

"Goodnight, mommy," Colby yells.

I lie in bed and cry myself to sleep. I wake up and check my phone, and it's 3 o'clock in the morning. Porter is completely out of it, and so is the rest of the house. What am I going to do to get the money? I have money in the bank but not enough to cover the whole thing. I quietly slip on some sweats in the basement. I grab my keys and creep out of the house.

Not knowing if Doc is anywhere around or still watching me, I look around the neighborhood before I step out. I quietly get into the car and back the car down the driveway on neutral before turning it on. I have to get this money, or Doc is going to kill all of us. I never knew him to be a killer, but from the look in his eyes, he is willing to do whatever to get his money or revenge. Porter has a safe in our house. One day he took me to the attic where it was hiding. He said that if something ever happened to him, that I knew the code.

I've been sitting in here for an hour, and I haven't figured it out yet. I look around the room to try and get an idea. Then it came to me. I punch in the numbers. 2-7-1-0, and the safe opens. When we were in college, that was my college dorm number. One day Porter came over, and he said that he saw that number four times that day. He would joke that he was going to play the lottery and win millions. It was an inside joke of ours.

"What!" I panic instantly. The safe was empty. All of the money was gone. All of it! Every bill!

My nerves are so high. I'm going to have to go to Porter. I have to, or someone is going to get hurt.

The Day of Porters Accident

The next morning, I wake up and take a look in the mirror. I look like hell… I have to come clean to them today about Grant, and I have to figure out what to do about Doc. I think the best thing to do is keep it quiet and work something out with him. I don't know what the outcome will be if Porter gets involved. I can't lose control of the situation.

"Trish!" Aubrey yells down the hallway. Oh goodness, I hope she is not in labor. I race down the hallway to Aubrey's room.

"What's wrong? Are you contracting?" I ask nervously.

"Girl, no," she says in a nonchalant tone.

"Can you get me some ice cream today?" She pleaded while lying in her bed with her legs spread open. Her belly looks like she's carrying twins. I'm sure she went from one hundred forty pounds to a bit over two hundred - ten. She has shrimp in one hand and a bowl of Frosted Flakes in the other. Her room smells like everything she has eaten in the past week and gas. It's too pretty to smell so disgusting.

"Aubrey, no! I got you a bucket of vanilla bean yesterday and butter pecan at the beginning of the week. That is too much damn ice cream, and that is too much shrimp in that bowl. You need to get up and go for a walk."

"Bitch, did you just call me fat? I know you didn't just call me fat!" she cries. Like, real tears, though? She is emotional as shit. I can't stand it. A few days ago, I told her that her room smells like a pound of ass, and she burst out in tears.

"Are you crying real tears?" I try not to smirk.

"Yes, because that's fucked up that you would call me fat. Do I look that bad?" She brings on the puppy dog eyes and the drawn-up lip while still holding a full bowl of cereal and shrimp. What in the hell do you think, sis?

"Aubrey, the words fat never left my lips." She's as big as a house.

"Look, okay, I'm sorry. I will get you a smaller portion of ice cream, but this is the last day."

"And a ginger ale soda, I have heartburn, it helps. I think the baby may have a lot of hair." No, the baby probably has high cholesterol. I rolled my eyes and left that embarrassing ass room.

"Thaannkkkss!" she screams down the hallway. Porter and Colby are gone; this gives me enough time.

I hop in my car and call Grant.

"Hello," he answers.

"Hey... Can we talk?"

"About what?" he says in a melodramatic tone.

"About everything, look, Grant, I just need a few minutes of your time. Can you meet me on President Street at our spot at noon?"

"I'm already here, and I have a meeting in an hour," he says sternly.

"I'm on my way. Grant, please wait for me." He hung up in my ear without speaking another word. First, I stop by the bank and empty my savings. The lady at the counter looked at me like I was nuts. I did 85 miles per hour all the way down 83 highway until I reached downtown Baltimore.

When I got there, I could see him seated at a window seat sipping on what looked like a glass of cranberry juice. I walk in, and my heart is beating out of my chest. I have so much to say, but my nerves are so bad I can't get Doc out of my head, and I don't know how Grant is going to respond to what I have to say.

"Grant." He stands up and hugs me. He smells so good; I can't take it.

"Hey babe, how are you doing?" he asked in his mellow tone.

"If I could be honest, I'm not doing well. So much on my mind. So much going on... But the one thing I know is how much I still love you. Grant, I love you. I've loved you since the moment you got up on that stage and the world erased. It was just us. Every touch, every kiss, your heart pulls me in and nourishes my soul. When I left before, it was because I was scared and wounded. I didn't understand how a man could love me the way you did because I didn't love me. I didn't know me. I didn't know what it meant to surrender my heart to someone and just let them love me. I don't want to be confused and making decisions. I just want to be with you, just you! I am willing to risk what I have if that means having your love and your friendship because I know you love me more than anyone else has ever loved me." My eyes are filled with tears. I can't control them.

"So, what are you saying, Trish."

"I'm saying that I want to be with you more than anything in the world, and I'm asking… If you would accept my proposal and be my husband."

There is a long pause, and the longer I wait for a response from him, the sicker I feel. I feel like my heart is about to erupt. Please don't leave me like this, standing here in the wilderness. He stares out of the window and sighs.

"Of course, I will. I got it bad for you." He smiles softly and reaches over the table to kiss me on my lips. Overwhelmed with joy, I squeeze him tight. In less than a second, I can feel the weight descend from my body. I feel light as a feather. Then I look out of the window, and Doc is standing there across the street. Far away not to be seen, but close enough for me to notice.

"Babe, I'm sorry. I need to go out to my car and put more time on the meter," I say.

"I got it," he responds.

"No! I got it… Can you order me something to eat?" I walk out as calm as I can so that he doesn't expect anything.

I walk across the street to the machine to get another pass or at least act like I am. Doc walks up behind me. I felt his presence so strongly. I knew Grant would not be able to see me behind the machine, so I turned around.

"You got my money?" he asks in a low, relaxed tone.

"Doc, I just need a little more time. I tried to get it all, but," he interrupts.

"Porter looks like he is running a real lucrative business. I've been watching how he moves. Same thing every day, pretty much. I'm sure he-"

"Porter doesn't have anything to do with this… Don't you touch him!" I order with my finger pointed in his face. Remembering that Grant can see out of the window, I put my hand down and play it cool.

He walks away with a mischievous grin on his face.

"I won't," he replies.

"I'm gonna get it," I yell as he walks away.

I go back inside the restaurant.

"Can we take this to go?" I say as the waitress is putting my food down on the table.

****

I can't sit here and enjoy this food in this hotel room without thinking about everything that is going on. Grant falls asleep.

"Where are you going?" He wakes up while I am leaving. I can't tell him about anything that's going on. I have to keep things as normal as possible.

"I need to get to Aubrey's house. I haven't called her all day."

"Where is Porter? Can't he check on her?" he replies with irritation.

"I am not sure the last I spoke with him; he was at his mom's with Colby."

"Okay... So now what?" he asks. I sit on the edge of the bed and gaze into his eyes.

"So now I tell everyone my truth." Relief fell over him. He kissed me on my forehead and pulled my bra strap up on my shoulder.

"I love you, Tree," he smiles.

"Oh, you know I hate that! But I've missed it." I kissed his lips.

"I will see you later," he says.

"Yes, you will," I respond.

"Oh, one more thing... I have been asked to go to California for six months. I won't need to leave until the beginning of the summer. I would love for you and Colby to go with me. I know she has school here, but maybe for just the summer. If that's okay with you and Porter."

"Grant, she would love that. I would love that. I don't know about Porter, but let me throw one thing on him at a time. I love you."

"I love you too." I grab my shoes and head out of the hotel room. There is no way I'm adding that to my plate. I need to figure out what in the fuck I am going to do.

Finally, I spoke my truth. I needed Porter to know how I felt. He needed to know what was going on. It's only fair to both of us. I don't know if telling him about Doc is the right thing to do. I was able to get a loan for the remainder of the money. I will only owe him thirty thousand now. I can get him that by the end of the week, hopefully. Doc isn't going to hurt anyone. If he were, he would've done it already. I just need to get him his money so that he can disappear. I just need him to hold off.

****

"I don't know why you are trying to hide the smell with those vanilla candles. It is not working," we both laugh.

"Girl, I don't know what it is? I'm trying to kill it!" she laughs. My guess is it's the plate of food that she has had sitting on her nightstand or the bag of Doritos on her bed. She has become a pregnant slouch.

"So… Aubrey… I need to talk to you…" I take a seat on the edge of her bed. She turns down the reruns of the tv show "The Game."

"What's going on? Is everything okay?"

"For the most part, no, I'm not okay, but… So, I will start with this… I have someone…"

"Someone like… What do you mean?" She looks complexed and thrown off.

"Before I came back to Baltimore, I was with a man named Grant. He is a good man and was great with Colby. Everything I could ask for. We were engaged, but one day I got scared, packed up Colby and me, and we left Chicago without me saying a word. I wasn't ready for what he was willing to give. I couldn't trust that a man could love me the way that he did. It was too perfect. The way things happened with Porter and I back then really messed me up. At that time in my life, I had no one. It was just Colby and me. My parents disowned me because I had a baby out of wedlock. We struggled for years. I had to do whatever I could to make money. My job didn't cut it. I came in contact with good and bad people. There was this one guy. I worked for him for a little bit. He ran a few illegal operations, and I was his number one go-to. He paid me well, but then he was arrested. So, I used the money that I made working with him to stay afloat. When I met Grant, he showed me something that I had never seen before. He loved me, and he loved Colby so much!" I weep. I would not dare tell her more about Doc or what played the biggest part in me leaving Chicago.

"Trish, I had no idea that you went through all of this!" Tears begin to stream from Aubrey's face.

"No one did…" I wipe my eyes and take a breath.

"Anywho, I don't know how I got there, but… Oh yes… My pain sparked fear in me. I didn't believe there would ever be a man to love me as Grant does. We reconnected not long ago. Although I left him, I took my chances and reached out. His energy didn't change. He came back to me and was open to trying again. So, we did, and as of today, we are engaged." I let the words flow out of my mouth without any restraint and effortlessly.

"Wait. What?!" Confusion is all over Aubrey's face.

"What do you mean you are engaged Trish, what about Porter, does Colby know?" she rants.

"No, but Porter does. I broke the news to him right before I came here."

"So that's why you've been so distant?" she asks.

"Yeah, I guess." Besides the fact that this man is out to kill me possibly.

"Look, Aubrey, all of this has happened for a reason. Even if our circumstances are a little unorthodox."

"A little?" she jokes.

"Well, a lot!" we laugh.

"You have become a great friend of mine, and I wouldn't take that back. Colby adores you, and so do I, but I think it's time for everyone to live their truth. My truth is that I am not happy in this situation. I want love, not convenience. Real, true, heart-bursting love, and Grant gives me that." I feel the breeze in every word I speak.

"Oh, goodness! Trish, well, I can't say that I'm not happy for you, because I absolutely am. Everybody deserves to know what real love feels like." She moves close towards me and tries to hug me with her big belly in the middle.

"Thank you, Bre. I knew you would understand. Now someone else's truth. Although he hasn't said it. Porter is still in love with you. Everything that he did and is doing is for you and Colby. I can respect that. He wanted us together so that Colby could experience a real family. I knew that I didn't play a big part in the equation, but he wants us to see that he messed up big time and just wants to be a better man. If you are still in love with Porter, the bottom line is, don't worry about what everyone else thinks. You have my blessing; we are all free now to do what is best for us." I gently smile at her, and once again, she looks like she has been caught off guard.

"Oh... Wow... This is a lot... Like my life is a soap opera. I love Porter. I mean, we have been through a lot... What about Carter? I can't do that. Not after all that he has been through. I love him too. We have something different than what Porter and I had," her words fall all over the place as she tries to explain herself.

"Well, I guess this is between you and God. I'm sure he will work it out as he sees fit. But for now, I am done, before we have burnt lasagna. Aubrey, thank you for understanding." I get up off of the bed and walk out. She sits in her bed, quiet as a mouse as I walk down the hallway.

I get a text from an unknown number.

"Aubrey, I'm about to run to the market to get something to drink for dinner. I will be right back."

I pick up the phone to call, but the line is silent. I get in my car.

"Look, I have thirty thousand dollars right now. I can–" I plead, but he interrupts.

"Porter makes more than that a night. This bill just went up. I need an extra twenty thousand. Doesn't he make his drop tonight?" He sounds like he is up to something.

"Wait, just let me try to get it from him, first. Please!" I plead.

"Time is up–" He hangs up the phone—my mind races. I start the ignition and head back to La'Rose. Porter's phone keeps going to voicemail.

Moments later, the phone rings.

"Trish, my water broke!" Aubrey screams through the phone.

Before I knew it, my foot was on the breaks, and I was busting a U-turn in the middle of the street. I drive as fast as I can back to the house. I get out of the car and run into the house. My heart is racing out of my chest.

"Bre! Oh my God, what do I do?!" I rant.

"I don't know! Haven't you done this before? Would you calm down!"

I pace the floor as I try to gather my thoughts.

"Okay, how far apart are your contractions?"

"I don't know, about seven minutes, maybe."

"Seven minutes? Oh, goodness, we have to go!"

I help Aubrey up off the bed and help her down the stairs. "Did you call Porter?" I ask.

"Yes, but he said he would meet us at the hospital."

"Okay, great."

"Ahhhhhhhhhhhh, shiiittttt," Aubrey shakes the house with her scream.

"Okay, Aubrey, we are almost down the stairs."

"Let me go," she says.

"I don't want you to fall down the stairs," I respond firmly.

"Let me go!" she screams again.

"Okay fine." I let her go, and I walk down the stairs and grab the baby bag that has been sitting on the chair by the door for two months now. I open the door and get the car started. By the time I open her car door, she comes wobbling out of the front door. She tries to control her breathing as she makes her way to the car. Finally, she gets in, and we are on our way.

On our way to the hospital, there is a detour. It looks like a bad accident. The rain is coming down so heavily that I can barely see out of the window.

"Oh my God, Trish, please hurry up! I can't hold it!"

I cannot deliver this baby in this car. First of all, I just got my seats cleaned, and Aubrey's ass is too big to spread across my car.

"We are almost there."

Finally, we get to the hospital, and Aubrey is rushed to labor and delivery. I call Porter, but I don't get an answer, so I leave him a message.

"Porter, we are at the hospital. Where are you? Look, something is going on. I need to talk to you. Please call me back asap."

Aubrey's contractions have gotten close.

"Okay, Ms. Bryant, it is time to push!" Dr. Richardson is at the bottom of the bed.

"No, No, No! Porter isn't here yet!" Aubrey cries.

"Ms. Bryant, this baby can't wait! Now push!"

After a few pushes, baby Porter arrives, and he is the most handsome little boy I've ever seen. He looks just like his dad, but more like Colby. I watch as

Aubrey bask in her bliss. The whole world is forgotten, and it's just her and baby Porter. She has yet to mention the baby's name, but she and I held the secret that she would name him Porter Jr. and surprise his daddy if it was a boy.

Torin and Eric arrive bearing gifts. I wish they were here when it was going down. All I keep thinking about is Doc and the last words he said to me. I can't leave Aubrey.

"Hey girl, are you okay?" says Torin as she rubs Aubrey's head.

"I'm fine. I'm good." I feel like I'm about to pass out. This was a hell of a day.

"Aubrey, did you call your parents?" ask Torin.

"I did. They said they would be on the next flight."

"Girl, your parents are living it up! Traveling here there and everywhere!" Eric responds.

We've called Porter a thousand times, but still no answer. Something is wrong; I can feel it, but I can't mess up this moment for Aubrey by worrying myself. I give Aubrey a piece of mail that has been sitting around and walk out of the room to call Porter.

Eric turns on the news, and there is an accident exactly where we were today. I knew at that moment...

Chapter 3
Tell Me What I Need To Know

Four days Before Porters Accident

Aubrey

As I sit at the top of Federal Hill, my creative juices are flowing. My pen hits my notebook and glides across the paper as light as a feather. It's been a long time since I've been able to write from a happy place. It's the perfect day outside. The ideal day to grab a blanket and indulge in the best parts of Baltimore City. Unfortunately, if my big ass gets on this ground, I will have a time getting up. The sun is shining. It's a good breeze. The perfect Sunday. Now that we are closer to the baby's arrival, I think it's time for us to talk about our living arrangements. I can see that Trish isn't happy, and I don't blame her at all. It's a lot for all of us. Porter means well, but I don't think that he sees it.

"Hey sis, do you mind if I sit next to you?" A short older woman sits down next to me. She reminds me of my great aunt Sarah. She passed some years back. A short petite woman with a natural short haircut.

"Yes, ma'am, you can," I reply with a smile.

She pulled a plastic bag out of her bag. My nose can catch smells like a hound dog. She opens the aluminum wrapping and got damn! A big juicy cheesesteak! By the aroma, I knew it was from Lexington Market. My daddy used to take me there when I was a little girl. He'd pick me up from school early, and we would grab a cheesesteak and sit on the top balcony of the market. Those were the best cheesesteaks in Baltimore City.

As I inhale the scent of the cheesesteak, the baby is doing flips in my stomach. I try to ignore it and keep writing.

"Every day is a blessing, you know? I've come a long way. I used to run these streets; me and my brothers. Baltimore City was my playground. They used to call us 'The Hot Dugs.' I stop writing to give her my attention.

"I've done some good and some bad, but it was God's grace who allowed me to get this far. Life doesn't always pan out the way that we want it to, but we have to go through to grow through. You feel me? There is a lesson in every experience." She takes a big bite of her sub and looks off into the scenery.

"Let the past go, my dear, and look into your future. You will have what you need... Aubrey, right?"

"How do you know my name," I ask surprisingly.

"Well, your necklace says so, sweetheart," we both chuckle. Porter bought me my name necklace for my 18th birthday, and I still have it.

"Oh, yes, yes, my name is Aubrey," I giggle with embarrassment.

"Well, Ms. Aubrey, you keep your head up and stay strong for that piece of heaven in your belly. Remember, life ain't always what we want it to be, but it will be what it's supposed to be one day. Enjoy the rest of your day." She gets up and walks towards the back of the park.

"Hey! What's your name?" I ask.

"Hattie Ophelia; Hattie Ophelia Hill," she smiles.

"Well, it was nice talking to you, Ms. Hattie Hill," I smile pleasantly at her.

"The pleasure was all mine, sweetheart." She smiled so peacefully and walked away. Ms. Hattie bopped off as she sang. "This little light of mine, I'm gonna let it shine. This little light of mine, I'm gonna let it shine, let it shine, let it shine, let it shine."

I listened as her voice faded away. When I looked up, she was gone.

My mother used to sing that song to me as a little girl. It made me feel unstoppable. Like I could do anything. I haven't felt that way in a long time. Unstoppable, I mean.

It's funny how life can take you for a loop. I remember when I used to sit on this hill with Porter and look at the city's backdrop. I used to fantasize about having my own publication office in one of these buildings. Life is a lot more different than I dreamed, but I will have to make the best of it. I've sat here long enough; it is time for me to eat! I wiggle myself to the front of the chair and stand up. Immediately my phone rings.

"Hello"

"Bre! I'm hungry. Let's eat!" screams Eric.

"E, I am supposed to be on bed rest right now."

"But you're not. I hear helicopters and cars, so you are damn sure NOT in the comfort of your own home. Plus! I saw Trish at the coffee shop, and she said you snuck out of the house," that damn Torin interrupts. She clearly has me hooked up to her car's annoying ass speakers.

"Plusss! We got some juicy, juicy, juicy ratchet news, and it calls for brunch and mimosas," says Eric.

"Ugh, Trish gets on my damn nerves!" I yell jokingly.

"First of all, Ms. Thang, don't act like you don't want to see us," says Torin.

"We don't want to see you an-ny WAY. We want to see how oversized your belly is and how your big ass tilt forward when you walk and wobble!" Eric laughs.

"Oh, that's messed up. I didn't say all of that, Bre!" laughs Torin.

"Ugh ugh, I'm sick of the weight jokes," I cry.

"Oh Lord, girl, I was just playin. I forget how emotional you are these days. Gees!" says Eric.

"But let's be real, soon we won't want to see you anyway, it's going to be all about our new baby. So, you best be grateful," says Torin.

"Our?" I say sarcastically.

"Yes, OUR, God Parents are like thirty percent of the baby's parent, right," says Torin.

"Speak for yourself bitch- I'm like... two-point-five percent. I'm not changing no shitty diapers, and I'm not staying up all night. I'm the uncle with the money. Gifts and candy and shit. That's where I come in. Thirty percent? That's a big number; you mind as well move in. You're trippin," we all burst out in laughs.

"Ya'll are a mess, but at least I know ya'll got me," I say.

"Of course!" says Torin.

"I got this meal! Cut the small talk; where are we eating?"

"How about Sugar, Honey, Iced, Tea?" I request. Sugar Honey Iced Tea is one of my favorite places. Porter and I spent all of our time there in high school and college.

"Oh, yes, those honey biscuits are the bomb!" says Eric.

"Okay, I will meet ya'll there." I hang up the phone and get into my car. I can't believe I took that long walk back to my car. Thank God I was distracted by the phone call.

****

I arrive at Sugar Honey Iced Tea, and I can barely get out of the car. Thanks to the gentlemen that works at the ice creamery next door, I had some assistance with getting all of this body out of the car.

"Bre!" Torin yells from a booth in the back of the restaurant. Eric is stuffing down honey biscuits like there is no tomorrow.

"Hey, girl, hey! I saved you a biscuit," he says with a mouth full.

"Barely," says Torin as she rolls her eyes at him.

"So, what's the ratchet news? You know I can only take an hour of gossip a day." I say with a grin.

"Girl! You didn't hear?" Eric throws down the last bite of his biscuit. He is always prepared to spill hot tea.

"No, what?"

"Girl! Thomas… and Lisa… eloped to Turks and Caicos," says Torin as she allowed the anticipation of my response to build up.

"Ugh, ugh heffa! That was my line," Eric snarled and gave Torin the side-eye. Torin ignores him and keeps going.

"And Lisa is pregnant," she shouted.

"Oh, hell, no bitch we are about to fight! You are just taking all of my glory!" Eric is about to throw a bitch fit. Torin and I both indulge in this hot tea!

"You are lying!" I yell.

"Nope! Girlfriend has been impregnated!" Eric joins in.

"Honey, Thomas, didn't waste a drop of time. Lisa must've put a hex on the 'D.' She got the good goods," Eric laughs frantically.

"I'm sure it's better than Lana's dry vagina," laughs Torin.

"Speaking of Lana, how is therapy going, Aubrey," says Eric.

"It's going... I keep having these same dreams about her. Over and over again."

"What are they about?" ask Torin.

"It's an entire replay of the night everything went down. Accept Carter isn't hit. Porter is."

"Maybe, subconsciously, you wish it was Porter instead of Carter," says Eric.

"No... I don't feel that way. At least, I don't think so. It's crazy because, in my dream, Lana doesn't look like she wants to do it. She looks forced. There is a voice, a woman's voice. I don't know where it's coming from, but it's telling her to do it. She looks at me, and she is shaking. Finally, she shoots, and Porter jumps in front of me. Every time he takes his last breath, I wake up in a cold sweat. And I've been having dreams about our childhood. Images of her and Porter together. Images of us hanging out. I feel like it all means something, but whatever it is, I don't want no parts of it."

"Damn Bre, that's crazy. Have you talked to your therapist about this?" ask Torin.

"Yeah, I have but-"

The waitress walks up to the table, ready to take our order.

"Hi, my name is Tia. I will be your waitress for the day. Are you all ready to order?"

Eric starts to order first. "I guess ladies first went out of the window," I say.

"Girl, please. I'm ready to order," Eric responds as he rolls his eyes and waves me off.

"I'm ready. I would like a peach mimosa with a stack of banana cream pancakes, hickory smoked bacon, not turkey bacon darling, turkeys don't make bacon, and a scrambled egg with cheese."

Next is Torin. "I would like the red velvet pancakes and a peach mimosa as well."

"Can I have a honey buttered Belgian waffle, one slice of brioche french toast with the vanilla cream on top, a slice of smoked salmon, two slices of turkey bacon, home fried potatoes, and two scrambled egg with extra cheese, salt, pepper, and a side of ketchup?"

"Scratch that extra cheese; you will not be gasing our table up," Torin laughs.

I continue with my heavy order, "Oh, and can you bring the butter pecan syrup? A cup of water with lemon and a glass of cranberry juice? Thank you!"

Eric and Torin both look at me with their jaws dropped to the floor.

"What in the holy hell just happened?" Torin questions.

"Girl, did you just order the whole damn menu? I guess all of our hard-running days are gone out of the window," Eric rolls his eyes and takes another bite of his biscuit.

"It's not me; it's the baby," I cry in my most innocent voice.

"Bullshit, sis, that baby didn't make that long ass food order. You better slow down before that baby weight becomes YOUR weight," Eric teases.

"Oh, Eric, hush! Ain't nothin wrong with a little meat on your bones," Torin adds.

"Correction, ain't nothing wrong with a little meat on YOUR bones. There is nothing wrong with being body positive. Seriously, but Aubrey's mind isn't set up to gaining weight. She will lose her mind if she can never get back into that fully stocked closet of hers. I mean, let's keep it real. You have pieces in there that you haven't even worn yet," Eric points his fork at me.

"Well, they say the weight drops easily after birth if the baby breastfeeds," I try to defend myself.

"Girl, please, I don't believe in statistics. Where is the proof? I guess it just didn't work out for a whole lot of chicks." Of course, he follows up.

"Eric, that is so mean. Don't discourage her," Torin chimes in.

"I'm not! I'm just saying we are going to have to get back to work when that baby drops. Me, you, and the baby carriage," we all laugh.

Finally, our food arrives, and it is taking everything out of me to not eat like a pig. Eric, on the other hand, is eating like he hasn't eaten in years. How can he talk about what's happening with my weight but cannot seem to slow down with his own damn fork and mouth placement?

"So, what did your therapist say," says Eric with a mouth full of food.

"She wants me to go visit Lana. She feels that I need closure and that something is being left out of the past that I need to clear up."

"Like what?" ask Torin.

"Girl, how in the hell should I know? All I know is that I have no desire to talk, look, or be in the presence of Lana. Everything about her gives me bad energy. I know I should've felt it earlier, but seriously. I don't want anything or anyone to distract me from the joy I have right now. I'm finally feeling optimistic about life. When this baby comes, my life will fall in place, and I will finally do all of the things I've wanted to do. It's not an ideal situation, but it's the cards I was dealt, so I have to make the best out of it."

"Well, I'm happy that you are looking at things from another perspective," says Torin.

"When you feel the time is right, I'm sure you will be led to go see her. I get it. It's best to stay as far away from toxic energy as possible," Eric adds.

"My thoughts exactly," I reply.

****

Aubrey tosses and turns in her sleep.

"He's weak, Aubrey... He is fucking weak. Just... like... you..."

Aubrey paces back in forth in her room with a bottle of wine. She cries frantically and tosses the bottle of wine at her mirror. The mirror shatters. She stands silently in tears as the wine runs down the glass. She glances at her reflection. She tosses and turns in her sleep as the visions come to her dreams. Aubrey, Porter, Lana, and Carter are all standing on the lawn. The night of Carter's shooting replays in her dream.

"Aubrey, Aubrey! What in the fuck is so special about Aubrey? I can end all of this crying and whining over Aubrey," Lana says threateningly.

She points the gun towards Aubrey and shoots. Porter jumps in front of Aubrey and falls to the ground. "Porter!" Aubrey screams.

Aubrey wakes up.

3 Days Before Porters Accident

"Good morning Aubrey! Mommy is making some pancakes. Would you like some?" Colby stands at the edge of my bed with her doll in her hand.

"Hey, Colb! Yes, please. I will be down shortly." She twirls out of my room with her tutu around her waist.

These dreams are kicking my ass. I need to talk to my therapist, but if she tells me to go and see Lana again, I'm going to flip out on her. Seriously, why would I want to visit the person who tried to kill me? What more could she say? She made it clear in court that she is a lunatic, and she has it out for me. Lana messed up, and she is a lost cause. I would rather dream these dreams every night than be in the same room as her.

I step out of bed and throw on my robe. My room is a complete mess. I've never been this messy in my life. Clothes are everywhere, plates with old food residue. I spend way too much time in this room. Trish used to come in and clean it for me, but I guess she saw how out of hand it was getting, and she quit.

I step out of the shower and can smell the aroma of breakfast. That is my Que!

"Good morning, ladies!" I sing loudly.

"Well, aren't you in a jolly mood this morning," Trish smiles.

"Yes, I am. I'm not going to let anything change my mood. My baby will be here soon." I grab a plate full of pancakes and smother them in syrup.

"Aubrey, that is way too much syrup. Didn't your doctor say to stay in bed and chill on the sweets?"

"Girl, I am not staying in that bed. My body cannot take it. I will be fine."

"Okay, miss thang, you know it all," Trish shrubs.

"Whatever, Trish, pass the butter," I laugh. "What's on your agenda today?"

"I have a closing today. Do you mind keeping Colby for me?"

"Sure, we can hang out today."

"Yayyy, what are we going to do, Aubrey?" Colby jumps up and down, awaiting an answer.

"I don't know. I'm sure we will figure something out." She runs upstairs singing.

"I will be back later on this evening. I have food in the fridge for dinner if Porter doesn't bring anything home by then," Trish tells me.

"Trish, are you okay?" I ask.

"Yeah, I'm fine," she mutters.

"You know you can talk to me, right? About anything. I know all of this is weird. It's crazy for me too, but I am always open, and I will not judge."

"Thank you, Aubrey, but I am fine." She takes her cup of tea and walks upstairs without saying another word.

****

"You wanna go for a walk?" I ask Colby as we drive through downtown Baltimore.

"Yeah, sure. It's not a long walk, is it because my knees are bad," she says.

"Your knees are bad? Colby, you are too young for bad knees!" I laugh.

"You are never too young for bad knees. Ballet can do a number on you!" She has definitely been here before.

We pull up to Fort McHenry and park the car.

"Have you ever been here before, Colby?"

"No, I haven't." We walk the passage into the park and arrive at the open water.

"Wow, it's so pretty. A little windy, but pretty." She smiles as she gazes over the large body of water.

"Aubrey, who are you to me?" Wow, I didn't see that question coming.

"Um, well… I am your brother or sister's mom," I answer in confusion.

"So, you're like what to me, though?"

"I don't really know how to answer that, Colb. It's kind of a complicated question. Who do you want me to be?"

"Well, you are almost like my best friend, but you are also like another mom. Like my mommy is my mommy, and you are like an extra mommy," she explains with hand demonstrations.

"Ok, like a bonus, mommy?" I ask.

"Yeah! Like a bonus, mommy!" she shouts.

"I am okay with that as long as it's okay with your mom and dad. I would wear the title of your bonus mommy any day." Colby has a smile that lights up a room. She brings a sense of serenity wherever she goes, but of course, she doesn't know that. She's just a kid.

We walk around the park and watch the boats sail by.

"Aubrey?" says Colby.

"Yes," I answer.

"Are we going to live together when our new baby comes?"

"I don't think we will, sweetheart."

"Why?" If I don't get out of here soon, the questions are going to become a four-page letter. I think the water is calming her mind a little too much. She has room for a lot of damn questions.

"Well, your mommy and daddy would like to go back to their house. You all will come over to see the baby, come and pick the baby up for dates, and maybe even stay the night at my house with the baby as long as it's okay with your mom. Of course, you can keep your room and decorate it; however, you please."

She picks a dandelion from the grass.

"This is a very complicated situation," she replies. I burst out in tears of laughter.

"Little girl, what do you know about a complicated situation?"

"I don't know, but daddy says it all the time. When I ask him questions like this, he always says it's a complicated situation."

"I totally agree with him. These are definitely questions and concerns that you should talk to your parents about." I laugh at the seriousness of her face. She seems to be passionate about where her life will end up. But what's even crazier is that her questions are relevant. They make a lot of sense. I feel like God put words in her mouth for me to figure things out that I didn't realize it may actually be a problem or concern.

"Let's head back home before your parents come looking for us."

"Yes, that's a great idea. The wind is blowing way too hard, and mommy just did my hair." She throws her hair back, takes her sunglasses off of her head, and put them on her face, and prances in front of me as I follow her lead.

****

Aubrey toss and turns in her sleep. She is struggling to open her eyes.

"He's weak, Aubrey! He's fucking weak! Just... Like ... You...," screams Lana.

Aubrey can't wake herself up out of her dreams. She breaks out in a sweat.

"Aubrey, Aubrey, Aubrey. What the fuck is so special about Aubrey?"
Lana aims the gun at Aubrey.

"I can end all of this crying and whining over Aubrey."
Lana's gun goes off, and Porter jumps in front of Aubrey to shield her.
"Porter!"

Aubrey

I wake up out of my sleep, and I can barely catch my breath. It feels like I've been running miles. There is no way I am going to be able to fall back to sleep, so I turn the television on. For some crazy reason, television relaxes me.

I can feel my eyes getting heavy again, but I want to go downstairs and get some ice cream. I think my eyes are winning.

****

Lana aims at Aubrey, and her gun goes off. Porter jumps in front of Aubrey to shield her. He drops to the ground as the blood rushes out of his mouth. Aubrey runs over to him. Aubrey cries out, "Porter, Porter, please!"

Lana walks over and stands over top of them. Aubrey looks up at her, "Why Lana? What do you want?"

Lana replies with a vengeance, "He was mine first. He was always mine."

Aubrey wakes up out of her sleep once again drenched in sweat. She goes downstairs to the kitchen and grabs a bottle of water out of the refrigerator. When she turns around, Lana is standing there with a gun and points it at Aubrey's belly.

"Just admit that you were wrong." Vengeance is written all over Lana's face. Lana looks into Aubrey's eyes and pulls the trigger. Aubrey drops to her knees.

****

"Stop!" I scream after waking up out of that nightmare.

Before I could process it all, I hopped in my car and drove to my parents' house. I grab my phone off of the passenger seat and call my dad.

"Daddy, I'm coming over."

"Is everything okay?" he asks.

"I just want to come over, that's all."

"Okay, I'll see you when you get here."

It's like he timed my arrival. He is standing in the doorway in his robe and slippers. When I pull up to the driveway, he walks out to open my door and greet me. My daddy has always treated me like a princess. When I finally get me and my belly out of the car, he pulls me up, hugs me tightly, and gives me the softest kiss on my forehead.

"Hi, daddy." I close my eyes to take in the sensation of his kiss on my forehead.

"Hey, Bre- Bean." His arms are the warmest and safest place I've been in a long time.

"Come on in." He takes my purse and leads me to the front door. I head straight to the kitchen and raid the fridge. What are you doing out here in the middle of the night? It's 2 a.m. Bean.

"I keep having these awful dreams. I can't sleep, and sometimes I can't wake up out of them. It's like I'm being forced to stay in until the end."

As I am searching through the refrigerator, Dad walks over and pulls the door handle out of my hand. He reaches all the way to the back of the freezer and grabs a box of butter pecan ice cream.

"Jackpot," I laugh.

"Shhhh, I'm hiding it from your mother. She says it gives me gas," he giggles.

He grabs two spoons, and we both sit on the island stools and eat out of the box of ice cream.

"So, tell me about these dreams," he asks as he takes a big scoop and stuffs it in his mouth.

"Well... All of them are about Lana." He drops his spoon back in the bucket of ice cream, and his facial expression gets serious and concerned.

"Oh... Lana... Well... What was the dream about?"

"It's not a dream; it's multiple dreams. Sometimes they are back to back. I keep having replays of the night she shot Carter. Accept in my dreams; Porter is the one who gets shot. He shields me from the bullet. But in the same dream at a different time, she aimed at my belly and shot me. But before she shot me, she said, 'Just admit you were wrong.' I keep replaying it all in my head, but I can't think of one time that I've done Lana wrong. I've always supported her. I've always been there for her. I don't understand why she would do any of this to me. To everyone else, she is a bitch, but even though she has done me wrong, I still can't shake that she was my best friend, my sister."

Before I knew it, tears were flowing from my eyes, and I could barely catch my breath. My dad pulls me close to him and wraps his arms around me.

"I know these dreams mean something, but I'm afraid to find out. I can't take any more bad news, daddy. I just can't. My heart can't take it. I just want to live a normal life and get out of this daytime soap opera, better yet this nightmare."

"Oh baby, it's not a nightmare. You are holding on to the past. You have to open your eyes to the best part of your life. Yes, it's been a little messy, but you've made it through. Now you are on the better side of it all. You didn't hurt anyone or commit a crime. You were the victim in all of this. Now allow yourself to be free and stop stressing out my grandbaby before he comes out bald like his grandpop," we both laugh.

"What makes you think it's a boy?"

"I don't know, but I got my girl, so I'm just praying that's my little man swimming around in there." He rubs my belly and smiles.

Me and daddy sat on the sofa and watched reruns of Martin until we both fell asleep.

2 Days Before Porters Accident

The first thing I do when I open my eyes is check my phone. Porter and Trish have called me over twenty-two times. I put my phone back in my purse and go upstairs to give my mom and dad a kiss, but my mom wasn't there. I walk up to daddy to kiss him on his cheek. But when I get close, he jumps up out of his sleep.

"I'm sorry!" he yells. He looks like he has seen a ghost.

"Daddy, it's me. Are you okay?" He gets himself together.

"Oh, goodness. Yes, Bre- Bean, I'm okay." I give him a kiss on his forehead.

"I love you, daddy," I smile.

"I love you to daughter. See you later. Oh, don't forget me and your mom leave for our trip tonight."

"I didn't forget, as long as you are back before the baby arrives."

"We will be. I wish we hadn't booked the trip so early. I should have listened to your mom and got some insurance protection."

"Oh, it's okay, daddy. Don't stress yourself over it. Everything happens as it should, right?"

"Right."

Before I could shut the door to my car, the phone rings again.

"Aubrey, where in the hell are you?" screams Trish.

I can hear Porter in the background, "She answered? Where the hell she at?"

"Ugh, first of all... I'm grown, so relax. Secondly, I went to my parents' house last night and stayed."

"In the middle of the night?" yells Porter.

In the most nonchalant sarcastic voice, I answer. "Yeah, Pops. I'm grown, remember."

"Aubrey, we were just crazy worried about you. Is everything okay?" says Trish.

"Yeah, everything is fine. I'm on my way home.

Chapter 4
The Beginning to My Ending

Aubrey

"I tossed and turned all night. I have not slept in days. Days! This morning I woke up on my parent's sofa because I was too scared to fall back asleep in my bed last night."

Dr. Powell sits in her plush magenta pink wing back chair. She crosses her legs at the ankle. She is a bomb ass therapist, and she gives me more attention than she gives her pen and pad.

"I love this red sofa, by the way. Your room feels like Valentine's Day," we both laugh.

"Well, I'm happy you lightened the energy in here with that remark, and thank you. Now let's get back to these dreams. Are they about Lana still?"

"Yes, they are. I've had dreams of Lana killing my baby and me. Last night she said things in my dreams that keep replaying in my head. After she shot Porter, she says, 'He is mine. He always has been.' And in the second or third sequence of my dream, she said, 'Just admit you were wrong,' or something like that. The same dream replays almost every night. That night on the lawn. Sometimes I can't wake up out of it."

"Why do you think that is?" Dr. Powell is so focused that it looks like she's watching a juicy television show, and I'm starring in it. Shit, she might be on to something.

"Why what is?" I ask.

"The dreams. Why do you think you keep having them?" She follows up with as if she is trying to get me to figure it all out.

"I don't know." I am so confused. If I knew why I had them, I probably would not be in this expensive ass therapy session.

"You know what I think? Don't get upset. But I think you need closure. And I think the best way to get it is to visit Lana. Something is missing in all of this. You need to sit down and have an open, honest conversation with Lana. And no matter what she says, you can either take it with a grain of salt or see it for what it is. All I ask is that in that space, you have complete control of your emotions."

"Dr. Powell, I am pregnant if you haven't noticed. There is no way that I can have complete control of my emotions."

"I'm probably asking for a miracle, but the only way you will get an understanding and hear everything is by keeping your feelings intact. You have questions, and you need answers. Why does she hate you so much? Why didn't she just leave you be? What happened between her and Porter? All of this stemmed from something deeper than a little crush. There is something else deeper, and you need closure."

"I don't want answers! I want all of this just to go away! Disappear! This has taken complete control of my life, and it's making me crazy. Lana is locked up in a jail cell, and she is controlling my life. Everyone thinks that I am fine. I'm playing it cool, but what if something else happens? What if she gets out? Or what if Carter never wakes up? Carter is lying there in a hospital bed because of me. He had nothing to do with any of this. I don't need closure. I needed this to have had never happened in the first place."

As my tears fall, I can feel the anxiety raging in my chest. Seeing Lana will place me in a serious panic attack. I know it.

"Aubrey, there is nothing you can do about what has already happened. Unfortunately, there is no button to delete or change the past. This is what you get. These are the cards that you have been dealt with. Now the question is, what are you going to do with them? I don't want to upset you, so I am apologizing in advance, but your reality is that your best friend tried to kill you over a man that you both loved, and she could have possibly had an added motive. I don't know, but what I do know is your life will never have peace until you know the truth."

There is something in me that wants to visit Lana, but I'm afraid at the same time. Afraid of being vulnerable. Afraid of new lies she may have put together in her deranged little mine, but more than anything… I am afraid of what could possibly be the truth.

"What if the truth is worst than what has already happened?" I ask.

"But what if it's only that… the truth… Unfortunately, there is a possibility of more secrets coming out. But what's better? To face the truth and move on. Or to keep battling with your mind and not getting any rest.

I hate that she is right.

"Does Porter know about these dreams?" she asks.

"No, he doesn't… I don't want to share it with him. Everyone seems to be in a good place. I want to keep it that way."

"Well, I am not going to put a rush on things. I believe you will know when it's the right time. Well, it looks like we've gone over the hour again today, but it's always a pleasure. Let's play our next appointment by ear. It looks like you are going to bust any day now."

"It feels like it too," we both laugh.

****

All night all I could think about was the day I would visit Lana. With this big feast of seafood in my face, there should be nothing distracting me. Between the sadness on Trish's face and my crazy thoughts, the energy at the table was shot. Trish mopes upstairs, barely saying a word.

"What's going on, Porter?" I ask.

"I don't know, man. She has been very distant lately. Maybe she is just tired of this setup," he answers.

"Maybe, and I wouldn't blame her," I add.

"What set up?" asked Colby. She was so quiet eating crabs that we forgot she was there.

"Nothing, babe, go upstairs and get yourself cleaned up. I will run you a bubble bath," says Porter.

"Okay, daddy." Without hesitation, Colby gets up and runs upstairs. I love to see how his face lights up when he speaks to her. I've never seen him this gentle with anyone. She is changing him.

"Porter, it is okay for you all to go back home? I am going to be okay; it's not like we live too far away."

"No, no, no. I'm not missing the birth of another child of mine. I'm not missing the moment he opens his eyes. Or the screaming and violence against my hand while you push. I'm not missing it. We are at the home stretch now. You're due any day now. I can't leave you home alone now," he argues as if he is standing in front of a jury.

I like this new Porter. He cares about everyone, if not, more than himself.

"Okay, Porter, I want you to be there too." I back off of the subject.

"Porter, I want to ask you something. Did you and Lana have something before you and me?"

He took a sip of his beer before answering. I can see the hesitation on his face. Here comes the lie.

"No, I mean, I saw her around," he answers before stuffing a shrimp in his mouth.

"And that's it?" I ask. I was trying my best to read him to see if he was lying.

"Yes, that's it." I watched him while he drank the last sip of his beer and cracked open the last crab, which I'm confused about.

"Yeah, so I'm confused," I say.

"Confused about what?" He dropped the crab. The look on his face says, "What now!"

"What made you think that the last crab was yours? That's petty."

He smiled and silently tossed the crab to my side of the table.

The Day of Porter's Accident

I can't take it! I don't want to be pregnant anymore! This is ridiculous. I can't see my feet or my vagina. I need a fucking wax! It's hot, and I make funny pig noises when I laugh and cry. And I'm always crying! Yeah, it's been great around here. Porter has been taking care of me. Trish makes sure that I eat, and I cheat with a box of ice cream every now and then. Colby rubs my feet and, Eric and Torin decorated the nursery. But I'm still in this body, and I want out! After lying in this bed for an hour, I finally manage to get up. Of course, the phone rings.

"Hello," I answer in the most irritating disturbed voice possible.

"Aye, Bre. You alright this morning?" Porter sounds a little down.

"Yeah, I'm good. What's wrong, Porter."

"Man, I just found out some of the craziest shit."

"What is it?"

"I will have to explain it to you later. Right now, I'm just trying to get to the bottom of some things. Look, I have Colby. We are on our way to my parents' house."

"Your parents? Really? Well, tell them I said hi."

"I will... I will be back in a little bit. Listen, Aubrey, I know I've said it a million times, but I just want you to know, man. I'm going to do everything that I can to take care of all of us. I love ya'll. Ya'll are all I got. I know we have been through a lot, but I love you for real, Aubrey, and if I could take all of that stuff back, I would. You are the only person that ever really believed in me or saw my true potential. You are the only person that never lied to me or wanted something from me."

It sounds like he's crying by the change in his voice.

"Porter, babe, what's wrong? I ask.

"Nothing, nothing is wrong... I just need you to know that you are a good woman. You deserve so much more than what I've offered to you. So, I pray that when Carter wakes up and all of our new lives begin that he gives you everything that I couldn't. Just love him as you loved me."

"Okay, Porter," I sigh.

"Alright, I will hit you back later and lay off of the ice cream; your room stinks."

"Bye, boy!" I giggle and hang up.

****

I've taken three naps today. This baby is kicking my entire ass at this point. The phone is ringing on my bed, somewhere between my hot

Cheeto chips and my blanket. Never mind, it's under my thigh that I can barely lift.

"Hello."

"Hello, who is this?" I repeat, but the phone is silent. And then...

"Hey Aubrey, how is everything? How is the baby?"

"Who is this?" The voice sounds familiar, but I can't make it out because it sounds more like a whisper. Then boldly, she says, "It's Demari."

"Demari? Girl, what do you want?"

"Damn, Aubrey. I didn't know it was like that?"

"Yeah, it's like that. You are fake and a phony, and you can't be trusted. So, lose my number bitch."

I hung up the phone and blocked her number. She has some nerve calling me. Porter told me everything, and so did Eric. I don't know what her motive is, but she is like a baby Lana. I don't need her in my circle or my energy.

Trish comes to the door. Bre, can I talk to you about something?

****

How in the hell did we go from Trish spilling all of her dirty little secrets to rushing to the hospital?

"I think you sent me into labor!" I yell from the passenger side of the car.

"Why do you say that?" Trish yells back in panic.

"Because you came in my room, spilling your guts and all of these dirty little secrets. My body couldn't take it. Slow down, Trish, it's raining!"

"Okay, okay!" Trish looks like she is about to lose it. But if she hits another bump, she will be delivering this baby.

She picks up her phone to call Porter.

"He's not answering!" she yells.

Chapter 5
The Day After The Rain

Aubrey

They say that when life comes into the world, another leaves. I pray that's not in this case. Porter is lying in this hospital bed, nearly lifeless and barely breathing on his own. This dream quickly turned into a nightmare. What is all of this about? I find myself questioning God all of the time. I just don't understand. What did any of us do to deserve all of this tragedy? We are not perfect, but we are good people. Why is it so hard for us to just live regular, happy lives? What does that mean anyway?

Porter was turning the page in his life. He was trying to change.

I stand over him and examine his still and bruised body.

"Porter? Porter, I am here. Porter, I am so sorry that this has happened to you. To us. Porter, he is here. PJ is here. And he looks just like you. He has your eyes and your nose. He is strong, Porter; I think he is going to be solid and strong like his daddy. Porter, you hear me? You are strong, and you can beat this. We need you to beat this."

I wipe my tears as I raise his hand to interlock it with mine. Porter, no matter what, I'm never leaving you. Never. I feel a slight squeeze from his hand.

"I love you, Porter," I cry.

As I exit the hospital room, I hop over and sit in my wheelchair. I see Porter's parents walking towards me.

"Wait." I signal the nurse who is pushing me and PJ.

"Aubrey," says Mrs. Garrett.

"Yes, ma'am." I try to pull out a smile with tears in my eyes. She leans down and tries her best to hug me tight without squeezing the baby too.

"Oh, my goodness, Aubrey. I'm so happy to see you. I'm so sorry we were not here for all of this," she cries.

"It's okay, Mrs. Garrett," I reply.

"No, no, it's not. We should've been here for the birth of our grandchild and our son. We are sorry," Mr. Garrett cries out.

"May I hold him, Aubrey?" says Mrs. Garrett.

"Yes, ma'am."

She picks him up from my arms and cuddles him in her arms while Mr. Garrett leans over her with a soft smile as he glances down at PJ.

"This feels like Deja Vu'. He looks just like Porter when he was a baby. So strong and solid," she says without taking her eyes off of PJ. I smile, knowing that those were my exact words.

"Aubrey, we are here for whatever you need. You may get tired of us, but just know that we are here," says Mr. Garrett.

"Thank you so much. I'm upstairs on the 5th-floor room 2222. You are welcome to come by. We are supposed to go home in two days."

"We will be there," Mrs. Garrett replies as she passes PJ back to me.

When I get back to my room, I see I have fifteen missed calls from my mom and dad. I lay PJ down and call them back.

"Hey, mommy."

"Dear, we are on our way! How is everything, how is the baby?" she yells. By the sound in the background, they are still at the airport.

"PJ is great, but Porter..." I can barely get my words out without crying.

"Porter, what baby?"

"Porter got into a bad car accident last night. I don't know if he is going to live! He had surgery, but he is still in intensive care. They wouldn't even let me take the baby to see him at first. I just don't know what to do, Ma," I cry out.

"Oh, my Lord! Baby, we are on our way! We are on our way! Just hold on until we get there." I hang up the phone and lay PJ in his cradle next to my bed. With the ounce of energy that I have left, I get in the bed and try to curl up in a fetal position. My body is tired, and my spirit is exhausted.

Trish

I'm trying my best to get this house cleaned up. I don't want Aubrey and the baby to come home in a mess. Colby is upstairs playing in her room, and I don't have the guts to tell her what happened to her father. Or even worst, telling her that Grant and I got back together.

The number I had for Doc is going to voicemail. He has not popped up since all of this happened. I know he did this to Porter, but I am too afraid to go to the police.

While I am cleaning the countertops, the doorbell rings.

I run to the door before Colby comes running downstairs.

"Who is it?" I whisper.

"It's Grant." What in the hell is he doing here?

"Grant?" I opened the door, and he was standing at the front door in the flesh. Dressed in a tracksuit, I can tell it's a down day for him.

"Babe, what are you doing here?" I asked, puzzled.

"And how did you know where I lived?" I continued.

"Well, I'm here, because you didn't answer any of my calls and I was very worried. And I got your address from that last car ride you booked on my phone. So, what is going on? Is everything okay?" I can tell he was worried because his hands slightly tremble when he is under stress, although he won't admit it.

"No, everything is not okay. Last night Aubrey went into labor, and Porter got into a really bad car accident that has him in intensive care." I break down in tears.

"What? Wait, what are the doctors saying?" The concern on his face is more than I expected.

"They did the surgery, and now we just have to wait and see how his body will respond. Right now, they have him sedated. It's bad, Grant. It's really bad!" He pulls me towards him and kisses me on the forehead.

"Everything is going to be okay. Porter is going to be okay. Where is Colby?" Before I knew it, Colby was parading down the stairs.

"Mommy, can I..." She stopped in her tracks. Her face lit up with the biggest smile. She raced down the stairs to jump into Grant's arms.

"Grant!" she screamed as he hugged her so tight. They are both lit up with joy. I watch as a tear drops from Grant's eyes while he squeezes her tight. You would think that Grant was Colby's dad. He treats her like his own, and she loves him like crazy.

"Where have you been, big head?" Colby smiles while poking Grant in the forehead with her index finger.

"I've been away for work for a very long time, but I'm here now," he smiles and glances at me.

"I'm so happy to see you. Now I have you and daddy. Have you met my daddy?" she smiles.

"No, I haven't, but I hear he is quite the gentlemen," Grant replies while giving Colby his undivided attention.

"Well... I must say, I agree," Colby replies. Grant burst out laughing as he puts her down. Her vocabulary has grown rapidly since the last he saw her.

"Well, it looks like we may be seeing a lot of each other," he says. I elbow him to be careful of what he says to her.

"Okay, so maybe we can go on a date sometime. Mommy, I guess you can come too." She turns to me with a bossy stance as if she is calling all of the shots, or we are sharing yet another man.

"Well, I guess I will be there! Colby, go upstairs and get yourself cleaned up. You and I are going to hang out a little. We need to have a talk," I say.

"Okay, Mommy! See ya later, Grant the Ant." She runs up the stairs.

"Later, C- Baby," he replies.

"So, what now?" Grant turns to me.

"I don't know. All of this is so unexpected. Porter and I had a conversation about you and me before all of this happened, but we didn't talk about California yet. I really don't know." I take a seat on the sofa, and he joins me.

"Shhh. We still have time, and if it doesn't work out how we planned, I understand as long as I know that you are in this with me still. Take the time you need to get things on track, and I will support you the best that I can."

I grab him close to me and kiss him soft and sweet.

"I am so happy you are here," I whisper.

"I am not going anywhere, I mean, except California," we both laugh.

****

Colby and I pull up to our favorite yogurt spot.

"Honey Rush! Honey Rush!" she starts ranting.

"Welcome to Honey Rush Frozen Yogurt!" shouts the young teenage girl, cleaning the candy bar with her mouth filled with gummy worms.

Colby grabs a cup, and she goes to every yogurt machine and fills her cup with a sample of each. Then she goes to the toppings bar and gets a scoop of snickers and gummy bears.

"$8.75, ma'am!" says the girl after weighing Colby's giant cup of yogurt.

"8.75? You better eat every drop, little girl." She shy's away with a smile.

We take a seat at one of the empty tables. I watch her devour this large cup of yogurt. I figure this may be the best time to tell her about Porter or not, but I'm going for it.

"Colb, mommy has to tell you something."

"Please don't tell me we are going to one of those big department stores after this because my stomach can't take it," she sighs with vanilla yogurt covering her face.

"No, silly! It's something a lot more serious. So last night, Aubrey had the baby."

"Yayyyy! Finally, I have someone to boss around! Was it a girl or a boy?" she shouts.

"It's a boy, and his name is PJ, Porter Junior."

"That's the best she could come up with?" I am so used to Colby's dramatic, playful yet sarcastic personality that nothing she says surprises me.

"Listen, Colby; there is something else I need to tell you. Last night… Um… Last night… Your dad…" I am trying with all of my might to hold back my tears.

"Mommy, don't cry. What's wrong?" She drops her spoon and moves closer to put her arms around me.

"Last night, your dad got into a really bad car accident. He is in the hospital right now."

"Well, is he okay?" Her face changed instantly. I can feel her heartbreaking through my chest.

"Baby, I don't know. I did not want to be selfish and keep this from you. I would like you to decide to see him in the hospital or not."

"I want to see him. Can we go now?" she asks in a peaceful tone.

"Yes," I cry while wiping my eyes.

****

"Daddy? Daddy, I'm here." She walked into the room where Porter is resting with no hesitation. She spoke to him in the softest, most angelic voice, like an angel. I stood behind her in the doorway and let her have her time with him.

"Daddy, I love you. I know you are scared, and I know that it hurts, but it will be okay. Grandma said it's all God's plan. I don't know what that means, but she said it so… Daddy Grant came to see us. Remember when I told you about him? Mommy's friend? He is so nice, like you, Daddy."

She stood there, silent for a little while. I could hear her quiet sniffles. She grabbed his hand and placed her tiny little hand in his.

"We haven't been together that long, Daddy, so I hope you decide to stay." I walk up to her and grab her by the shoulder. She dives into my arms. I wish I could tell her that it is going to be okay, but I just don't know. Porter looks like he is barely holding on.

"Would you like to go see baby Porter?" I ask.

"Yes, please." She wipes her eyes and climbs up on the chair to give Porter a kiss on the cheek.

"See you later, Daddy. I love you, Banana Head." With all of his might, Porter smiles a little.

I give him a kiss on the forehead, and we leave the room.

"Mommy PJ is in this hospital?" She looks up at me while we walk towards the elevator.

"Yes," I answer.

We catch the elevator to Aubrey's floor and run into Eric and Torin.

"Hey, Ms. Colby!" shouts Eric.

"Hey, Mr. Eric! Do you like my purse?" She gives him a big hug.

"Of course, dear. It is stunning," Eric replies.

"How is she doing?" I ask Torin.

"She is doing okay, given the circumstances. She has a full house right now with all of the grandparents, so we dipped out, but I'm sure she will be happy to see ya'll," she replies.

"How are you doing?" ask Eric.

"I'm not sure yet. This is a lot at one time. I don't know how to feel or how to help. I just don't know," I cry.

"It's going to be okay. We are here for ya'll whatever you need," says Torin.

"Thank you."

"Bye, Ms. Colby!" says Eric.

"Bye!" she shouts.

When we walk into the room, Aubrey is sitting up laughing at her mom, dad, and another older couple.

"Grandma!" Yells Colby as she runs towards the other woman.

"Colby Bear!" The woman yells back. She jumps into the woman's arms. It's very clear that these are Porter's parents. So, I walk up to them with my hand out.

"Hi, I am Trish. Colby's mom."

"Well, Trish, we don't shake hands. We give hugs. It is so nice to meet you finally. We heard so much about you in so little time. I am Darlene, and this is my husband, Sam." She gives me a big hug, and Mr. Sam does too.

"Thank you for getting her home earlier. I'm sorry I didn't make it downstairs this morning. I had a hard time."

"We understand, baby. It's a lot on all of us," says Mr. Sam.

"Colby!" says Aubrey with a huge smile.

Colby jumps up and goes over to Aubrey's bed. She reaches up and gives her a big hug.

"I've missed you, my Colby." Aubrey squeeze Colby extra tight.

"I know right, I've missed you too. Is that my baby?" she smiles when she glances over at the baby bed.

"No, that's my baby, but your brother," Aubrey laughs.

"Well, you know what I mean." Colby walks over to the bed and leans in to get a good look.

"Wow, he looks like a doll. Can I hold him?" says Colby.

"Yes, you may, but only with help, okay?" says Aubrey.

"Okay…"

"Oh, Trish, this is my mom and Dad. Mom. Dad, this is Trish."

"Nice to meet you, Mr. and Mrs. Bryant."

"You too, Trish. Thank you for helping to care for my baby," says Mrs. Bryant.

"You are some kind of woman," she continues.

"Trish, how are you feeling?" Aubrey asks.

"Well, right now, I feel like I'm in the twilight zone. So much is happening. So much is going on at one time. I am… I'm sorry, I just don't know. I'm feeling so many emotions."

"That's understood. You don't have to explain yourself. I think we are all feeling the same," she replies.

"Have you seen Carter?" I ask.

"Yes, I have. They are still working on his memory, and he will start therapy in the next two weeks. His mom is here with him right now," Aubrey answers.

"Trish, I know we just met, but if you need anything at all, please know that we are here for you too. All of us. Something as small as dinner. It's not a problem," says Mrs. Bryant.

"Yes, this is all new to all of us, but we are here. I would love to have Colby for a few more days if that is okay with you? I know we are like strangers, but we are family now," says Mrs. Garrett.

"Um, yeah, sure. I do need to get some rest," I answer with relief.

"Ok, well, it's settled; we will pick her up after we leave here," says Mr. Garrett.

Mr. Bryant sat in the corner, so quiet. I recognized his face from college. I remember seeing him drop Lana off back on campus one night, freshman year. I remember because I was walking back to my dorm room after an evening class, and she was crying when she got out of the car. I didn't know who he was then, but I know now.

"I'm going to go grab a bite to eat from downstairs. Is anyone hungry?"

Everyone replied, "No."

I walk out of the room and get to the elevator.

As the elevator door shuts, a hand sticks in to stop it. On steps Aubrey's father. We are both silent while we watch the numbers drop on the elevator door. Then he says...

"I know we've met, but not formally. I know it was a long time ago, but please. I beg you; please do not say anything to Aubrey. Please."

I glanced at him sideways and exited the elevator without saying a word— the nerve of him. I am not in the business of bringing on more pain to Aubrey. She has already gone through enough.

****

"Hello, may I speak with Trish?" says an unfamiliar voice.

"This is she. How can I help you?" I reply.

"This is detective Charles Brass. I am a friend of Porter. I heard about the accident, and I want to just take some time to speak with you. Do you know of a Lana?"

"Yes, I do. She is in jail."

"Yes, I am aware. Before I got off the phone with Porter yesterday evening, he mentioned that Lana was calling and sending him letters, threatening him. I'm concerned that his accident may not have been an accident." I don't know if he is looking in the right direction.

"Is that possible? Because Lana cannot communicate with Porter, Aubrey, her ex-husband, or his wife. If so, she immediately gets time added to her sentence."

"Are you sure about that?" he asks.

"I know this was a part of her sentencing, but you never know. Lana is very sneaky and strategic," I answer.

"Okay, please keep my number if anything comes to mind. I just want to make sure there is no foul play going on," he responds.

"I will, and thank you, detective, for your concern." I have to find out what's really going on.

Chapter 6
True or False?

Aubrey

"It's been two weeks, and Porter is still sedated. Not much has changed. The doctor asked us to prepare for the worst, but Porter opened his eyes for the first time. He finally got the chance to meet PJ. Life is still crazy, but I appreciate the help I've been getting between Porter's parents and my parents. Trish and I have been getting a lot of free time. Trish finally broke the news to Colby that she and Grant are back together and getting married. The poor child is so confused. I hope she has a better understanding of relationships when she gets older because she has no hope right now.

Carter is moving around during his physical therapy. Thank God for that. He didn't lose as much memory as the doctors thought he would. He has lost mostly short-term memory more than anything, but he remembers everything that happened that day. Every day I'm making my rounds to check on him and Porter. I often wonder why God gave me this life. You know what I mean? What was so special about me that he figured I could take one hit after another. I'm so tired that I am tired of being tired."

I sit on this sofa and spill my entire life once a week, hoping that one day I will have nothing left to say. Per usual, Dr. Powell sits there in her wingback with her legs crossed, looking unbothered, waiting for a chance to speak.

"Aubrey, I know this has been a roller coaster of emotions, but you are one of the strongest people I know. Have you had any bad dreams?" she asks.

"Yes, I have. But now they are about Porter's crash. Me watching the whole accident but not able to help him. That is how I feel about everyone and everything right now. Helpless. The day Carter got shot, I felt guilty, and I felt helpless. It is so hard for me to look him in the eyes because I know that he is thinking, 'You did this to me.' And it's true. I did! I caused all of this. It's a miracle that he even woke up!" I can barely catch my breath. It feels like my heart is fluttering through my chest. A stream of tears run down my face.

"Aubrey, none of this is your fault. Lana did this to you. She built this devastation in your life. I'm not asking you to hate her or not to forgive her, but I am asking you not to blame yourself." She takes off her glasses and set her big brown eyes on me.

"Have you been to see her yet?" she asks.

"Dr. Powell, no. No, I haven't. I can't face her," I cry like a scared little girl, afraid to face her bully.

"You can, and you will, Aubrey. Do not let her defeat you. Take your power back." She balls up her fist to demonstrate strength.

"I will think about it, Dr. Powell. I'm going to head out. It's time for me to pick up PJ." I get up and grab my purse.

"Aubrey, please think about it." I see the concern on her face for me, but it's hard for me to face Lana.

****

The house is empty and quieter than it has ever been. PJ is still asleep after that ride from my parents' house. I want to drink a glass of wine so bad, but it showed up in my breast milk the last time I had a glass.

You know what? What the hell? I've pumped enough milk to last a lifetime. I take PJ to his nursery and lay him in his crib. I turn on his speaker to the sounds of rainstorms and his diffuser to shoot out a little eucalyptus mist. I turn on his small adapter and take the monitor with me. After making a bubble bath and turning on the sounds of Snoh Aalegra, I emerge my body in the water and pour myself a glass of wine.

Dr. Powell is right. The only way I can move past all of this is by facing Lana head-on.

****

I can barely open my eyes, but PJ's cries pulled me out of bed. I walk into the room to Porter, cradling PJ. He looks up and smiles.

"He's beautiful, Bre. We did a good job."

"Porter, what are you doing here?"

"I'm going to always be here, Bre."

I wake up and run to PJ's nursery. These dreams have to stop. I know I have to request through my lawyer to see Lana, so I give her a call.

"Aubrey, are you sure this is something you want to do?" she asks.

"Yes, yes, I am sure," I answer with hesitation.

"Alright then, I will call the jail to get you a visit for one o'clock this afternoon."

"Perfect, thank you."

"Not a problem, Aubrey. Guard your heart," she responds.

"Thank you for that." I hang up and call my mom.

"Mom, can you watch PJ for me? I have something I need to do."

"Of course, drop my sugar biscuit off." I can feel her smiling through the phone.

"Okay, we are on our way."

I hang up and call Eric while I am on the drive.

"I'm going to do it," I say when he picks up.

"You're going to do what?" Eric replies.

"I'm going to go see Lana."

"Oh, goodness, girl, did you pray?" he responds in a brass tone.

"No, but I should, huh? I'm so nervous."

"Girl, don't be. It's just Lana. She bleeds like you bleed. You walk in there boldly, just prepare yourself for whatever comes out of her mouth, because Lord knows she can twist your whole world upside down."

"Eric, I can do this. I can face her. I will call you when it's all over."

"Please do, because I got a feeling this is going to be a game-changer. And Aubrey, you may want to sage, meditate, pray, and take some garlic. Bless up, sis!" he laughs.

"Bye, Eric!" I laugh.

We pull up to the house, and my mother is at the door waiting for us.

"Hey, Ma." I pass her the car seat and diaper bag.

"Baby, are you alright? You look a little bothered," she asks.

"I'm okay, Ma. I just have to handle some business. I will be back in a few hours." I quickly get back into the car and pull off without waiting for a response from her.

I drove almost an hour to the prison in Jessup. And the anxiety in my belly has not calmed down a bit. I walk into the front entrance, and the guard is standing there like today is her last day on earth.

"Name?" she says without looking up at me.

"Aubrey Bryant," I respond.

"Identification?" I pull out my driver's license and hand it to her.

"Who are you here for?" she states in a dry, uninteresting tone.

"Lana Jackson," I answer as she passes me my ID.

"You mean Lana Cortez?" She must've changed her name back to Cortez when she signed those divorce papers. Her last name is Smith, but that is another story.

"Yes, Lana Cortez," I reply.

"Place your things in a locker and take a seat. She will be down shortly."

My anxiety is off the charts. My heart is beating out of my chest, and I feel like I will throw up. Every minute is worse than the last one. Finally, they call my name. I can't let her see me like this, so my poker face is on. The guard leads me to the room and set me at a booth with a telephone. I am the only other visitor in the room. Finally, she walks out, and my stomach drops. I could barely recognize her without lashes and makeup. Her hair is braided in two cornrows going straight back. She looks like hell.

She doesn't blink, not once when she looks at me. She stares me dead in the eyes as she sits down in her seat. I pick up the phone. I was anticipating for her to pick up her line. Finally, she slowly picks up.

"I was wondering if this day would ever come," Lana says in a sarcastic tone as she taps her fingers on the table.

"Hello Lana, how are you?" I ask, barely wanting to say anything.

"Oh, it's all sunshine and palm trees in here. I am living my best life. Hair done; nails done. You know…" she says sarcastically as if it's my fault that she is in here.

"How am I? Is that a real question? How do you think I am, Aubrey? I am in prison," she snarls at me as she pierces her eyes into mine.

"Well, Lana, you put yourself there. You did that," I respond.

"You're right, I did. So how is the new baby? I would've called you to say congrats and all, but you know… I am restricted from calling you, Porter, and my weak-ass husband."

"You mean your ex-husband."

"You know what I mean. Look, why are you here?"

Before I can speak a word, I have to build my words together in my head.

"Lana… I came here for answers. I can't sleep without seeing your face, and I want to know, I need to know what happened? Of all people, why did you come for me? Why did you try to kill me? I've done everything I could to be a good friend to you. Why, Porter?"

"Why, Porter? Why Porter, what?" she seemed thrown back.

"Porter is in the hospital. He was in a bad car accident. I know you had something to do with it." When I walked in here, I knew that Lana was behind all of this, but the way her expression changed. I just don't know.

"Aubrey, I didn't do anything to Porter or anybody."

"I don't believe shit you say, who sent the letters to me."

"What? I cannot have any contact with you. I'm surprised they let you in here. I'm being set up."

"I don't feel bad for you. Because all of this started because of you. What did I ever do to you, Lana?"

For the first time in a long time, I didn't see vengeance in her eyes; I saw something else, but I am bewildered. Her eyes feel up with tears, but they never fall.

"You just don't get it, do you? Or are you so caught up in your shit that you can't see mine? You have no idea how it feels to be me. You let this happen. You let all this happen!"

"I don't know what you're talking about, Lana." I am eager to know what's going on. What am I missing?

"You know exactly what I am talking about. You knew... You knew everything! And you laid in that bed and never said a word!"

"Lana, what are you talking about?" My heart is beating so fast, neither one of us can control our breathing. She looks like she wants to bust through the shield that's separating us.

"He came into my room every night and told me he would love me the right way. Give me what I deserved because I was a woman. That man! Your sweet DADDY came into my room almost every night that I lived in that house. And put his di-!"

"What? No, no, no, no- You're lying! You're a fucking liar! You will not pull me into another one of your lies! Liar!"

I slammed down the phone and jumped out of my seat.

The correctional officer standing behind me walks up to me and taps me on the shoulder.

"Okay, ma'am, this visit is over."

Lana sat there in her seat with the monitor still in her hand. When I turned around, I finally watched a tear drop from her eyes. At that moment, I knew the truth.

****

"So, how did it go?" Dr. Powell sips on her tea. I sit there quietly, still in shock.

"What part? The part when I go to see Lana, and she tells me that the entire time she lived with me in high school, my father was raping her or the part when he actually confesses?" I try to hold back my tears once again, but I can't. I'm so fucking angry. I'm facing betrayal once again.

Dr. Powell put down her cup of tea. "Oh goodness, Aubrey, oh goodness... I know this has to be a lot on you. If you don't want to talk about it, I understand."

"I get in my car and drive to my mom's house. When I walk in the door, my mom is holding PJ and rocking him to sleep. 'Ma, where is daddy?'" My heart is still racing from earlier.

"He is upstairs in his office. Is everything okay, baby? You look a little shook," she asked me while putting PJ in his basket.

"No, I'm not okay." I race upstairs to my dad's office.

"When I get to his office, he is at his computer typing. He looks up at me and takes off his reading glasses. I feel like a little girl again confronting my father. This is my dad; he has been my best friend, my everything. The only person that truly understands me, my angel, my knight. I pace his office floor, forcing myself to speak what I've just heard, but the words just won't come out."

"Daddy, I have to ask you something."

"He gets up from his seat and comes around to the front of his desk."

"Bean, what's wrong? Is everything okay?"

"Daddy, I need you to tell me the truth." He leans back on his desk. His eyes drop to the floor. I stop pacing and walk up to him. Before I could say anything else, he takes three big breaths and…"

"Yes, I did it," he says.

"You did what?" I say with anger.

"You did what, daddy?"

"I." My mother walks into the room and interrupts.

"She wanted it. I saw how she would look at my husband. That little sneaky bitch, she wanted it." My mother slowly walks into the room with pride and anger all at once.

"Ma… You knew?" I think daddy is as shocked as I am. We both stood there in shock. I am lost for words. He looks as frozen as ice.

"Yes, I knew! You nasty bastard," she said to dad and me.

"I snuck out of bed every night. I had a video camera set up in Aubrey's room just in case you tried my baby. When I replayed it, there was nothing there. One night, you turned over to check to see if I was asleep. You snuck down the hallway to Lana's room. I thought I would catch you on top of her, but instead, she was in control. I tried to walk into the room, but I couldn't. I was frozen. I could've called the police, I could've killed you, but I knew my position, and this wasn't rape. You were fucking a sixteen-year-old. Besides the fact that I didn't have my own income, because you so-called 'Wanted to take care of me.' - Aubrey would have died if she knew you were having an actual fucking affair with her best friend! So, I let you have your fun, but I had mine too. Ask your golfing buddy Jake. As soon as I saw fit, I put that little slut out of my house and went on a few mini vacations with Jake. 'Girls trip' my ass."

"I couldn't believe what I was hearing. I felt like the room was spinning."

"I guess you think you saved the day? Ma, what kind of woman would allow her husband to rape a sixteen-year-old girl? Consent or no consent, it's rape! You are just as bad as he is! Ya'll are fucking disgusting!"

She walks up to me and points her finger in my face. "Listen here, little girl, it wasn't rape! She was fucking my husband!" she trembled as tears fell from her blush cheekbones."

"It was rape," he interrupted. It looked like his soul broke the moment he said those words. Like he was relieved to say them but disgusted at the same time. Tears streamed down his face, and his eyes were bloodshot red.

"It was rape from the very beginning. The moment she came to live with us, I had my eyes on her. She was vulnerable. She would cook breakfast in the morning when you were gone to work. She said she used to cook breakfast for her father, but he would just throw it away. Some days, I would bring her to my office and have one-on-one therapy sessions with her before seeing my other clients. She needed someone to love her. Instead of loving her like a father, I took total advantage of what I wanted her to be. I wanted her to love me as my wife should. One night I went into her room, and I seduced her. I told her that if she wanted to stay here, she would have to play along. And that's what she did. I taught her. She wanted to stop. She wanted to leave, but whatever I had to do or say to make her stay, I did. I knew she didn't have anywhere else to go. When you put her out, I knew there was nothing else I could do to keep her there. She couldn't go back home. When she was gone, I started to lose it. It became an obsession. Like I had to have her. She was staying from place to place. I knew that she would call me sooner than later. After graduation, she finally called. She said she needed money and didn't have anywhere to go. I rented her an apartment downtown. It was her place. I told her we didn't have to do what we were doing again, but I don't know. I just couldn't control myself around her. I took it even when she didn't want me to. I did it. I did all of it. I'm so sorry, Aubrey."

I could barely move. I was frozen. My mom charged at him, kicking, hitting, and screaming.

"You son of a bitch! Get out of my house! Get out! You bastard! Why? Why did you do this?" She breaks down and swings until she is out of energy. He stands there and takes every punch.

"Still unable to move, I stood there. No thoughts. No feeling… numb… unable to speak… unable to feel… just… still. Tears fall down my cheek. My heart rate slows down. It felt like it was stopping. I am the cause of all of this. I am the center. This all started because of me. My mom ran up to me and grabs a hold of me. She puts her arms around me to hug me, but I refuse to hug her back."

"Aubrey, I am so sorry, baby. Baby, I'm sorry. Please forgive me." When she releases me, I walk away without looking at her. My dad walks by the both of us, runs down the stairs and out of the door. I can hear the car pull off. I slowly walk down the stairs and pick up PJ. I put him in his car seat and grab his diaper bag. "Will you be bringing him by tomorrow?" my mom asks in desperation.

"Aubrey, please don't keep me away from my grandbaby," she starts crying frantically. Without saying a word, I walk out to my car, buckle PJ in, get in, and pull off.

"Aubrey, please!"

She is standing in the driveway. I look in the rearview mirror until I can't see her anymore.

Dr. Powell sits there like she is in a trance. Finally, she breaks her silence.

"Wow… Aubrey… You just cannot get a break. Aubrey, it's time for you to start completely over. I don't know how and I don't know exactly when, but it's time for you to step out of all of this dysfunction. It is total mayhem."

This will probably be my last therapy session with Dr. Powell. She doesn't know that, but it is. I don't need my life to be entertainment for her, and that is what it feels like. I need help. Yeah, she's right; I need to start over. I need a fresh start, but it won't be here. She can find someone else to view as a blockbuster movie.

Lana

"Hi, Lana. How are you doing today?" My therapist's name is Ms. Jean Conard. She is a very put-together woman. Word in the prison is that she served a few years in prison, but her record was expunged. She got a Masters's in social work and came back here to become a therapist for the prisoners. What she did was noble. I get it, but once I leave these grounds, I'm never coming back.

I walk into her office and take a seat on the sofa. As always, she is sitting there waiting for me with a cup of tea in her hand and peppermint tea for me. She has a peaceful expression on her face as usual. I play with the string hanging from my jumper.

"I don't know how I'm doing?" I finally answer after spending at least a minute in silence, trying to gather my thoughts.

"I heard you had a visitor."

"Yes, I did."

"Well, who was it?" She scrambles for answers waiting to hear my response.

"It was Aubrey."

"Your best friend, Aubrey?" She takes off her glasses and unfolds her legs.

"That's right. My best friend, Aubrey." I roll my eyes at the "best friend" title she put on it.

"Okay, well, how did it go?"

"I shift gears on her. I just want to talk. I want to say everything that I've held on to. Everything that I should've told Aubrey. Everything that I wanted to remind her of."

As my mind flashes back into the past, all of my feelings come back as if they never left:

"It was the last day of school, before summer. I was walking down the street on my way home. Aubrey and I had just split off. She lived a few blocks away from me. My mom said she would be picking me up from school, but she didn't show up, so I just walked. On my way home, I stopped in the store to grab some gummy bears. There were a group of guys walking down the street. It looked like they were coming from the basketball court. One of them had a basketball in his hands. Before they could get closer, I started walking so that we would be a little further apart. I opened my gummy bears and got on my way. The guy with the basketball walked up to me."

"Hey!" he said. He was so damn fine, tall brown skin, charming, and a beautiful smile.

"Hey," I answered in the most uninterested tone I could come up with. I kept walking and didn't break a smile at him.

"Why are you walking so fast?" he asked while trying to keep up with me.

"I got somewhere to be," I said.

"Where?" he continued to question.

"None of your business creep. Why do you have so many damn questions?" I reply.

"Oh… You are feisty. I like that."

He jumps in front of me to stop me in my tracks and put out his hand for me to shake it. With a big smile, he says, "My name is Porter. What's your name?" I walk around him.

"Lana is my name." I roll my eyes and proceed with my walk.

"Okay, Lana Is My Name… I like you."

"You don't even know me. So how could you like me?"

"Okay, you got it. Well, I like what I see at the moment. So how about we cut the anti-social act and get to know one another?"

I look up at him, and he smiles again. I honestly couldn't resist him. He was beautiful and charming, but I didn't want him to know that.

"I will think about it," I reply.

"Well, how will I know that you are thinking about it if I can't contact you?" he asks.

"You won't."

"How about this. Let me take you out. If you don't find me as interesting as I find you, you will never have to speak to me again. And I won't bother you. Deal?"

He stuck his hand out to seal the deal.

"Okay fine. Deal." I shook his hand and kept walking. I was already into him the moment he walked up to me.

"Later on, that week. Porter and I went to the summer carnival. We had so much fun. Aubrey and her family went to visit family in Virginia for half of the summer, so I never had the chance to talk to her. Porter and I spent our whole summer together. One night Porter's dad let him borrow his car. Porter had just got his permit. We drove all the way to D.C. We walked around the monuments, went to the white house, and ate a shit load of ice cream and tacos. That night was like a dream. Porter took me away from my problems. The shit I was dealing with at home. He took me from all of it. We sat in his father's car, listened to music, and talked about our plans after high school. The next thing I know, Porter and I were in the back seat of his daddy's car. He was the first man to ever touch my body. It didn't feel like sex. It felt like I was floating on air. I forgot it was my first time because the pain only existed for a moment. He made me feel safe. Like nothing I ever felt before. Afterward, he told me he would be headed to North Carolina for basketball camp and would be back a few days before school started. I was devastated, but he assured me that we would pick up where we left off.

The rest of my summer went downhill from there. My mother left me with my dad. And he reminded me every day that she hated me and he hated me more. I sat outside every night after that, waiting for Aubrey to return home from Virginia. Two weeks before school started, she finally returned. One day my father beat me up so bad, I ran to Aubrey's house and knocked on the door. Aubrey's mom opened the door."

"Hi Lana, what's wrong?" she asked as she opened the screen door and welcomed me in.

"Can I speak with Aubrey?" I asked.

"Sure, you can. Aubrey!" Aubrey came running down the stairs.

"Hey, Lana!" She was so happy to see me; her face lit up until she got closer and saw that I was not happy at all.

"Lana? What's wrong?" We sat down on the couch, and I poured out my heart like a flood.

"My mother left us. She moved to Las Vegas with her boyfriend, and she didn't even say goodbye. My father has been beating me every day since then. I can't go back, Aubrey. I can't," I cried.

"Oh, my God!" Tears weld up in her eyes, then she laid my head on her shoulders.

"We will figure out something."

"That night, I went back home. My father was at the door with a belt in his hand. I could smell the liquor on his breath. He drank so much the scent was coming out of his pores. He beat me for almost thirty minutes. I remember looking up at the clock on the stove. He swung that belt, not caring where it landed. When he was done, he drank another bottle and passed out. I went to the bathroom to look at myself in the mirror. It hurt for me to do so much as blink, so I knew my face was in bad shape. I had cuts and swollen whelps on my face from the belt. So were my neck and arms. I slowly went into my room and packed my bags and suitcase that my mom bought me for my birthday. She said we were going to take a girl's vacation this summer, but of course, that never happened. I had so many bags, and I didn't want to walk back and forth to get them. I knew that would wake him up. So, I threw them out of my room into the back yard. The only way he would hear them is if the back door was open. I crept down the bottom of the stairs, and he woke up."

"Lana, come turn on this tv for me." I turned on the television, and before I got to the movie channel, he was back out like a light. I didn't take chances with sneaking back up the stairs to grab anything else, so I went into the kitchen and quietly snuck out of the back door. I picked up my bags, and I ran as fast as I could until I got on Aubrey's block. I knocked on the door until I got an answer. When she opened the door, she pulled me in with all of my bags.

"Oh my God, Lana. Look at your face!" She grabbed half of my bags and headed upstairs as I followed.

She took me to her room. "You can sleep in my room. I will sleep in the guest room. Don't worry, Lana, you won't have to go back there. I will talk to my parents in the morning."

"The next day, Aubrey's parents agreed to let me stay there for as long as I needed to. They gave me the guest room. While I was unpacking, I heard a knock at the door. I knew it was my father. I walked to the top of the stairs, too afraid to go down. I stayed there. Aubrey opened the door."

"Where is Lana?" Before she had the chance to answer, Mrs. Karen was at the door.

"She is here, and she will not be leaving with you." She stood boldly in his face. My mother had never stood that firm with my father.

"Lady, that is my child, so if she doesn't get down here, I am going to call the police and have you arrested for kidnapping," he yelled.

"Oh yeah… Let's see what they think about all of the scars and bruises that poor child has across her face. Then we will see who's going to be arrested." I didn't hear another word from him. All I heard was the door shut. I was relieved. It felt like a weight was lifted off of my shoulders. I went back to my room and finished unpacking. Mrs. Karen walked up to my room and said,

"You are safe here." She closed my door and walked away.

"I felt safe. I felt like I finally had people who cared about me.

A few weeks later, school started. Mrs. Karen took me and Aubrey school shopping. Colin was barely home during that time. I barely saw him. He was a therapist, but he traveled to a lot of conferences during the summer.

I knew Porter would be home from camp, but I didn't know how to get in touch with him. He went to William G. High School. My plan was to stop by his house. I told Aubrey a little about him, but not much. I never told her his name. I just called him P. He was special to me, and I wanted to keep him to myself. A few days after school started, I walked into the lunchroom and sat down with my tray, waiting for Aubrey to come out. Then, who walks in with a basketball cuffed under his arm? None other than Porter. My eyes glowed up. My first thought was, what in the hell was he doing there? I got so excited I dropped my tray and walked towards him. But then... Aubrey walked into the cafeteria. I watched him watch her. When she walked by, he pulled her by the arm. She turned around and looked at him, and I knew she was as hooked as I was. I watched them fall head over hills for each other in seconds.

I went back to the table, grabbed my backpack, and went out of the back cafeteria exit. I left school that day and went home. I played sick for a whole week. Aubrey came to check on me every day, but I brushed her off by turning over and pretending that I was asleep. I never told her that Porter was the guy I fell stupid for, and neither did he. When she finally introduced us, he acted like he didn't know me. Like I wasn't the same girl he took to DC and had in the back of his daddy's car. It hurt until it didn't hurt anymore. She asked me a million times about P. I just told her he moved away. In my mind, the guy I knew as P did move away because Porter wasn't the guy I fell so hard for."

She put down her pen and pad. I can tell she was so drawn in. It was like watching a movie. Her expression was of a mother who wanted to cuddle her child.

"A few months later, Colin approached me. It started with a tap on the shoulder, then a rub on the knee, then deep stares. When I first moved in, I saw him as a father figure, someone I could trust and confide in. I had enough pain, enough people that I couldn't trust, but he treated me like he cared about me and what I was going through. He took the time to listen to me. Until it became all about what he wanted. One night, he came into my room. I remember looking at my alarm clock. It was 4:22 in the morning. Everyone was still asleep, including me. First, he woke me up with a tap on my shoulders. Then he asked me how I felt about him, and I told him he was a good person. He said that he loved me in a different way. I knew this was going somewhere, but I didn't want it to. He said he wanted me to make him feel like a man again. He pulled off my pajama pants, and he went down on me. I kept saying, "please don't do this." I jumped up and pushed my body to the top of the bed. I squeezed my legs tight and tried to cover myself. I could see in his eyes that he was going to fight for it. I couldn't believe what was happening. I saw a different person when I looked at him—like his soul died. He got close to me and put his hands in between my legs. He whispered in my ear, "I will make sure you are taken care of if you make sure I am taken care of. You know what I'm saying?" He pulled my body down and got on top of me. Without saying another word, he opened my legs up and put his-"

Before I knew it, I'm in tears. I have never told this to anyone.

"From that moment on, it turned into a consistent thing. He would even pick me up from school and take me to an apartment he had during his lunch break. I often wondered if this is where he took all of his girls. Sometimes I wouldn't show up, but he would threaten to put me out. Our relationship never got physically violent, but he made me feel like I had no one else in this world. He forced me into sex plenty of times until I just stop fighting it. I think he enjoyed the fight in me. He was right, though; I didn't have anyone else. The one thing I learned from Colin is how to manipulate to get what I want. After Karen put me out, I had to figure things out for myself. Sometimes I would use sex; other times, I would just play the game. Like a man. I made him feel needed, he made sure I had a place to live, but my breaking point came when-"

"Oh, goodness. I'm sorry, Lana. We have to finish this up at our next session. We have gone over, and I have other patients waiting to see me." She looks at her watch and immediately picks up her pad.

I get up off of the sofa without speaking another word.

"And Lana… Thank you for sharing today. This is a good start to your recovery."

I walk out of her office and down the hallway. All of the other inmates are in the auditorium for some talent bullshit that they put together. I take this chance to go outside to the garden and dig up the moonshine I had sitting for the last month. A few sips and I'm inebriated. I hear everyone leaving out of the auditorium, and as soon as I see fit, I join the population and go back to my cell.

I get on the top bunk and pass out.

Aubrey

"So, I know you are wondering where I've been. You know it's hard for me to come into hospitals since my dad died, man. It's hard for me to see you like this. Ryan said he would be by to see you again. You know that fool is getting married. He keeps saying that he hates that this accident inspired him to grow up and settle down, but it's true. That fool is actually getting married. She's beautiful too. Hopefully, he doesn't screw this one up. Look, man, I'm gonna get out of here. Stay cool, P, and come back to us." Preston leans over and kisses Porter on the forehead. I stand in the doorway and let him finish his visit before I interrupt.

"Hey, Preston." He turns around.

"Hey, Aubrey! What's up, girl!" He moves in to give me a hug.

"I'm good Pres… It's so nice to see you."

"Yes, you too. You don't even look like you just dropped a baby. You're looking, good girl. How is PJ doing?"

"He is doing good. He is greedy, that's for sure. He is starting to look like his daddy more and more."

"Look, I meant to call you. A detective came to talk to me about Porter's accident. They were asking me about Lana. I think they think she has something to do with it."

"I thought so too, but I went to see Lana, and she had no idea all of this happened to Porter. She even denied the letter I received. She was ordered not to have any contact with me, Porter, or her ex-husband. If so, she would get a longer sentence."

"Then who would do something like this?" he asks, just as puzzled as I am.

"I don't know, Preston. Maybe this is all a coincidence. Maybe I am being paranoid. It was a rainy day. That could've been anybody. There has been a lot of hit and run accidents going on lately."

"You might be right, Bre, but I don't know my gut is telling me something different. You just make sure that you are careful. Take care of my nephew, and if you need me for anything, just holla. Babysitter, diapers, whatever. I got you." He gives me a big hug.

"Thank you, Pres, I appreciate it. Porter is lucky to have friends like you and Ryan."

"No, he was lucky to have a woman like you. Look, I'm going to head out. Take care of yourself." He gives me another hug and leaves.

"Man, this has been some kind of week, you wouldn't believe. Well, maybe you would believe it. I need one of your 'tough love' talks right now because I feel like I'm about to bitch up and crawl up into a dark hole. I feel so alone, and I feel betrayed. I'm back to feeling like everything about my life is a lie. I can't get a break."

"You are not alone; I am here with you." Carter is standing in the hospital room door with a cane in his hand when I turn around. He uses it to walk until he is fully dependent on himself. With a big smile, he says, "I used to love that song."

"You are terrible," I laugh.

"That song was the shit back in the day. No, but for real. I know it took me some time to come around and get back right, but I appreciate you staying by my side Aubrey. And that's solid when I say I'm here for you."

"Carter, I'm the reason you are here in the first place. If anything, it should've been me spending months lying in that hospital bed."

"Naw, don't say that. I wouldn't wish that on my worst enemy."

"Yeah, but that is how I feel. I'm so sorry that I pulled you into all of this mess."

"I pulled myself in. I came to you. I may have forgotten a few things, but the way I feel for you hasn't changed. I still love you, Aubrey. I'm here for you, and I'm here for PJ. Even when Porter is back on his feet. I'm here." It feels a little awkward with him pouring out his heart while Porter is lying in this bed, but I guess this time is better than any other.

****

"Lana, wake up." I open my eyes, and Officer Kelley is standing over me.
"What? What time is it?" I say.

"It's eleven." She looks at her watch.

"In the morning?" I ask.

"Yeah, you slept all through the night. I told Officer Kelley you weren't feeling well." My bunkmate Cassie replies. She is in here for stabbing her husband after she caught him cheating with his coworker.

"Thanks, C," I say after I jump down off of the top bunk.

"Lana, you got another visitor today." Officer Kelley is leaned up against my cell. She's cool. I couldn't stand her funny looking ass when I first got here, but she grew on me.

"Must be my lucky week." I shrug without any care at all. I follow Kelley down to the visiting area.

"So, who is it?" I ask Kelley. She turns around with a tight look on her face.

"Do I look like your assistant?" I just ignore her smart-ass remarks. She must be in a shitty mood.

I enter the room, and I immediately stop in my tracks. It feels like all of the wind has been knocked out of my body. He has got a nerve showing up here. My heart is racing. I feel all of my emotions going crazy. This son of a bitch! What is he doing here? He looks like he has lost his best friend. Like his life is over. Well, join the fucking party, bastard. I sit down at the table and stare at him with as much hate as I can build up.

"It's just like Aubrey to try and clear her own conscience of guilt. What in the actual fuck are you doing here? I guess they figure since no one was on my visiting list that everyone was invited."

"How are you doing, Lana?" Colin's words tremble as he speaks. I hope he is not expecting this to go well.

"Please don't act like you give a damn about me. What do you want?" He sits there in silence for a few minutes. Tears roll down his face.

"I'm sorry," he whispers.

"I'm sorry for what I did to you. Please don't blame Aubrey for this; she didn't know." I felt my heart plunge into the pit of my stomach. I had finally come face to face with pieces of my pain. So much time has passed, and so much damage was done. I have damage on top of damage.

"So, what do you want from me? HUH? Permission to not feel guilty? Advice on how to move on with your life? FORGIVENESS? If this glass weren't in between us, I would kill you myself. I would watch life escape from your body. I had two, not one, but TWO abortions and a miscarriage because of you and that other motherfucker. I couldn't carry a baby if I wanted to. You will never understand my pain! You will never understand how it feels to be rejected, disrespected, and taken advantage of by every man you ever loved. You did this shit to me! You, my daddy, and that bastard Porter! I had a man that loved me. Thomas really loved me. And I used and abused him until I had nothing left, because how could someone actually love me? Right? Not me... I've been worthless to everyman who has been in my presence. But I thank you because you taught me how to use my pain to get whatever the fuck I wanted. You taught me that. You're the MVP. So, you can keep your tears and your apology. You are a piece of shit on a stick, and I hope you die a lonely death, you son of a bitch!"

"Guard!"

I drop the phone, wipe my overflow of tears, and carry my power back to my cell. When I turn around, I can see him still sitting at the phone booth with the phone to his ear.

Fuck that! Fuck his apology! Fuck how he feels! He got what he wanted! He didn't care about what I felt, neither did my coward ass father, neither did my mother, and damn sure not Porter. So, fuck them all! I am who I am thanks to them. They didn't give a rat's ass if I would be okay or not. They need my forgiveness; I don't need there's. So, to hell with them all.

I get back to my cell, and Cassie is packing her things.

"What's going on, Cas?"

"I'm being transferred. I don't know what in the hell is going on." She pulls all of her pictures off of the wall.

"Damn, is everything okay?" I ask.

"I don't know, L. I want you to keep your head up. I know you say that you have a bad rep on the outside, but you are not half bad in my eyes. Relearn yourself, find out who you really are without all of that shit."

"Thank you, girl." She gives me a tight hug, grabs her things, and leaves the cell.

Aubrey

I step out of the shower to a knock at the door. I call for Trish to answer, but I forgot that she and Colby have been spending most of their time with Grant. He has been staying in a hotel until he finds a place. I throw on a tee shirt and sweat pants and rush down the stairs before the knocks wake up PJ.

I open the door, and a tall, handsome, dark skin man built like a linebacker; is standing in my doorway.

"Can I help you?" I ask as I profile him.

"Hi Aubrey, I am a friend of Porter. My name is Detective Charles. On the day of his accident, we were on the phone. He was receiving calls and letters from a woman named Lana. He was being threatened by her."

I open the door to welcome him in.

"Come on in. You can sit anywhere. Would you like something to drink? I am making tea for myself."

"Tea is fine." He takes a seat on my sofa. I walk into the kitchen, put on a pot of water, and grab two mugs from the cabinet.

"From my understanding, she is the same woman who is in jail for attempting to kill you and shooting your friend Carter." He pulls out a writing pad to refer to for information.

"Yes, she is, but there is no way that she had something to do with Porter's accident."

"How are you so sure?" He turns around to face me in the kitchen.

"Well, to be honest, I'm not sure… Her past has proven that she can manipulate people to do whatever she wants them to do. That is very clear, but I went to see her. Two things were clear to me. During court, she was ordered not to contact Porter, myself, or her ex-husband and his wife. She would receive more time if she did. I doubt that she would send those letters in her name, knowing the consequences. I also doubt that she got someone to do it because she would have covered her tracks and used them as pawns instead of calling and writing letters herself."

"So, what are you suggesting?"

"After sitting down face to face with Lana, I realized that she is holding on to some pain. I can't say that she is remorseful, but I do believe that she is tired of hurting others and being hurt. I just don't think that is who she wants to be anymore. I think she may have been setup. My question to you is, why do you think that someone hit Porter purposely?"

Charles goes into a folder and pulls out a letter from Lana.

"Porter sent a picture of this letter to me the day that we were on the phone. He was complaining about a phone call he had just received from Lana. He wanted to do something about it. He never said if the call came from a jail phone or a regular phone. He just mentioned that she was in jail."

"Can I see that?" He walks into the kitchen as I am preparing the cups of tea and hands me the letter. I hand him his mug.

"Whoever wrote this knows everything about Porter and Lana's relationship dynamic or at least a good amount of it," he exclaims.

I read over the letter a few times, and it is very similar to the letter I received from Lana. I kept it just in case I needed proof if something crazy happened.

"Give me a second, Charles. I will be right back." I rush upstairs to grab the letter out of my nightstand. I hear PJ cooing in his room, so I pick him up and carry him back downstairs with me.

"This is the letter I received from Lana. Trish gave it to me after I delivered PJ."

"Oh, wow, is that Porter Jr.? Can I see him?" I lean PJ down so that Charles can take a glance at him, but of course, I am not going to let him hold him. I don't know this man from a can of paint. I do remember Porter mentioning him when all of this went down. He was the guy who got him out of the confession room when he and Lana were arrested.

"Man, he looks just like Porter. No offense, but you had nothing to do with this," he laughs.

"It's okay; I've heard it a million times." He opens the letter.

"You said Trish gave it to you, right?" he asks.

"Yes, she did."

"Well, what is her involvement in all of this?"

"Trish doesn't have any involvement in anything. The letter was in an envelope never opened. She bought me all of my mail. It was difficult for me to get to the end of the driveway and back, further into my pregnancy. So, every day, she went for me."

"Okay, I understand." He took a sip of his tea and analyzed the letters a little more.

"The handwriting is different." He put both letters on the kitchen counter, and he took a good look at them again.

"Can I see?" He slid both letters closer to me.

"Yes, I see. And neither one of these are Lana's handwriting," I say as I quickly notice the change in her signatures.

"Well, how could you know for sure? People change their signatures all of the time," he replies.

"Yeah, that's true, but I used to work for Lana when she first opened her magazine company. She has two different signatures, and neither one of them look like that. Also, she makes the edges of her letters more rounded than sharp. Even when writing fast, she wrote the same way. This is not her writing at all." I walk away from the letters and pick up my tea.

"Wow, you have a good eye. You should've been a detective," he says with a grin.

"Yeah, maybe," I smile humbly.

"Do you plan to go and see Lana?" I ask.

"Not just yet. Something is telling me to hold off. She's not going anywhere," he cleverly suggests.

"Well, Aubrey, it looks like we have a full-on investigation that is about to begin." Charles puts down his half-full cup of tea and picks up his folder and the letters.

"Is it okay if I take your copy?" he asks.

"Yeah, sure, and please keep me updated on the case." We walk towards the front door.

"I will… Thank you for everything." I open the door to let him out.

"No problem, Porter is my boy. Take care of that King you have right there."

"Will do." I shut the door and get back to my tea. But I can't stop thinking. Who in the hell could've done this?

Chapter 7
Always, Always

"He is walking a lot better now, Aubrey. You should be proud." Nurse Patricia walks me into Carter's room. He is packing up and preparing to leave.

"The day has finally come!" I say to Carter as I pick up his bags.

"Are you ready?" I ask.

"I've been ready to go. Is my mom here?" he asks.

"No, just me. Your place in Harlem is still the way you left it. Thank God you owned the place, because otherwise, your landlord would have been on your ass," I laugh.

"That's not funny... Am I that far behind?" He sits down in the wheelchair, and I push him down the hallway.

"No, actually, you're not behind at all. I was just kidding. While you were in the hospital, your amazing secretary, whom I must say should get a raise when you decide to go back to work; has been holding it down since I was unable to get there every month."

"Oh damn, she paid my bills?"

"No, actually, Porter did..."

"What?" He looked so complexed yet relieved. From that point to the elevator, he was silent.

"Hey, Bre, can we stop by Porter's room, please?"

"Yeah, sure we can. The nurses were cleaning him up when I left, but I'm sure they are done by now."

When we get to the room, Carter gets out of the wheelchair.

"Do you mind giving me a minute?" he asks.

"No, sure. I will be right here." I stood on the outside of the door and waited for him.

"Hey, man. What's going on? This shit sucks, right? Man, listen. I know we've had our differences, but I just want to say... Thank you. Thank you for holding me down when... when I was down. The nurse kept mentioning that my brother came to see me every day. I didn't realize it was you until I heard her mention to Aubrey that my brother wasn't doing too well. I don't know what will happen or how this will end, but just know that I got you. Whatever you need. I'm going to take care of Aubrey and PJ while you're here. I met your daughter Colby. She is beautiful man. You lucked up—all of these beautiful women in your life. I will watch out for her too. That's my word. I'm praying for you, man. I appreciate everything you did for me. Stay up."

I peeked in the room, and Carter was squeezing Porter's hand. As he walked towards me, he wiped the tears from his eyes.

"I'm ready now." He sits back in the wheelchair.

"Okay, give me a sec." I walk into the room and kiss him on the forehead. Now that he is on life support, he is no longer breathing on his own. His lips are so chapped and dry. I reach into my purse and take out my Chapstick to rub across his lips. I slide back one of his eyelids just to take a look at his eyes, and they look lifeless. His eye color has lightened.

"Porter, I love you. Your mom and dad are both on their way here to stay with you again tonight, so I will see you in the morning. I love you, P." I leave my Chapstick on the table next to him. He hates to have dry lips; he would say that they make you look thirsty. I notice his urine holder is empty. Maybe they dumped it out earlier today.

"Alright, let's go," I suggest.

****

When we get back to my house, I help Carter out of the car.

"I'm good," he says when I try to assist him with standing.

"Are you sure? Don't fall back on me now!" I smile.

"Yeah, yeah, I'm good. I got this," he says. He stands up out of the car and shuts the door.

"Oh, okay big man!" I laugh. When I open the door, the lights come on.

"Surprise!" everyone shouts. My living room was filled with people.

People from our old neighborhood, Carter's mom, Julisa, Trish, Colby, Eric, Torin, and Carter, friends from his marketing firm in New York. Julisa made sure everyone he knew was here. I have no idea how my mother found out, but she's here. I hope she won't be here for long.

Everyone runs up to Carter, giving him hugs and kisses. I walk over to Julisa to give her a big hug.

"Julisa! Thank you so much for bringing everyone together!"

"Girl, not a problem. It was my pleasure. I'm just so happy to see that he is okay, you know?" she smiles as she glances over at Carter.

"Yes, girl. I do. This part is over; now, I'm waiting for Porter to come home."

"Oh yes, how is he doing?"

"Julisa… I don't know… All I can do is keep praying and being there for him. He is on life support. The doctor says that he may start breathing independently, but it is not a guarantee. So, we straddle the fence and just wait around, but I'm not giving up on him. I have so much on my plate with PJ and Carter, some other stuff, and Porter. Porter is now at the top of the list."

"I'm praying for you, Aubrey, I really am. You are as strong as an ox! It's unbelievable. If you need me at all, please call me. I love Baltimore, so I have no problem coming down, even if it's just to babysit," she smiles and gives me another hug.

"Thank you; I appreciate that." Trish walks over, holding the hands of this beautiful chocolate man.

"Well, hello. And who do I have the pleasure of meeting?" I say jokingly. Trish is smiling so hard that it looks like it hurts.

"Aubrey, this is my fiancé… Grant."

"Hi Aubrey, it's nice to meet you finally." He sticks out his hand. I pull him in for a hug.

"Grant, you are family now, honey. We give hugs," I embrace him tightly.

"You take care of my family, okay?" I whisper to him.

"Will do," he smiles.

"It looks like Colby is over there, entertaining my mother. Let me go say hello," I say.

I walk towards her, and my smile breaks instantly.

"Hey, Colb!" She jumps into my arms.

"Bre! I missed you!" she smiles while looking up at me with those beautiful brown eyes.

"I've missed you too! Can you do me a favor?" I ask.

"Yes, I can. What is it?" she replies.

"Ms. Julisa has been watching your baby brother all day long. Could you please play with him? He is in his car seat. Now, don't try to pick him up without asking for help, okay."

"Okay, I won't." She runs over to Julisa and tugs on her dress.

"Ma, what are you doing here?" I turn back to my mother, and instantly I am back to the broken mug on my face.

"Carter is like a son to me. Of course, I am here," she answers in defense.

"Ma, I am not ready to be in your presence right now. I would appreciate it if you would leave." I try to be discreet so that no one can hear or see what I am saying.

"Please, Aubrey. I haven't seen my grandson, and you won't answer my calls. I'm sorry. I made a mistake, a huge mistake, and I am truly sorry."

"We can talk about this some other time, but not right now." She gets up out of the chair and grabs her purse.

"So that you know, I haven't seen your father since the day he left. What he did was messed up, but I'm worried about him." I had no idea that he has not been home at all.

"I will look into it, Ma." She walks towards the door—my phone rings.

"Aubrey!" Mrs. Garrett is frantic on the line.

"Mrs. Garrett? What's wrong?" I spoke loud enough that the whole party stopped moving, and everyone was looking at me. I could hear the distress and her voice. It was cracking like she could barely breathe.

"Aubrey, this is Sam. Please get down to the hospital now." Mr. Sam took the phone out of Mrs. Garrett's hands.

"Mr. Garrett? What is going on?" Filled with anxiety, I pray it's not another horror story.

"Aubrey, I don't think we should speak over the phone, Sweetie. So please, get here," he pleads.

I hang up the phone and grab my purse. Trish walks up to me.

"What's going on?" she asks, with her eyes bulging out of her head.

"I don't know, but we need to get to the hospital. Now!" She grabs her purse and walks over to Grant.

"We have to go to the hospital; something is going on with Porter," she says to Grant.

"Julisa! We have to get to the hospital. Would you mind keeping the kids? The party can keep going. Just tell Carter I was called to the hospital. I don't want to disturb him from catching up with all of his friends." I walk past my mother and out of the door.

"I'm coming too," she says.

"Whatever." I breeze by her and out of the door.

****

When I walk into Porter's hospital room, Mr. Garrett is holding Mrs. Garrett while she cries uncontrollably. Dr. Hill is standing over Porter, along with his nurse. Porter's breathing is heavier than normal. As if he is fighting to breathe.

"What's going on?" Everyone stops and turns to me.

Dr. Hill walks up to me. His aura is different from normal. I can tell something is wrong.

"Hi, Aubrey... Porter... Porter's organs have shut down. All of them... He is now brain dead and has appeared to become a vegetable. I spoke to Mr. and Mrs. Garret already. There are not many options. The only options we have are to let him stay on life support until he stops breathing or take him off and let him go on his own."

I feel like my heart has stopped beating. That feeling I felt the first time I saw Porter like this has returned with a vengeance. I stare at him, lying there. Lifeless... In an instant, our whole life together flashes before my eyes.

Everything... Before I know it, my legs turn into spaghetti, and I fall to the ground. Before I hit the floor, I feel someone pull me up. When I look up, it's Carter. Trish and Grant are both standing behind him.

"I got you," he whispers as he pulls me up.

"I can't... I can't! No, no, no, no," I cry.

"Porter, please! Fight! Porter!" I scream. Mrs. Garrett walks over to me and holds me by my face as tears run from her eyes. She smiles gently with sorrow.

"Baby, his fight is over... It's time for him to be free," she hugs me as my cry breaks.

"Shhhh, let God have his way, Aubrey. Let my son be free."

At that moment, I felt like I fell into a trans. I saw his soul rise from his body, and peace came over me.

****

A few hours have gone by. We all came to the hardest agreement of our lives. We decided to let him free. Mrs. Garrett called her Pastor to come and pray over Porter. Trish decided that Colby's last time to see her father would not be as he took his last breath. And I agreed. I called Preston and Ryan. They are both on their way to the hospital.

The respiratory nurse walks in with two other nurses. We all stood around as they removed the equipment and breathing tube from his throat.

"Are you all sure you want to stay in the room for this?" one of the nurses ask.

"Yes, I am staying," I answer.

"I can't do this!" says Trish as she stormed out of the room. Grant went after her. Carter walks up to me and holds my hand.

"I'm not leaving you," Carter exclaims. My mom walks up and grabs the other hand.

"I'm not either," she leans her head up against mine and squeezes my hand tight.

"Thank you," I whisper. I walk over to Porter and kneel to whisper in his ear.

"Porter, it is okay. We are okay. I know you gotta go, and I understand. I will never let PJ forget you... It's okay to let go...Porter, I love you forever...

Always, always… Go to sleep…" I kissed him on his lips and held his hand. He squeezes my hand with all of his might. It was so weak and fragile, but I know he heard me. When we were in high school, I would sit in between his legs while playing video games, and he would say to me.

"I love you… Always, always…" Those five words would light up my world.

I look up at the heart monitor, and his heart rate started to drop. Then he breathed. 1…2…3… I watch as his lifeline runs flat… And there it is… He's gone… And so, has the air in my lungs and the beat of my heart. Gone…

I can't take my eyes off of him. I stand in this spot with his hand in mine until it's cold. I can't let go. He did it again. For the very last time… He broke my heart. Mr. Garrett walked to the other side of the bed and kissed Porter on the forehead.

"I love you, son. You are still my MVP." Tears roll off his face and onto Porter's cheek. It looks like Porter cried a tear himself. Mrs. Garrett stands at the end of the bed with her arms wrapped around her body. She cries in silence, weeping with her eyes on Porter. The examiners walk in to escort Porter's body out of the room. My mom walks up behind me.

"Baby, they have to remove Porter from here now," she whispers.

"His body is getting cold." She softly removes my hand. I can't bare to let go. I just can't… This is forever… There is no more… My hands tremble as I let go. For the very last time… He held on to me.

Chapter 8
What Now?

Aubrey

Dr. Powell's couch is the only place I have privacy right now. I thought I would never come back, but who can I turn to?

"The hardest part of all of this was telling Colby that her dad has gone to heaven. When I walked in the door, Trish was already there. I walked up to her, and she looked like a ghost. Like she was empty, no soul. I will never forget the look; I didn't see her. I don't know who I saw.

Before we arrived, I called home to tell Julisa that Porter passed. The children were already asleep. Trish went into Colby's room and slept in the bed beside her. Without saying a word, I went to my room, and Carter went into PJ's room. I didn't sleep the entire night. Porters last breath replayed in my mind over and over again. Whenever I dozed off to sleep, I relived that moment: 1...2...3...flatline. I cried until my face started to hurt. Until my eyes were too tired to shed another tear. I feel empty, and the only beacon of hope that I have left is Porter Jr.

The sun had finally risen. I forced myself from out of my covers to take a hot shower. I could still smell the hospital on me. I sat in that tub and let the water hit every part of my body. Until the water was cold. My body feels so fragile and weak. When I got downstairs, Torin and Eric were there cleaning up and cooking breakfast. Carter was holding PJ and feeding him. No one noticed me. I guess they were so busy trying to take care of everything for me that they didn't hear my footsteps, so I quietly walked back upstairs. I walked past Colby's door, and there she was; Trish was breaking the news to Colby. I sat in the hallway and listened in."

"Colby, mommy has something to tell you… First, I want to tell you that I love you so much, and I promise that no matter what, you will always be loved and cared for. Last night your daddy… your daddy… he went to heaven," Trish weeps.

"Like to live with God?" Colby replies.

"Yes," Trish replies.

"So that means that he died, right?"

"Yes, baby, it does," Trish continues weeps.

Colby is silent for a second, and then she says, "But that's not what heroes do…"

The innocents in her voice melted my heart completely. It literally made me sick to my stomach. I've never lost a parent, and I am dreading that experience, but those words spoke volumes on the love Colby and Porter had for each other in such a short amount of time."

"Did Porter's friends come to the hospital?" she asks.

"Preston and Ryan got to the hospital as we were all walking out of the front entrance. As soon as Ryan saw us walk out, he dropped to his knees. It was like he already knew. Preston tried to pick him up, but he was crying and was too weak himself. Ryan screamed, 'We're too late, he's gone! Why did he stop fighting?!' I'm still in shock. I don't think it has hit me yet. You know what I mean? It's only been a week, and I haven't been alone yet. I had to get away from everything and everybody. At least I tried, but Carter is in the waiting room, waiting for me."

I take a sip from my blueberry tea. Dr. Powell sits there in her wingback chair, waiting for me to continue. I still think she looks forward to my drama every week. She could easily write a book or a movie about my life, and it would be a hit.

"Aubrey, I cannot express how sorry I am that all of this is going on in your life. I wouldn't wish this sufferance on anyone…"

"Dr. Powell, I need all of this to be over."

"I understand, Aubrey. How are the funeral arrangements going?" she asks.

"Well… they're going… Pretty cut and dry. No one has any objections. I've been working with Porter's mom to work everything out with the insurance companies and funeral directors." Dr. Powell takes out her planner.

"When is the funeral?" she asks.

"It is tomorrow… Noon." My eyes fill up with tears. I am tired… Worn out and exhausted, to say the least. It's a lot going on, and for the million and one times, I've lost control. Dr. Powell walks over to me and takes a seat on the sofa. She wraps her arms firmly around me.

"Aubrey… I know this may not be the best time to say this because you have been very strong. You deserve a chance to be weak. To just scream and shout and let it all out, but right now… I need you to be strong. Here, you can let it all out. I will allow you to be as weak as you need to be, but I need you to get through this. It's not just you anymore. You have PJ, and he needs you," she says softly.

"You're right. But I am tired, Dr. Powell. I don't know who came up with, 'God doesn't put more on you than you can handle.' Because it is a lie!" I cry.

"Aubrey, you have been in some of the worst situations that one can bear, but you still have your health and freedom… so does your son. Those are both blessings. These tragedies that have happened in your life are also your testimony. I'm sure you are not looking for a preacher right now, but you should know that your pain will not go in vain or be forgotten. Please believe that a new chapter in your life will begin when you come out of all of this. It will be better than ever before." She grabs a tissue and daps my eyes, trying her best not to smudge my makeup. Although I'm sure I'm covered in black mascara. I take a deep breath to try and control my emotions. Then I get up, grab my bag and give Dr. Powell a big hug.

"Thank you, Dr. Powell. You have no idea how much you have helped me through everything."

"My pleasure," she responds with a smile.

On the ride home, I am silent most of the way. Carter stares out of the window, barely speaking a word. He is finally gaining his weight back. He lost a lot of weight since the shooting.

"So, I know you've been in a rush to get back home, but-"

"I will stay as long as you need me, Aubrey," Carter interrupts. I had a whole monologue ready. I thought I would have to put up a big fight.

"Under one condition… You marry me…" I press the breaks in the middle of a crosswalk. I look over at him, and something about his face says he is bluffing.

"Are you serious?" He breaks a smile.

"I mean, the aura was so tight, I had to find a way to break it." When we were kids, he did the same thing.

"So, you're not serious?" I'm not sure if I am disappointed by the joke or not.

"I am serious about the way I feel about you, but no. That's not the condition. I wouldn't put an extra load on you like that." Without responding, I pulled off.

"What's the condition, Carter?" Clearly, he has made me a little salty.

"You and PJ would come to New York at least once a month to stay with me. It would be like us having two homes."

"Us?" I say.

"Yes, us… Aubrey, listen. I may not have been your first choice. I may have only been your 'Best Friend,' but you and I both know there is another chapter written for us. With all that has happened… the shooting… Porter dying… It has taught me one valuable lesson. Life is too short to bypass your blessings. And you are my blessing Aubrey. I want to be yours… but… no pressure."

No pressure, huh? My life is based around pressure. The car is silent. I look in the back seat and watch PJ sleep through the reflection of his little mirror. He deserves a dad, and I deserve to be happy. One thing for sure, Carter has been there through it all. I love him. He jumped in front of a bullet to save me. He was willing to give his life for me. He deserves to be loved just as I do. I pull the car over into a gas station.

"So, we're doing this?" I say. Carter looks at me, and his eyes glow up.

"If you will have me," he answers.

"Is this another fake proposal?" He laughs, and it makes me laugh as well.

"No, this is a… 'When the time is right, that door will open, but at this moment, I will still love you, cherish you, support you, be your friend, and your love.' I want to be official with you. No one has to know. It's just us… me, you, and PJ. I'm ready to step in and be his missing link too. I made a promise to Porter, and I'm not going to break it. Whether we are together or not." Tears run down my eyes. I lean in to give him the softest, sweetest kiss, and he returns the favor.

I finally come home to an empty house. Trish has not been here in three days. Colby has been staying with Porter's parents. Breaking the news to her was very hard. Trish struggled. My house feels empty and cold, or maybe that's just me. Carter takes PJ out of his car seat and walks to the kitchen to grab a bottle from the refrigerator.

"Don't forget to heat it up," I say.

"I got this, how about you go and take a hot bath and relax? You have a very long day tomorrow," he responds as he tries to juggle the baby, a diaper, and the bottle.

"Are you sure?" I reply.

"Yes, I am sure. We will be fine. I'm going to feed PJ, make us some dinner, and put him to sleep." Carter is filled with energy. I must say. I appreciate it.

"Uh, okay… well, I am going to go upstairs." I hear Jay-Z's *Black Album* playing from the kitchen. He's being playing Jay-Z music nonstop since we were young. I go into my bathroom and run my tub water; before I can lay my head back on the edge of the tub to relax, my phone rings.

"Hello…"

"Bean? It's dad…" I freeze… Unable to speak a word… I just freeze…

"Baby, I know you don't want to hear from me… I just wanted to let you know that I was okay. I'm staying at the Four Seasons downtown for now."

"Oh, you did it big, huh? I guess you needed to be comfortable while buried in shit," I reply.

"Aubrey, I am still your father, don't disrespect me," he responds in a fragile tone. It sounds like he is drunk.

"Don't disrespect you? You have spent years humiliating me behind my back. Disrespecting my friendship with Lana, disrespecting her, disrespecting yourself, my mother, your legacy! Now you want to talk about respect. I am not a child anymore. You will have to use that line somewhere else. As a matter of fact, I don't have time for this. I am mourning the loss of my sons' father. I don't need you to remind me that I am your seed; it's painful enough. Good night 'Father!'" I hang up the phone and get out of the tub.

When I walk into the bedroom, Carter stands next to my dresser with a glass of water in his hand.

"I prefer wine, but thanks." I take it out of his hand and sit on my bed in my robe.

"But PJ doesn't so… Water it is." He sits down next to me.

"Was that your father, Aubrey?" he asks.

"Yes, it was…" He sighs. I can tell he is about to come on pretty strong when he sighs.

"I know you're angry with him. I'm angry with him. He was my only father figure growing up, but remember forgiveness if you haven't learned anything from all of this. What he did was totally fucked up. I don't know the whole story, just what you told me, but at least give him a chance to be a grandfather."

With coldness in my heart, I respond. "He has to earn that title. Shit, he has to earn the title 'dad' again. Fathers don't do what he did, period."

"Okay, you're right. Well, do you need anything?" he asks.

"I do…" I move closer and kiss him on his neck.

"Get inside of me," I whisper in his ear. He gives me a kiss on the forehead and says. "When this is all over, I will make love to you, but let's get through all of this first. You need some rest."

Did he just reject me? He walks me to the top of the bed and tucks me in.

"I'm not rejecting you, babe. I just want you to be clear about everything that is going on so that we can move forward."

What in the hell happened? Did he have a whole "coming to self" conversation downstairs? It doesn't matter if he did or didn't, though, because he is right.

"I understand Carter, let's start fresh when this is all over." I give him a kiss and turn over. He shuts the door behind him.

****

"Hey, girl… Are you at the salon yet?" Torin promised to do my hair for the funeral. It's seven o'clock in the morning. My eyes can barely open.

"Hey girl, I'm on my way now. I will meet you there."

I walk into PJ's room, and Carter sits in the rocking chair sleep with the television on.

"Carter, I am going to get my hair done. I should be back early enough to get PJ dressed."

"Don't worry about it. I will get him dressed. The blue suit, right?" he points to the closet.

"Yes, thank you," I walk over and give him a kiss.

"I will see you in a few hours," I smile.

****

I get to Torin's salon, and I absolutely love what she has done with the place. Black marble floors, black walls, big chandeliers, and pops of beautiful vibrant art on the walls. Her style is written all over it. I walk through the salon to find her.

"Aubrey! I'm in the shampoo room!" she yells. The place is empty. No one comes in for another hour.

Torin is leaned over the shampoo bowl rinsing the conditioner out of her hair.

"Hey, girl! How are you feeling?" she says with water running over her face.

"I'm okay. Just... I don't know... ready for this to be all over... and dreading it all at the same time. I don't know how I feel."

"Brey, can you pass me a towel, please." She reaches out for the towel.

"Take a seat right here. Let's get you started." I sit down at the shampoo bowl.

"Girl, I can't imagine what you are going through. You have the right to feel; however, you feel."

"Last night was the first time I slept in the last two months. Honestly, I haven't had a good sleep in almost a year. From the day I found out about Lana and Porter, to the shooting, Carter in the hospital, pregnant, then Porter's accident. And now... this. I'm laying Porter to rest today. Like... forever." I start to hyperventilate. Torin quickly turns off the water and grab a towel.

"Aubrey! Breathe! It's going to be okay!" She kneels down and hugs me tight.

Two hours go by, and Torin is finishing up the touches of my hair. The salon is packed.

"I am going to finish up my hair and head to the church. My clothes are in the back," she says.

"Did I tell you about my visit with Lana?" Torin turned me towards the mirror to view my hair.

"No, did it go as you expected?" she asks with a smug tone.

"No, not what I expected at all." She stopped doing my hair and looked at me with a serious look through the mirror.

"She told you, didn't she?"

"Told me, what?"

Torin pulls up her stool and turns me around to face her. "Okay... Aubrey, first I want to say that I didn't tell you because I didn't know if it was true or not. Lana is a liar and a manipulator, and I didn't think it made sense for me to carry on what could be a rumor and mess up everything in your life."

"Everything in my life is already messed up. It's been that way for some time, Torin."

"This was before all of this mess started happening. During our second year of college, I was at an event, and I heard Lana tell Demari that she was moving out of the dorms because Colin got her an apartment. One day I saw her leaving the dorm, and I recognized your dad's car from that time we all went to your parents' house for Thanksgiving."

"And why did you feel this was something you should keep from me?"

"Aubrey, I didn't know if it was true. Those were feathers that I didn't think should be ruffled without facts. I mean, Demari said some shit that Lana told her, but nothing about Lana speaks the truth to me. I didn't think it was worth putting your whole family in jeopardy."

"You know what, Torin? I'm a big fucking girl. I am tired of all of the secrets and bullshit going on behind my back. I'm sick of it! Everyone around me has lied, cheated, or kept some kind of secret. I am sick of this shit. All of you can go to hell." I pick up my purse and storm out of the salon. What makes her think this is something to keep from me. We could've been past all of this shit a long time ago.

I get back to the house, and PJ and Carter are both dressed. They look so handsome in their slightly similar three-piece suits. Porter would be so proud to see his son dressed like a boss. I put on a smile, trying to forget what just happened with Torin and me.

"I'm going to go get ready." I head up the stairs.

I look out of my bedroom window, and I see Trish and Colby getting out of a car I've never seen before. The limousine pulls up in front of the driveway.

I walk downstairs, and everyone is sitting there waiting for me, including Mr. and Mrs. Garrett.

"Aubrey! I've missed you!" Colby runs up to me and jumps in my arms.

"I've missed you oh so much, Colby Bear." I give her a big hug.

"Can I stay with you tonight? Pleeeaasssee!" she sings, awaiting my answer.

"Yes, baby, sure you can." Mr. Garrett walks up to me.

"Are you ready, dear?" he asks with a peaceful grin.

"Yes, sir, I am." He takes Mrs. Garrett and me by the hand and leads us out of the door towards the limousine. Carter is behind us, carrying Porter Jr. in the car seat, and Trish and Colby come out last. Trish shuts the house door. She has not said one word since I laid eyes on her.

When we enter the church, the seats are packed. There are so many people that some are standing up in the back. I didn't realize how many people knew and loved Porter. People are weeping all over the building. Old basketball teammates, staff, and customers from La'Rose, even that kid he met at the basketball court some time ago. Porter started mentoring him after seeing him at the court a few times. I didn't find that out until the day I met the kid at the hospital. The closer we get to Porter's casket, the harder my heartbeats. This all feels like a dream, a nightmare rather. I can't believe I am here. Mr. and Mrs. Garrett are standing in front of me. I watch as Mrs. Garrett squeezes her husband's hand tight as if the pain is too unbearable. She rubs her hands across Porter's chest.

"My baby!" she shouts. Mr. Garrett grabs hold of her and walks her towards the seats.

I guess I'm up. Carter gives Mr. Garrett PJ. He walks behind me. I can feel my legs getting weaker and my heart beating harder as I walk closer to the casket. Wow… He looks like he is resting peacefully. He was dressed in one of his favorite Sean John three-piece suits. Navy always looked great on him. As I stand there, our life together once again flashes before my eyes—all of the good times. Before I know it, my legs give out on me. Carter catches me.

"Porter?" I whisper.

"I love you; I promise I will be the best mom to PJ. I will never let your legacy be tarnished. All is forgiven, Porter; all is forgiven." With the strength I have left, I lean over and kiss him on the forehead. I swear it looks like a glow comes across his face.

So many people got up to speak about their relationship with Porter. It seems that the funeral went on forever. And now it's my turn. Colby took me by the hand and walked up with me.

"Good afternoon, everybody. Thank you all for being here. I didn't realize how many people loved Porter. Hopefully, none of you hated him." The crowd laughed a little.

"Porter and I have been through many tough events. Some that challenged our love for one another. But in the end, I knew that we truly loved each other. I knew that his flaws could be forgiven. We all have flaws; we all make mistakes. Porter taught me that life is about growth. That we may start off on a bad foot, but we have the opportunity to change and become better. We have the opportunity to turn our wrongs into rights. And when you get that opportunity, you should take it. My life has done a total three-sixty in the last year or so, but through it all, I am grateful for the chance to start over again every day that I wake up. In Porter's last few months of life, he taught me that. He was a great father to Colby and was preparing to be a great father to PJ. He turned the other cheek and started to help and forgive people who he may have turned his back on at one point in his life. Although he didn't receive the opportunity to explore the 'new him,' he didn't leave here without making an effort. I just wanted him to know that I am grateful for our time together, the lessons learned, and I will hold his legacy to the highest standard. I will love and care for Colby as my own. That is my promise to him. I love him and will forever keep him in my heart." I looked down at Colby, and she smiled at me. Then she whispers.

"Can I say something?"

"Sure…" I pick her up and put her mouth to the microphone.

She looks over at Porter.

"I love you, Super Man," then she whispers in my ear.

"That's all I wanted to say."

"Okay," I reply with a smile. We walk back to our seats.

****

As I walk around the repass, I get so many hugs and stories about how people met Porter. I'm exhausted. I've been watching Trish all day. I walk up towards her and notice a guy whispering in her ear.

He walks off as I get closer to them.

"What was that about?" I ask. She has barely said a word to me since all of this has happened. I've noticed how distant she has become.

"Some guy. He was just paying his respects." Once again, silence...

"What's going on?" I ask.

"You've been pretty distant," I continue.

"Nothing, just sitting here trying to stay out of the way," she answers.

"No, I mean, what is going on with you, Trish? You have been distant. You haven't called, and you haven't been to the house. You didn't even want to help with Porter's obituary. This isn't like you."

"Look, Aubrey, I just have a lot on my mind. It's so much going on. I've just been taking some time alone."

"Okay, I understand. I can't hold that against you."

"I know this may not be the best time to ask," she says.

"What's up?" I can tell she is a little troubled. It's all over her face.

"I may need you to keep Colby for me. I will let you know when. I am going out to the West Coast with Grant for a few days. Just to get a feel of the lifestyle over there."

"Of course. That's not a problem... I will make sure she gets to school." She hugs me as if I granted her the last wish. There is a strange woman sitting behind her. I noticed her earlier today. She looks at me and then turns away.

"Do you know that woman over there?" I ask Trish.

"No, not at all," she replies.

"Okay, I will be back."

I walk over to the strange woman and introduce myself.

"Hi, my name is Aubrey. Have we met?" She stands to her feet.

"Hi, Aubrey, I'm Celia. I'm Lana's mother." Wait. What?

Chapter 9

Reunited, and it feels…

Aubrey

I agreed to meet Lana's mother a few days after Porter's funeral. Which got us here… In the visiting area… Waiting to see Lana…

"Do you think she's going to want to see me?" Ms. Celia is as nervous as a hoe in church.

"Ms. Celia, honestly, I don't know. I can't tell you. Just tell her what you told me. I will stand out here, and please show her this."

Finally, they call her back; I can only see through the door. They've changed the waiting room around a bit. People are able to sit face to face without glass between them.

"Wish me luck," says Ms. Celia with a nervous smile.

"Ms. Celia… It will be okay." She walks through the doors with her head held high.

****

Celia could barely breathe. Her heart goes through a state of panic as she enters the visiting area. She sits at the table and waits for Lana to arrive. She taps her feet against the leg of the table. Minutes go by, and finally, Lana walks in. She was dressed in a t-shirt and green pants with her hair in a ponytail. She looks around, wondering who is there to see her. Finally, she stops in her tracks when she sees her mother sitting at the table. She walks towards the table, and Celia stands up.

"Lana..." Celia walks up to Lana and rubs her hand across her face. She breaks down in tears and grabs her close, but Lana doesn't hug her back. Finally, Celia lets go, and they both take a seat across from one another. The table is silent. Finally, Lana speaks.

"So, you're not dead? You just forgot about me."

"I never forgot about you, baby. Never..." Celia weeps with joy, but nervousness in her voice.

"You left me for a man. You did more than just forget about me." Anger builds up in Lana's face. She tries to hold her composure.

"Wait... what? Is that what he told you? Lana, do you remember when I brought you that suitcase?"

"Yeah, for my birthday."

"That suitcase was for us to run away. I had it all planned out. My girlfriend from the hotel where I used to work; moved out to Texas. She was the only person that knew that your father was abusing me. She told me that we could come out to live with her whenever we were ready. One night your father got drunk, and he beat me so bad I could barely recognize myself. I didn't go to work for a week."

"I remember," Lana listened with her undivided attention.

"During that time while your father was at work and you were in school. I made phone calls to find a job and get you into a school in Texas. I found a job and school on the same day. The only problem was that I didn't have enough money. My girlfriend was going to be in Las Vegas with her husband and said she would send us tickets to meet her there, and then we could fly back to Texas with them. She told me not to worry; they would cover everything. Your dad saw the tickets for our flight in my jewelry box, and he tore them up. He beat me worse than the time before. This time I went back to work, and I saved everything I made in tips. That next week, the night before our flights, I booked us a room near the airport. I packed our bags and hid them outside behind the trash cans. After he had a few drinks and fell to sleep, I went into your room to wake you up. The moment I got to your door, he was standing behind me with a gun to my head. He whispered in my ear, 'Leave... but she stayin.' I cried! I begged and pleaded. He dragged me downstairs to the door and told me that he would kill me if I ever came back. The cab pulled up just in time. I grabbed my bags and got in the cab and left."

"So that was it? After all of those ass whippings, you couldn't take another to get me out of there? You just gave up?"

"No, Lana... Your father had a gun in my face. What was I supposed to do? I planned to get a job and come back to get you. I waited a week to call, but by then, he had changed the number. I didn't know what to do."

"You should've called the fucking police! You should've come back to get me! You should've never stopped fighting!" Lana cried.

"Lana, I came back! And I tried to find you! Your father moved out of that house. I gave up after a while... I did... I knew you would hate me. I didn't know how to face you. How to look you in the eyes and say I gave up. Lana, I'm sorry, I wish I could take it all back. I was a coward... I finally got up the courage to find you, and your name had changed. I ran into an old friend from our neighborhood who knew about your friendship with Aubrey. Evette; she lived around the block. Do you remember her? She took me to Aubrey's mom's house. She was generous enough to let me in. We went to Porter's funeral, and there is where I met Aubrey."

"Wait... Porter's- Porter's funeral?" Lana couldn't believe what she was hearing.

"Porter is really dead?" she wept.

"Yes." Celia pulls the obituary from her lap. Lana looks at it and breaks down in tears.

"Oh, my God," she cries.

"Aubrey asked me to give this to you." Lana takes a second to take it all in.

"I can't believe Porter's face is on the front of an obituary."

"She said you could keep it if you would like."

"Tell her, I said, thank you. You know... Everything that I have been through, everything that I've done, started in that household—watching my father beat you. You leaving me and my father using me as your substitute.

Do you know that he whipped my ass every single day after you left? Every day! Until I got the guts to run away. You saved yourself, but what about me? I carried those whippins' everywhere I went."

"Lana, baby, I'm sorry. I'm sorry that I haven't been there for you all of these years. I missed out on a lot, and I regret every bit of it... Aubrey told me everything. She told me about Porter. She told me about her dad. She feels guilty for the way that your life has turned out, but I'm sure that my guilt runs deeper than hers," Celia cries.

"I've been in therapy every day since I've been in here. It started out pretty rough. I started out telling her lies about Aubrey just to make myself feel better. The last thing I needed was someone else telling me about me. Nobody knows shit about me. They don't understand what I'm feeling. Or that I've tried to take myself out more times than once. Behind all my arrogance, the makeup, and the Chanel shoes... I was screaming! Dying inside... I was suffocating in my own body. I hated myself more than I hated Aubrey or Porter or Colin or my pathetic father. Even more, then, I hated you. Only two people loved me more than I loved me, and I betrayed them both. But I am in a different place right now. It's taking time for me to love myself again. To forgive myself for all of the pain I've caused. WHAT YOU DID HURT ME. I always thought that if my mother couldn't love me, I shouldn't look forward to love from anybody else, but I still searched for love, and every single time I was let down... but I forgive you. I have to start somewhere, so I forgive you." Tears streamed down Lana's face. She felt a release fall over her spirit.

"Visiting hours are over!" shouted the guard. Lana wiped her eyes and stood up.

"I will be back here to see you every week. I will never leave you again, dear. I promise." Celia grabbed hold of Lana and wrapped her arms around her. Lana wrapped her arms tightly around her mother and squeezed tight. Celia broke her cry, and so did Lana. The guards allowed them to have their moment. Finally, the guard calls Lana to the door.

"Let's go, inmate," the lady guard exclaims.

"I will be here next week, my baby," Celia says with excitement in her voice. Lana turns around and smiles peacefully.

"Thank you," she replies.

****

I wake up to puffy, red eyes, and my soul is drenched with heartache. I roll over to see Carter resting with PJ lying on his chest, sleeping peacefully. I peek into Trish's room, and she is still asleep, with Colby snuggled up under her. They stayed up all night watching movies. I go downstairs to the kitchen and make myself a cup of tea. Memories of Porter and I began to race through my head. I've been struck with boatloads of pain, but of all the things I've dealt with, this was the hardest. The silence in the house feels so cold and weary. I walk down to the basement, where all of Porter's boxes are stacked up on top of each other. Overwhelmed with emotion, the room starts to spin. I can feel my heart breaking all over again. I approach a box of his clothes. We never washed any of his dirty laundry. You can still smell his scent on them as I open the box. I pull out his college t-shirt that he wore on his lazy days. Tears fall down my eyes as I weep silently. This can't be real! I grab all of his clothes out. I lay them on the floor and wrap myself up in them. My tears turn into shouts, I try to control myself, but my emotions get the best of me once again.

"I can't do it!" I cry. I still can't believe that this is real! I will never be able to pick up the phone and call Porter again. After all that we have been through! Life was not supposed to end up like this!"

I can feel someone else's presence in the room. I turn over, and Trish is standing on the steps, watching me.

"I can't do it, Trish!" I blubbered.

Trish comes down the stairs and sits on the floor next to me. Trish is so much stronger than I am. She falls into silent spells, but she has done a lot better at keeping her shit together.

"I can't be here. I can't," she says as she stares into my eyes with a look of sorrow.

"Yes, you can. You have to; what about Colby?" I ask.

"No, I mean, I can't be here. In this house, I am not going to be able to wake up every morning in this house." She is holding on to Porter's shirt tightly as she observes the words and weeps. I get her up off the ground, and we walk up to the kitchen where Colby is sitting there, holding her head up with her hand as she is eating her cereal.

"Good morning, Colby," I say.

"Morning," she replies. The look on her face is breaking my heart even more. The energy in the house is nothing less than sorrow. I walk over to the refrigerator to grab some orange juice and my phone rings.

"Trish, can you get that?" I ask.

"Hi, may I speak to Ms. Aubrey Bryant?"

"Yes, hold, please." Trish hands me the phone, but I don't bother to reach for it.

"May I take a message; she is busy at the moment?"

"Yes, this is Karen Cosby. I am Mr. Garrett's attorney; who am I speaking with?" she asks.

"Trish, Trish Watkins," she responds curiously.

"Oh, Ms. Watkins, I was just about to give you a call! I am calling because I will need you and Ms. Bryant to come to my office as soon as possible, and I will explain everything when you all get here. How does noon sound?" she says in a pleasant manner.

"Okay, noon is fine. We will be there," I respond, puzzled.

"That was Porter's lawyer. She wants us to meet with her at her office today at noon."

"For what?" I ask.

"She said we would talk about it when we arrive." We stare at each other in the most anxious and confused way. We get dressed, eat our breakfast, and head out. Hopefully, this meeting will be as painless as possible.

We arrive at the attorney's office. Silence comes over both of us as we walk into the building. Trish has not said a word since we left the house. I don't know if she will be able to cope without therapy.

A tall, fair-skinned woman walked out of her office with a pleasant smile and well dressed in an all-black pants suit. "Hi, you must be Aubrey and Trish? I'm Karen," she says as she sticks out her hand.

"Yes, we are. I am Aubrey, and this is Trish," I answer. Trish doesn't say a word; she just walks into the office as we followed.

"First of all, please let me pay my condolences. Porter was not just a client. He was a good friend of mine. He spoke of you all, all of the time. I watched him grow into a man over the years. His priorities changed tremendously, and his actions showed it."

She hands both of us folders.

"What is this?" I ask.

The attorney smiled and said, "The wellbeing of you and the children were all Porter cared about. He came here once a week and added more to his will. I don't know if he felt his end coming, but he surely was prepared for it. Aubrey, he told me that the worst thing that he had ever done was watch you hurt and although you all had rekindled a friendship, he had a hard time forgiving himself for what he did to you."

I reminisced on our best times and how he will never have the chance to be the dad he wanted to be. Trish held my hand as I watched tears fall down her face.

"Trish, Colby was the reason he made the changes so that he could show her what a good man was. He wanted the best for all of you, and he had some big plans."

Karen tried to hold back her tears, but the moment was overwhelming for all of us. "As my client and best friend, I watched him change and flourish over a few months, and it was because of you all."

As we sit in silence to get ourselves together, I opened the folder.

"What is this?" I ask.

Karen smiled with excitement. "You are now the owner of Sugar, Honey, Iced T Breakfast and Lounge."

"What? How?" I almost jump out of my seat.

"Porter found out that they were selling the place. He said it was you two favorite spot when you were kids, so he bought it for you. He planned to surprise you the day the baby was born. Like a push gift."

That's one hell of a push present. I have no words. Nothing... I'm too full to speak.

"He also left each of you, including the two children ownership in La'Rose lounge. If you turn to page six, you will see that he has stocks and bonds for both you and the children. Trish, he left you the house and his car. He spoke about the interior design firm that you've talked about. Trish, he left you sixty-thousand dollars; this would be a jump start." Karen hands Trish more documents.

"Jumpstart? That's a leap!" we laugh. "Aubrey, he also left you sixty-thousand dollars. He talked about how great of a writer you are. Maybe it's time for you to finish that book he bragged about."

"I didn't know he read it," I mutter.

"There was a lot you didn't know... He left each child thirty-thousand dollars. The stocks and bonds are worth two hundred and fifty thousand dollars as of today. Porter has been trading stocks since his first year in college. No one can touch the children's percentage until they have reached the age of eighteen. Porter would like you to teach them about generational wealth and the value of money before they are allowed to cash out. He trusts that you will both make the right decisions."

"It sounds like Porter knew he was going to die," I say as I look through this folder, puzzled. Something just doesn't add up. What made him put a time limit on things that just don't seem right.

"I think he just wanted to be prepared one way or another," Karen replies.

Celia

I've been sitting outside of Davis's job for almost an hour, waiting for him to walk his big angry ass outside of the front door. I cannot believe what I am seeing! Look at him with some old heffa on his arm. This must be a new thing because his charm is shining through that monster in his soul. That's how he got me. He put on the charm, broke me down to dust, and built me back up with mud. I regret leaving my baby, but I thank God I got away from him. I get out of the car and quickly walk upon him as he woos her with all of his charm.

"Hello, Davis." Instantly, his smile broke as if he saw his own ghost.

"Davis, who is this?" the old skank asked while she profiled me from head to toe. I don't have time to look her way. I want him to stare into my eyes; he needs to see me.

"I am his wife... Sadly... And the mother of his child," I respond while giving him a hard look. He can barely move. He is stiff as a board, for once.

"You didn't tell me you had a wife or kids," she looks at him with an attitude and precedes to walk off.

"No, Suga, stay… It just might save your life." I walk closer to Davis so that we could be eye to eye. Close enough for him to see the vein in my eye.

"I thought that after all of these years… being away from you… would make this easy. That all of my hurt was gone but standing here looking at you… The pain hit me like a flood. I can feel every punch, every kick, every disgusting thing you have done to me. The best thing I could have done was to leave you, but the worst thing I've done was to leave my daughter there. I should've taken the bullet. She is lying up in a jail cell filled with anger and pain and grief because we failed her! That is my baby in there! You beat her like she wasn't your own! Like you didn't hold her in your arms or watch her through the windows of the nursery. You! You taught her how to ride a bike. You! But because you couldn't hurt me… You forgot that YOU ARE HER FATHER! The one man who should have protected her!" A pitiful tear runs down his cheek. He stands firm, without a blink, without any movement. The woman looked at him with disgust. Without saying a word, she walks away.

"You will reap all that you've sown. I promise you that." I walk back to my car and pull off. Through the rearview, he is standing in the same spot where I left him.

Aubrey

A week goes by, and I have yet to tell Carter about Porter's will. My mother used to say to me, "Never tell a man about all that you've got. Slowly, but surely you won't have it anymore." I don't know if that's true or not, but I will at least tell him about the restaurants. He is going to find out anyway. I just need time to think things through. A lot has hit me at one time. The manager Teddy, at Sugar Honey Iced Tea called me. I guess he got the news from Karen, who is now my new lawyer. She is a powerhouse. I understand why Porter has stuck with her for so long. She and my mom share the same name; I think that was a sign.

I still don't know what's going on with Trish. She is gone away with Grant for some business or something. All I know is that I've been a whole mom to Colby lately. I don't mind it, because Colby is a good kid and Carter can't get enough of her. She makes his face up every day, and he giggles all the way through it.

When everyone goes to sleep, I get in my car and take a long ride. When I finally get tired of driving, I pull over and cut my car off. When I look up, across the street from me is La'Rose Lounge. I get out and walk over. I go to the door and open it up with my key. I thought Porter would've gotten the locks changed after our breakup. When I walk in, the place is spotless. Everything has been closed since the day after he died. When I walk to his office and open the door, everything is exactly how he left it. A blank envelope was sitting on his desk. He never opened it. I sit down at his desk and open the envelope. I opened the envelope, and there's a letter. As I read it, I realize it is the same letter Detective Charles had. Porter must've faxed a copy over to him.

I spent a few hours walking around La' Rose. I tried to envision a new look, but nothing came to me. Finally, I made my way back home.

I walk through the door, and Carter is sitting on the sofa reading a book.

"Babe, what are you doing down here?" I ask.

"PJ woke up crying. I just fed him and put him back to sleep. Are you okay?" He gets up and wraps his arms around me.

"I'm cool. I just needed to get out and clear my head. I ended up at La'Rose."

"Oh yeah?" I sit down on the sofa, and he flops down next to me.

"Yeah, I don't even know how I got there. I was just driving."

"Maybe you were led there," he replies as he caresses my hair while I lay on his chest.

"Yeah, maybe…"

"I'm going to hop in the shower. I smell like baby throw up," he smiles.

"Well, you have been great to PJ, and we both appreciate you." I lean in to kiss him.

"I will be up soon." I make a cup of green tea and go into PJ's room to kiss him. I should be at home with my son. I've done more running around from here and there than I have spent just gazing into my baby's eyes.

I walk into the bedroom, and Carter walks out of the bathroom. His body is back! I guess he has eaten enough protein for all of us. We hadn't had sex since that night at the hotel many months ago. Although I didn't want to admit it then, we MADE LOVE. Nothing about that night was just "sex." I felt like I was the sexiest woman in the world. He makes me feel love- feel safe. My goodness, I can't let this one go to waste; besides, he is what my body needs.

"Can I have you?" I ask, standing next to the dresser waiting for him to come my way. Without saying a word, he drops his towel and kisses me softly on my lips and down my neck. Before I knew it, Carter was taking me for the ride of my life.

"Carter!" I moaned while he gripped my hips. I turned around to see his lip tucked into his mouth while he grinds with everything he had, from the bed to the chair to the floor. We blessed every angle of that room. He picks me up and nails my body to the wall with his body. I held on to the lifting rail he uses for pull-ups. Before I knew it, the soles of my feet were on his shoulders, and my river was running like Niagara Falls. He did things down there that I have never felt before—what a way to end it all.

"Damn Aubrey," he says as we both hit our pillows.

"It's been a long time," I say with heat breathing down his neck as I kiss him softly. I don't think I had enough.

"Was I your –"

"My last? Yes, you were… I mean, from there, I found out I was pregnant with PJ. I thought he was yours until I counted the months. Back then, I regretted that I was having Porters baby. I saw myself all alone, maybe co-parenting with him, but I knew that the drama in my life would not stop."

"You know, I think about that all of the time. What if PJ had been mine, or what if Porter was still here?" He turns over to be eye to eye with me.

"I don't know about 'What if's' I let go of thinking that way. All that matters is what is here right now and how we will build a future. I want to build a future with you. I want to have more babies, I want to write books, and I want all the great things that this life has to offer me because I've seen the bright side of darkness, and it's not so bright there. I just want to be happy."

Carter pulls me close to him and put his arms around me while I rest my head on his chest.

****

The sun is shining brightly through my window. I take a shower, get dress, and get PJ cleaned up. For the first time in a long time, I put on my jogging suit and dress PJ in his little sweatsuit. Porter bought him every sweatsuit he could find in every color he could find it in. His closet is loaded. I have no idea where he was hiding all of this stuff, but Eric and Torin made sure it was all put away.

"Carter? Carter? Wake up." He turns over and opens up one eye.

"Huh?" he answers.

"PJ and I are going for a run. Colby is still asleep, but please tell her to get dressed. We are going to go and get our nails done later."

"Okay." He turns back over and goes to sleep.

I walk past Colby's room, and she is still asleep. I walk up to give her a kiss. In her arms is a picture of her and Porter on the shore at his mom and dad's house. Goodness, my heart broke instantly. I know she is broken. I wish I could take the pain from her, but I'm suffering on my own. I pull the covers up on her and give her another kiss.

****

"Aubrey, enough is enough now." Eric is on my phone, rambling on about how friendships are hard to find.

"Look, Eric, I am enjoying my morning run with my son. I don't have time for this. What do you want?"

"You know what I want? I want your little raggedy-ass to come and join me and your FRIEND, Torin, for lunch. And bring my god baby, I got something for him." I know that's not who I think it is. I rush Eric off of the phone.

"Okay, fine, send me the address. I gotta go." I quickly hang up the phone. I start to walk towards her, but then I call instead.

"Hello," she answers after three rings. I watch her hesitate to answer the phone.

"Hey, Trish. How is everything going?" She didn't want to answer the call from where I am standing, but her tone is pretty convincing.

"Hey, Brey! Girl, yes, everything is fine. We will be flying back in tomorrow."

"Oh, okay… I was just checking on you. Call Colby later; she has been missing you," I say as I open up my camera on my phone to snap a few pictures.

"Okay, I will do that. Look, I have to go. I will talk to you later." She rushes through the conversation. Before I could say another word, she hangs up.

Chapter 10
I'm taking my power back

Trish

Aubrey can't know that I am in Baltimore. I hate that I had to lie to her, but this is the only way I can keep them protected. That bastard actually walked up in Porter's repast. This is over! It has to end here before he tries to hurt someone else. I transfer stacks of money from one bag to an overnight duffle bag. Porter left a lot of money for us, but it's not nearly close to sixty-eight thousand dollars in here. If I pay him now, he is going to want me to pay him later. It's never going to stop, and I will never have peace.

I pull up to the grocery store across the street from the motel and park my car. I put on my wig and glasses. Grab my bags, and walk across the freeway to the motel.

Knock, knock, knock. Doc opens the door and looks behind me to make sure no one was with me. "Put down your bags," he says sternly with a smirk on his face. I drop the bags on the table by the window. He walks up to me and put his hands on my breast.

"What are you doing?" I ask in full fledge disgust.

"Are you wearing a wire?" he asks.

"What? No!" He continues to run his hands over my body. From my breast to my back, between my legs all the way down to my ankles. I was disgusted. Don't get me wrong; Doc is a good looking man. Tall, brown skin, and athletic build. But he is a fucking ass hole, and I wouldn't give him the time a day. But today, I may have to make another exception.

"Look, I'm not wearing a wire. I came to fix this. Make amends and get the hell on with my life," I say.

"Oh yeah? You want to make amends, huh?" He gets close to me like he wants to rip off all of my clothes.

"Yeah... I do," I speak softly.

"You got my money?" He sits down on the bed.

"I know you robbed Porter the night of the accident. If you were watching Porter the way you say you were, then you knew that he made deposit drops from the lounge. So how much did you get?" I ask.

"I knew you would put that little mine to work. Yeah, I did... I got thirty-five thousand. That couldn't have been for one day," he says.

"Maybe it was... I have twenty-five thousand in this bag. I will have the rest of it to you by the end of this week, plus interest. Just stay the fuck away from my family and me. Enough blood has been shed," I say as I pick the bag up and drop it on his bed.

"Sounds good to me, sorry it had to go this way, but you know... Business is business." I want to spit in this bastard's face, but I have to do this.

"I brought your favorite drink; as a peace offering." I take out a bottle of cognac, open it up, and pass it to him.

"You're not going to drink it with me?" he asks.

"No... You know I don't drink dark liquor." I pull out a pint of Patron that I have diluted heavenly with water. He can still smell it on my breath, but I won't be drunk.

"Come here." He pulls me close to him.

"You know you should've been mine." I push him on the bed, and he lays up against the headboard. He leans over and grabs the bottle of cognac, and takes a big gulp.

Showtime... I kiss him from his neck all the way down to his little man. And when I say little, I mean just that. He is way too fine to have nothing to show for it, but I'm here, so I might as well... Go for it. I stroke as hard as I can. He grabs the back of my head and says, "I'm comin'." And so, he did.

He came and went at the same damn time. I watched as his eyes rolled to the back of his head. He foamed from the mouth and fell into a seizure.

"You killed him, you son of a bitch!" I get up and spit in his face. He tried to reach for the pillow next to him, but before he could get to it, he was gone. I watched the life fade out of his eyes. I picked up the pillow, and a gun was lying under the pillow. I think he planned to kill me. I got up and checked him to see if he was breathing. Oh shit… I actually did it.

I quickly packed the money up and took the disinfectant and bleach spray out of my bag to wipe down everything I touched, including his little situation. I searched the hotel room to see if I could find the money he stole from Porter. Of course, "genius" hid it under the bed. I packed up the liquor bottles and got out of there.

On my way back home. I stop at Gwynn Falls Park. I throw away everything the clothes, the wig, the bottles… Everything but the money.

Celia

I will sit in this chair until he walks through that door. The smell of this house makes me want to vomit. He moved to a new house with old habits. He is still a trifling son of a bitch. It didn't take much for me to get in. He has a habit of leaving the back door unlocked. When we were together, he would come home from work, get a drink out of the refrigerator, and go outside to drink until he was too drunk to stand up. Then he would drag his big ass back in the house and beat me until he was tired enough to fall asleep. He never locked the door. So, my grocery bags and I had no problem getting in here. I cook him up a fabulous meal: steak and onions, green beans, and garlic mashed potatoes topped with parsley and finely crushed glass.

When he walks in, I will be sitting at the kitchen table, which I have dressed up so nicely. The aroma of the meal is bursting at the seams. He won't be able to resist. He used to love my cooking. I'm sure he hasn't eaten the same since.

"What are you doing here?" Without taking a long look at me, he walks in and drops his bags.

"I thought we should talk." He walks to the fridge and grabs a cold beer and a bottle of Jack from the sink cabinet. Before he makes his way to the door, I get up and stand in front of him.

"Please, Davis. I've needed closure for years. You could at least give me that," I plead with him.

"Are those mashed potatoes?" he asks as he leans towards the stove.

"Yes, with garlic and chives, just how you like them," I respond in the most innocent tone possible.

"I haven't had your cookin' in a long time... Celia." He puts down the beer and Jack Daniels and walks towards the stove. Got you! You son of a bitch!

"Here, everything is ready. Let me make your plate." He sits down at the table. I make him a big hefty plate with lots of potatoes. I grab his beer and sit down across from him. I watch him scuff down the plate, barely looking up.

"You remember how we met Davis?" He shook his head without saying a word.

"Right after you returned home from working overseas. Those were good times. You wheeled me right on in with your charm. Everything about you gave me butterflies."

Before I knew it, the steak and mashed potatoes were gone.

"Would you like more?" He sucks back his beer and says, "Yeah, thanks."

With the same angry look on his face, he barely made eye contact. I happily got up and made him another plate of steak and crushed glass. I added the last bit of pebbles of glass into the mashed potatoes just to give it an extra kick.

I sat the plate back on the table and watched him devour the second plate.

"I don't know what went wrong, Davis. You came back one day after having a few drinks with your friends, took Alana upstairs, came back down, and beat me until you were tired. No explanation, no words. Just fist to face." As I relive the moment, I can feel my anger rising, but I have to control it. This will end with a dash of elegance and class. He looks up at me without speaking. No tears, no apology, just silence, and the same cold expression.

"After I left you, I got over it long after, but to return and hear that you did the same to my child? I thought that you would at least love her. Since you fought so hard to keep her, well, you can only imagine how outraged I was. How unforgiving an act of such could be?" I sit firmly as I watch him cough up blood over his empty plate.

"What did you do?" he manages to say as his eyes turn bloodshot.

"You remember how I used to read murder mysteries? They're still my favorite genre. There was one, in particular, that was my favorite. I used to get off while reading it. There was one scene that excited me most of all. Patricia found her husband Blake cheating with her secretary Kathleen, so she went home one night and made Blake a big dinner. She never mentioned what she saw. She was as graceful and as poised as can be, like Jackie O, I could imagine, kind of like I am right now. She crushed up a bag of glass so fine that it looked just like salt. Like what you just finish eating, but in case your tiny little brain missed it; you're Blake. See, the thing about reaping what you've sown is you never know how or when the reaping is coming. You can only pray that God has mercy on you. Maybe he will and maybe he won't but in this case... Vengeance... is... mine..."

He dropped to the floor in a pool of blood, withering in agony, dying a grisly and painful death. He will expire in a manner that will even have the most experienced medical examiners baffled. I'm not worried about anyone coming to this house. Especially not Ms. Skank from work; I'm pretty sure I've scared her off, but just in case, I wipe down every part of the house that I've stepped in and cleaned the dishes. There is no way that I will be able to drag him out of this house. He is 6'2", and at least two hundred fifty pounds. I am all of 5'2", a hundred and fifty pounds, give or take. I check the cabinets for lightning fluid. He loves to grill, so it wasn't hard to find. I drench his body with a full bottle of lightning fluid and use the excess to cover the house. I light a piece of paper at the stove and drop it on his body. He lit up like a Christmas tree. Without hesitation, I dart out of the house, out of the yard, and up the alley without making a patter of noise. Finally, I get to the park where my car was parked.

By the time they get to him, he will be toast. Round one... Done...

Trish

I thought that I would feel better the next morning, but my reality is that I killed a man. Rather he deserved it or not... I killed a man in cold blood.

I look over to see my Colby sleeping peacefully. I pull back her hair and give her a big kiss. "knock, knock…" I frantically jump up.

"Yeah!" I answer.

"Hey Trish, I'm just letting ya'll know, I cooked breakfast if you're hungry," says Carter from behind the door.

"Okay, thanks, Carter. We will be down in a few."

"Alright…" I hear him walk away from the door. I go into the bathroom and run the shower. I took one when I got in last night, but I'm sure no amount of showers can erase the stench of murder.

"Good Morning," says Aubrey as I walk past PJ's room.

"Good morning," I reply.

"How are you doing this morning?" The energy is filled with something that I can't identify. Maybe I am just paranoid.

"I have to go and sign papers for Suga, Honey, Iced T this morning. Are you still up for going to La' Rose today?" Aubrey asks.

"Yeah, sure, of course," I respond. It gets quiet. I stand in the doorway silent, and she sits in the rocking chair folding PJ's clothes. Then…

"I saw you…" My heart froze in place, not knowing what to say. Maybe she isn't thinking what I think she's thinking, but what if she is? How do I get out of this?

"You saw me where?" I reply, trying to play it cool, all while my heart is about to explode.

"I saw you downtown yesterday… While I was on the phone with you, I was staring dead at you!" she exclaims.

"Aubrey…" I interrupt.

"What in the hell is going on Trish, you have been so secretive lately. It is starting to worry me. Do I have to watch you too? I've been fucked enough. I can smell it a mile away…" She looks at me with desperation in her eyes. She was waiting for a response, but I just can't give her one right now.

"Aubrey, no… It's nothing like that. I'm sorry just… You're going to have to trust me. I can't explain right now." I walk away before she draws me in with more questions.

****

"So, are you just going to give me the silent treatment?" I ask Aubrey, trying to break the ice a little. She looks tensed. I am tensed, and I just want something to feel normal for a second.

"What should I say? It's a nice day outside?" with more attitude than I can handle, she replies. So, I get quiet. If this is what it's going to be, I can't...

"Pull the car over," I say. I take a deep breath and release.

"I killed someone," I blurt out.

"What! What the fuck are you talking about?" says Aubrey. She is totally thrown back by my statement.

"Aubrey, you are the only person in this world I can trust. The only person... I need you to keep this secret. Please..."

"Who was it? Was it Porter?" she asks with a blank stare.

"What? Hell, no, Aubrey! Of course not! And I was with you," I yell.

"That doesn't mean shit... Then who was it?" I sit in silence, reluctant to respond.

"Promise me, Aubrey." I look her into her eyes. She knows that she is all I have in a friend. I could never tell Grant. I don't know what he would say. Finally, she broke her firm facial expression, and I could see the honesty in her eyes.

"I promise," she replies.

"Remember when I told you that I had to do a lot of things to make money back in Chicago?"

"Yeah, I remember." She takes another deep breath.

"Well, there is this guy named Doc. He ran a lot of illegal operations in Chicago, from money laundering, drugs, insurance fraud, counterfeit money, I mean, the list goes on. I came on to help him out with somethings. Long story short, he got popped for insurance fraud. He did a few years, a lot less than I thought he would. Before he went in, he gave me sixty- eight thousand dollars to put up for him until he got out. Times got hard, and I spent it a little at a time. I pinched off a little from time to time, thinking I would be able to put it back, but before I knew it, time had gone by, and all I had left was a little under thirty-thousand dollars. I ran into him one night and snuck out before he saw me. Grant proposed around the same time. I couldn't tell him, no, but I couldn't stay either. So, before Doc found me and had us all killed, I packed up Colby and moved back home. I never told Grant what happened. I didn't want to get him involved. So, I made up a bunch of lies about why I left him."

"Where are you going with this, Trish?" she asks.

"Aubrey, I killed Doc... He found me. I don't know how and I don't know when, but he walked up on me in the hotel garage where Grant and I were meeting the day before Porter's accident. He said that if I didn't have all of his money in twenty-four hours, he would start laying down bodies. I went back to the house to get the money Porter put into the safe, but it wasn't there. I thought that Doc would level with me and give me some time, but he stood by his word," I cry.

"He stood by his word?" She tries to take in the story, complexed on what I mean by that.

"Oh my God... Porter..." She clenched her hands to her face and screamed.

"I tried to keep it quiet and keep him away from everyone, but he had been following our every move. He knew too much... When you called to tell me that you were in labor, I was racing to La'Rose to warn Porter because he didn't answer the phone. But when you called..."

"You came back for me instead," she sighs.

"I couldn't be in two places at once, and I couldn't have you go through all of that alone. I had to be there. I know what that feels like, for no one to be there when you are going through the closest to life or death situation you may ever have. I'm sorry! I'm so sorry!" I cry frantically, failing to hold back my tears. She reaches over to hug me.

"Oh goodness, Trish... It's going to be okay... We will get through this." Aubrey rubs my head while she tries to soothe me.

"I was so afraid to come around because Doc disappeared after that. I didn't want him to see me with you all. Then he showed up at Porter's repast. That is when I lost it!"

"That was the guy you were talking to?" she asks.

"Yes, I told him I would meet him. I told you I was going to be in California because I needed to plan. So, I flew out with Grant and took the longest train ride back. I was too scared that I would get traced through the airport camera returning."

"You watch too much crime tv," she jokes.

"I had to think it through as much as I could. I couldn't leave room for error. Grant stayed in California. I told him I had to get back because Colby wasn't feeling well."

"I met up him at a motel, and I took him out. I poisoned him... I thought it would make things better. He was going to keep coming even after I paid him. I knew it. I didn't want someone else that I loved blood to be on my hands. So, I wiped my tears and bossed up." At this moment, I realize I did the right thing. Yes, Porter's death is my fault. I took his money; he would have never had been here if it wasn't for me. But none of that matters now. What matters is that he is gone. I wait for Aubrey to respond. I know that I caused all of this, but it would kill me if she didn't forgive me for Porter, especially when I am struggling to forgive myself.

"I can't blame you..." I know that she partly blames me for Porter's murder. I blame me.

"But I have to say this, or it's going to fester in me... If you would've told Porter, he would've paid him, and his death would've been avoided," she says.

"I know! Aubrey! I'm so sorry! I didn't mean for any of this to happen or to follow me back home. I thought I was doing the right thing by keeping you all out of it. I thought I could handle it. Please forgive me, Aubrey, please!" I cry frantically. I need someone in my corner right now.

"It's going to be okay, Trish; everything will come together. Now let's get to La'Rose."

Aubrey

The car ride over was so quiet. After Trish dropped that bomb, I was lost for words. I love Trish like a sister. She has been through a lot, and even though this situation could've possibly worked out differently, she has always had to deal with someone's shit. So, I can't turn my back on her, and I surely can't turn my back on Colby. We are family now.

We pull up to La'Rose lounge, and it looks abandoned. It feels cold and weary, or maybe that's just us.

"La'Rose Lounge... I remember when Porter first came to me about opening La'Rose. His eyes were so lit up like he had the world's most brilliant idea. See, no one knew that Porter had other dreams outside of basketball. He was afraid of what people would think about him." Trish and I stand at the entrance and take everything in.

"Porter was always so confident," Trish says.

"That wasn't real. That was a persona he built. He thought that a basketball star had to be arrogant, full of himself, and a lady's man. That persona he built is what started to tear us apart. But it was always so hard for me to leave because I knew who he was under that persona. I knew how insecure he was. I knew he looked for validation in the people around him. He seconded guessed everything he did. When he came to me about this lounge, he was nervous and so excited. It's like he thought the whole thing through. The hardest part was him telling his dad that he didn't want to go to the NBA. His father invested so much in him to make him a phenomenal basketball player, but it was never a big dream of Porter. Whenever he came to see me, he had Fortune or Black Enterprise Magazine in his hand. Very rare, was it a basketball."

"Wow, I didn't realize how much I didn't know about him," she says.

"Yeah, he had his shit, but he really wasn't all bad," I say while we walk around the lounge.

"I picked out everything in here. He wanted the look to have a warm women's touch. He thought it would give it the sexiness he envisioned. We built this place together, but it was never my dream," I sigh.

"Well, what is your dream, Aubrey?" Trish asks.

"I'm a writer. That is what I do, and that is what I love. I want to write lots of novels and maybe even open my own publishing company. I want to build a team of writers and have an office in New York City, looking over Central Park. That is my dream. That is what I want. That has always been my dream. Then from there, maybe write and produce my books into films and television shows." I gaze off into a daydream.

"Damn, now that's a dream. I can see it," Trish smiles with excitement.

"It's not a dream; it's a goal," I respond.

"It's already done," I confirm.

"Well, with all that we have on our plate now. I believe we can do this and achieve our goals," she adds.

"What are your dreams, Trish? What do you want?" I ask her. She lights up even more as if her dream was standing right in from of her.

"Man, where do I start? I don't know... Real Estate was always the beginning for me. I want to buy and flip homes and commercial property. I want to remodel homes, flip them to sell or rent out. Then I want to start my own interior design company. I have great ideas. I mean, I want my company to specialize in remodeling homes, interior design, and custom furniture. Maybe even become a developer and build up the neighborhoods in the inner city. With all of this gentrification going on, we need people who will build up and give homes back to the community. Yeah... I know it's a lot, but it's my dream. It's what I've fantasized about for years. It has always seemed so far fetched. So far away," she smiles humbly.

"Well, now we have a chance to make all of our dreams come true... And maybe even a few for others. You just never know what doors your dreams will open for other people," I smile at her.

"I call that purpose," she adds.

"Yeah... Purpose... So, let's get started... First thing first... I've always loved the name La'Rose. Porter's mom gave it to him. But I think the name should pay homage to him," I say.

"Porter's...The name should be Porters," she says.

"Do you think he would approve?" I ask.

"Why not, it's his name, and it's a legacy for his children," she argues.

"I agree, well... Porters it is!" We stand there full of excitement.

"I will focus on the staff and promotions, you focus on the interior design, we will both focus on the menu and the books," I mimic my thoughts with my hands while we pull our thoughts together.

"You really think we can do this?" she asks.

"Yes, Trish, we can do this. Porter wouldn't have left us all of this if he didn't think we could handle it. Which reminds me, I have to check out Sugar Honey Iced T," I say... as I ponder through my never-ending to-do list.

"Are you going to redo that place too?"

"No, I'm not going to change anything. I think that place is perfect just the way it is. I may add a brunch buffet on Sunday with live music, but that's pretty much it. It just needs more people to know about it. Everything else will fall into place."

"Okay, well, let's get out of here. We have a lot to do," Trish adds.

****

We have spent the last month in this lounge, day and night. Doing everything we could to put this place together. Trish found a good contractor to open up the space a little more. We are doing so much more work than we planned, but it's coming together.

"When will the new furniture be in?" I ask Trish as she pouts her lips at the assistant who struggles to hang the art on the wall.

"Yeah, it should be here tomorrow, I'm guessing." She focuses on the art piece while talking to me. She definitely has good taste, because I would have never thought about this abstract painting. It's colorful, but it works.

"What do you think, Bre?"

"Beautiful. You have a good eye," I respond while filling out the inventory list.

"Cool. What are you about to do?" She gives the assistant the okay signal and walks away.

"Girl, I have no idea. My mom has PJ, and Carter is in New York for a few days."

"Perfect, let's call Eric and Torin and hang out for the night. I will meet you back at your place." She tramples out of the lounge in a hurry. A lot has changed in this last month. We put that Doc thing behind us. Trish and Colby moved back into the house Porter built, but Colby still stays with us from time to time. Trish and Grant have finally put a date on the wedding. I mean, it's only been a month, but we all needed some good news, so thank God they put things in motion. So, Hawaii is where I will be in a skimpy bikini once I get rid of all this baby fat I accumulated. I walk into the office. We both agreed that I would take Porter's office. I left my phone on the desk. I had a thousand missed calls from Carter and a voicemail from Detective Charles. I call Carter first because it must be important.

"Hello," Carter answers the phone taking deep breathes.

"Hey baby, sorry I miss your call. We've been working all day."

"I was just checking on you babe, how was your day?" he asks with a heavy breath.

"It's been good. It sounds like you are jogging."

"Yes, I am. Spring has definitely sprung in New York. It's a really nice day. I wish you were here."

"Yeah, me too… We will be there in a few days. I'm excited." I tap my fingers on my desk and smile like a high school girl talking to her crush.

"Alright, well, let me get back to it. I will talk to you later tonight," he replies.

"Okay, babe, I love you. I will talk to you later."

"Love you too," he says before he hangs up.

Carter and I have really flipped the script. Sometimes it's weird… Like… He is the same kid I used to give knuckle sandwiches to when we were kids. It has always been something there, but I never thought that it would be like this. Carter has shown me another side of him, and I'm in love with that man. Like "that's my King, I'm his Queen, friends, and lovers. My heart beats for the both of us" kind of love. He is my Brown Sugar, Love, and Basketball, Love of My Life like Common and Erykah. Porter was my everything, but that trip I took to New York to spill all of my pain on to Carter had me full of "what if's."

"Hello," Detective Charles answers the phone very upbeat.

"Hey, Detective Charles. This is Aubrey; I saw you called."

"Hey Aubrey, how is everything going?" he asks.

"Everything is going great. Just trying to get Porter's Place up and running again."

"Okay, that sounds great. Listen, I want to meet with you and Trish tomorrow. Are you all available?"

Oh shit… What is this about, and why does he need to meet with both of us? God, I hope they haven't figured anything out.

"Uh yeah, I don't see why not. Can you meet us at La'Rose tomorrow around noon?" I was a little reluctant and one hundred percent nervous."

"Okay, sounds good. I will see you then." He quickly hangs up the phone, and I immediately call Trish.

"Hello," she answers. It sounds like she's driving.

"The Detective called you, didn't he?" She says before I could speak. I can hear the tremble in her voice when she speaks.

"Yeah, he did. He wants to meet with us at La'Rose tomorrow," I reply, trying to keep my nerves intact so that she does not freak out.

"Oh shit... Shit! Shit! Shit!" I can hear her hyperventilating.

"Calm down! We don't know what this is about. You have to keep your cool, Trish, please. Relax! Look, go home and get ready for tonight. I will text Eric and Torin," I calm my tone to relax her a little.

"Okay, you're right -Okay..." She quickly hangs up the phone. There is one thing that I've learned about a person with a pure heart like Trish's. They can hardly fathom doing wrong, and when they do, it's a challenge for them to deal with it or keep it a secret. I would never rat on her or tell anyone because she did what she had to do to protect her family. I just pray that she can keep her own secret and keep herself out of trouble.

Chapter 11
Let's make it official

Carter

"I'm in love, man… It's been like that since we were kids." I couldn't go back to New York and not hang out with my guys Keam, Rai' and Jay. We've been coming to Domingos Bar and Grill since the day we met. Keam, Rai, and I started at the sports marketing firm the same day. We were all hyped about our new positions. Jay, whose real name is Jake, had been there three years before us. Jay is a white boy, and his name couldn't get any whiter, so we started calling him Jay. He's a smooth white boy, but he doesn't try to "act" black. He's just who he is, a cool white boy. Keam is straight out of Harlem and Rai' is straight out of Brooklyn, so you could only imagine how they feud back and forth. Me and Jay just sip our beers and enjoy the entertainment while those two go at it after a few drinks.

Everything that comes out of Keam's mouth is about how great Harlem was back in the day, and now it's being gentrified, and "black" barely exists. "Man, even the white girls are walking around in Dashiki's," he argues. Rai's more laid back. He is definitely Brooklyn all day. He's my voice of reason. Both of them are married men. Rai's wife is pregnant with their first kid. Keam is on his third kid with his wife. He makes marriage and family look like hell. He is the last person I would go to for advice. Jay hasn't jumped into the marriage thing yet. That dude has a new girl every few months.

"So, you think you ready for all that, though, raising her baby and all that?" Keam rubs the bottom of his beard while he analyzes my response and tells me why I shouldn't do it.

"He said he's ready! I mean, you keep asking him like he's going to give you a different answer!" Rai gets irritated with Keam because this is the third time he asked me the same question.

"Look, man, I'm with you one hundred percent. You've been talking about this woman and fighting for her; she must be worth it," says Jay in a mellow tone.

"Hell yeah, she must be special if you took a bullet for her. I'm not gonna front; I didn't think you were coming back from that man," Rai chimes in.

"It's always the white man... Being all supportive and shit." Keam turns towards Jay, and we all burst out with laughs.

"Yeah, you took a bullet. That was gangsta. Shit, I wouldn't even jump in front of a water gun for my wife. Now we're talking about marriage and another man's sperm? Shiiiid." Keam takes a sip of his beer.

"That's a damn shame." Rai looks at Keam and shakes his head.

"I'm just saying," Keam adds.

"Look, Aubrey isn't just any woman. She has been thee, woman, since the first time I saw her. She wasn't really feelin' the kid, though. My crush turned into a real friendship, something special and solid. It took a while for things to happen, but it happened on its own timing. Yeah, I would be raising another man's baby, but seriously man... I love that lil' boy. It's bad enough that his biological father is not here... Even if Aubrey and I didn't make it, I would still be his father figure. I made a promise to his dad." Every one of them is silent and staring at me. The noise from the other drunk happy hour victims takes over.

"Damn, Carter... Did you write that? That shit sounds like it came right out of a movie script," says Rai' as he chuckles.

"I'm going to do it, man. The night of the reopening of Porter's Lounge..."

"Porter? Oh, that's her ex, right? The kid's father?" Jay asks.

"Yeah, man. Porter left it to her and his daughters' mom. He gave her another restaurant and some property too." I try to speak louder over the noise from the happy hour patrons. It has gotten packed since we have been here.

"Damn! He left her all of that? You're rolling in the doe, man! But how are you going to compete with that?" Keam inquires.

"Man, I'm not trying to compete with anybody. And I'm not rolling in anybody's doe, but mine. I respect him for leaving them all of that. That is what a man is supposed to do. Leave a legacy for the ones he left behind. Isn't that somewhere in the Bible? That stuff doesn't mean anything to me. I'm just happy that she is stepping into herself," I reply to Keam, but he's looking at me like I'm full of shit. Rai and Jay seem to agree with me.

"So, you mean to tell me; you don't want anything? It never crossed your mind that you could get something out of the deal? I mean... After hittin' that you didn't roll over like, baby, can I get a Benz?" He asked with his lip twisted to the side and his beer in his hand. Clearly, he had a few. He always has a thousand questions and will swear you down that you're lying or don't know what you're talking about. Rai taps his Nike Jordan's on the bottom of the barstool; he is definitely done with Keam and his dumb ass questions.

"Nigga! No!" shouts Rai. Once again, Jay and I burst out in laughs. Rai has no patience for Keam what so ever.

"Aight, aight, look... I wouldn't mind a Range Rover out of the deal, but I'm damn sure not going to ask for it. I don't think I would accept it if she offered. The bottom line, I make good money. Enough to take care of all of us. What she has is just icing on the cake."

"Shiiiiidddd! I would accept it!" says Jay.

"I was with you until you said that bullshit. A Range Rover? There is no way in hell I'm turning down a free Range Rover," he continues while taking his beer back.

"Man, I get it, but I want her to see that I am genuinely here for her. Period."

"Aight, man, so what's up? You love her; you love the kid; you don't want her money... So, what's the move?" asked Rai.

"The Ring," I reply.

Aubrey

We are at our bitter end with the renovations at Porter's Place. Trish's nerves are shot. Her energy is completely off.

"Trish, seriously... You need to relax. Damn, he's probably just going to give us more information about Porter's case, which you have nothing to do with." I try my best to calm her down while we hang the picture of Porter near the front entrance.

"No, it's not that... Well... It is, but it isn't... I'm..."

She hesitates to finish her sentence, and quite frankly, I don't need any more surprises, so she needs to just spit it out. "You're what? Spit it out!" I demand. "I'm pregnant..." My face lit up like Time Square, but Trish doesn't look so happy.

"What! Oh my God, Trish! This is wonderful news!" I grab her and give her a big hug, but she is clearly not feeling it.

"Wait a minute... Is it Porter's?" I held my breath, awaiting an answer.

"No, I'm not that far along. Porter and I had not had sex for months. It's Grants." Without breaking a smile, she lowers her head as if she is ashamed.

"Then what is the problem, Trish? This is a blessing! You love that man, and he loves you."

"I know... He comes back to town tomorrow. I want to tell him, but I can't do it."

"Why not?" I ask. I'm so confused right now. I mean, seriously, is this not good news?

"Aubrey, I can't have a baby right now. I don't even think I should marry that man. What if I am found guilty? What if I end up in jail? It's bad enough Colby might lose me," she whispers.

"Don't you think you're overreacting just a little bit?" I ask.

The look on her face says, "Bitch are you serious?" "Okay, maybe not, but Trish, you are not going to jail. I promise you that. I don't know what will happen, but you are calling the weather before seeing the clouds."

"Clouds? Aubrey, what the hell... You are reading too many books."

"I mean, you are making assumptions you have no idea of what's going to happen. What happened, happened, and bottom line... He had that shit coming, so my advice to you is to ride this thing until the wheels fall off because that is what I plan to do. We have been through enough. We are going to be all right. Do you hear me? We're gonna be alright. We are all we got."

"Yeah, I hear you." She lifts her head and nods back at me. There is a knock at the door… Knowing who it is, we stand frozen in place as our eyes lock on one another. Then another knock… Neither one of us want to answer the door, but what else are we going to do?

"Are you ready?" I ask her.

"Yeah, I'm ready." I open the door and put on my pretty girl smile. I turn to look at Trish, and she has done the same. Fuck that… It's time to get away with murder.

I open the door, and Detective Charles stands firm in front of me with an envelope in his hand. I signal him to come in. "Hey Detective, how is everything going?" I ask as we all walk towards the bar. Trish looks so tensed.

"Hey ladies, how is it going?" he asks in his deep, scruffy tone.

"Hey, Detective, we are pulling through," Trish answers.

"Can we get you anything?" I ask.

"No, this shouldn't take long. I just wanted you all to know that we are making noise on Porter's case. It took some time, but we have finally got a clear copy of the photos from Porter's accident. Now let me warn you… It may not be easy to look at them. He is not in the photos, but his car is and the suspect." He pulls out the pictures, and there you have it. The first picture was Porter's car. Completely crushed… It's hard to believe he lived at all. Tears fall from both of our eyes instantly. It feels like we are reliving that night all over again.

As he flipped through the pictures, I noticed that a car pulled up next to Porter before the accident.

"This is the guy that hit Porter. He got out of the car after hitting him, walked up to the car, and grabbed what looks like a gun and a money pouch." Detective Charles continues to flip through the pictures.

"He gets back into the truck and pulls off. This vehicle was reported stolen later that evening. This was not a regular accident. This was clearly a robbery and attempt murder. Porter's car wasn't just hit. He tried to do damage."

We both sit there silently as we go through the motions. I look over at Trish; her face is bloodshot red as she cries in silence.

"Did Porter carry large amounts of money with him?" Detective Charles asked.

"Only when leaving the lounge for the evening... He was the only one that handled the drop off and deposits to the bank," Trish answers.

"Well then, that settles that. Whoever this guy was, he knew Porter's every move. Do you all have footage from the cameras of the lounge the week before Porter's accident? If this was a setup, I guarantee you that he was here at least three times out of the week." Detective Charles looks to analyze the cameras in every corner of the lounge.

"We should have it; we haven't done anything with the camera system, so everything should be the same," I say.

"Okay. Have either of you ever seen this man before?" Trish froze up as she stared at the close-up picture of Doc.

"No, I don't believe so," I answer.

"Trish, what about you?" he asks, but she doesn't answer. Her eyes are glued to the photo.

"Trish? Detective Charles is talking to you." I break her focus.

"Oh yeah, no I... I don't know him," she answers.

"Look, I know this is hard for you two. I'm sorry that you have to go through all of this. I'm going to put the footage from the cameras on my flash drive and get out of your way." He gets up from the barstool and follows me to the back room. Trish pours herself a glass of water and took it back without taking a breath. Sweat beads cover her forehead.

"This should only take a few minutes, and I will get out of your hair," he says as he takes a seat at Porter's desk.

"Take as long as you need. We just want all of this to be over with," I reply.

"Hey, let me ask you... Is everything okay with Trish? I know all of this is a lot on her; she just seemed a little off." How else can I cover up Trish's shady energy? Well, here goes a small sacrifice.

"Yea, she will be okay. She just found out that she is pregnant by her fiancé, so her emotions are out of whack."

"Fiancé? I thought she and Porter were together?" Oh shit, I think I'm talking too much.

"No, they broke up. It was mutual. They were trying to keep it together for their daughter, but they both decided to move on."

"Wow, that was quick…"

"Yeah, well… You can't help who you love, right?" I gotta get out of this conversation.

"Yeah, that's crazy. Porter said that to me once." He looks up at me. I'm going to assume that conversation was about me.

"Well, I'm going to let you get to it," I say.

"Actually… It looks like…. One second… Okay, it's done. See quick and easy." He pulls out the flash drive and grabs the photos off of the desk.

"Okay, great… Well, let me walk you out."

We get to the front of the lounge, and Grant is hugging Trish. I didn't even hear him come in. Trish is still scared straight.

"Hey, Grant!" I shout as we get closer.

"Hey, Aubrey! How is it going?" he replies with a smile. He is as smooth as smooth gets. Trish was crazy to ever let him slip away.

"Grant, this is Detective Charles; he is working on Porter's case. Detective Charles, this is my fiancé Grant." Trish smiles at Grant as she leans up against him. We may be in this crazy mess right now, but Grant does something to Trish. Every time she looks at him, it's like everything goes away. I am entertained by it. It's like a teenage love affair.

"Hey man, it's nice to meet you. Congratulations on your engagement and everything else." Did he really have to point down at her belly! Shit! She turns to me and squeezes her lips together like a mother chastising her child. I shrug my shoulders.

"Sorry," I whisper.

"You all be good. I will keep in contact." Detective Charles leaves.

"Wait… Why did he point down at your stomach?" Grant's dark-skinned cheeks turn rosy red.

"I didn't expect you to be home until tomorrow, but I guess any time is the best time. We are… Pregnant!" She puts on a fake smile. I wish she would just allow herself to be happy.

"What! Are you serious?" Grant's eyes get big, and joy exudes his face. He grabs her tight and hits her with a big kiss. She looks over at me, nervously biting her lip.

"It will be okay," I whisper as she reads my lips.

Lana

"Well, Lana. I think we should wrap it up now. We've been talking for the last two hours." Dr. Conrad closes her writing pad.

"Yeah, it has been some time. Look, I just want to say thank you. I know I've been a bitch to you in the past."

"Lana, it's fine. I never judged you, never. I just wanted to hear your story and find out where all of this frustration was coming from, but now I know. I don't condone any of your actions, but I understand your pain. And I appreciate that you have learned so much about yourself and the process."

"Could you please do me a favor? I'm unable to communicate with Aubrey through phone or letter. If you could send this letter off to her, that would be great."

"Oh, Lana, you know I can't do anything like that." She refuses and hands back the letter, but I refuse to accept it.

"Please… I don't know the next time I will see her and I really need her to hear what I have to say. I've done enough harm. I don't have anybody else." She glances up at me while reading the letter. Reluctant to say yes, she folds it up and puts it in her Chanel purse. She must be pretty comfortable with me around at this point. Usually, she has it locked up in her closet.

"I will send the letter off for you, but she will not know that this came from me. I can lose my job for this," she whispers.

"I understand, and thank you." I get up and walk out of her office.

Carter

"Thank ya'll for coming up; I appreciate it." Time Square is overcrowded, but Torin and Eric fit right in with the highly fashionable scenery of 5th Avenue.

"Thank us? Thank you! How could we turn down a free trip to New York City for the weekend," Eric grins while taking in the city.

"So, Carter, what is this all about? Men only call the best friends for one or two things," says Torin.

"MMMMM... Either you're in the dog house or..."

Torin interrupts Eric, "Oh my God! You want to propose!" screams Torin.

"Alright now... You know, the first one didn't quite work out- God bless his heart and rest his soul. So, don't let her down!" Eric points his finger in my face like an old broke down ass school teacher.

"Man, look, Aubrey has been the woman for me since we were kids. I know she is a little fragile right now, but I want to be a part of that healing. Her dad hasn't been around, but I got her mom's blessing."

"Damn... Well... uh... okay... So, what's the plan? Breakfast at Tiffany's?" asks Eric.

"More like lunch, but that sounds good for me. We can just check out a few places until we find one that she likes." 7th Avenue traffic is at an all-time high right now. People are racing back to work from their lunch breaks. It is impossible to stand in one place in New York City; you will get trampled.

"So, we can walk up to 5th Avenue and 72nd. It's really not that far away. The blocks are short," I say as I dodge oncoming foot traffic.

"I'm cool with that; it's a nice day," Torin agrees.

"Who? Hell no. Not in these new Jimmy Choo loafers... We will kindly catch a cab... Taxi!" He waves down a taxi, and one immediately pulls up.

"A taxi?" I frown up my face while he works diligently to be seen.

"By the time we get to the top of 5th Avenue in a taxi, the walk will be over," Torin says. I agree with her, and Eric shuts the door with a bougie attitude.

"Oh! Okay then! So, I guess new loafers will be a part of my travel," Eric adds as he takes his sunglasses down off of his head and places them over his eyes.

"This is the perfect day for a good walk. Me and my summer dress are enjoying every minute of it." Torin's hair slightly breezes through the light wind.

"Girl, you are going to regret wearing those damn sandals. This is New York City! Your feet are going to look and feel like you walked across a pile of fire. And a summer dress? Where in the hell? Your inner thighs are going to be on fire when this walk is over. I guarantee you that!" I crack up, laughing at Eric. Now I see why Aubrey can't be away from them long; they are hilarious.

"Eric, shut the hell up and worry about those tight-ass jeans you have on! Besides, I have on spanks, so my thighs aren't rubbing asshole." I look down at Eric's jeans, and they look like they might rip if he moves the wrong way.

Finally, after two hours of walking and stopping at every designer store on Madison and 5th Avenue and where ever else Eric saw a show and Torin saw a handbag, we finally made it to Tiffany's. Both Eric and Torin's hands are filled with designer shopping bags that they got for themselves. Eric complained about the entire walk, but he didn't pass up one store. From Burberry to Prada, he window shopped and purchased more than he could carry.

"Alright, fuck this! I quit! I've already spent 3g's!" Eric complains as we walk into the store. I keep quiet and listen to these two bicker back and forth.

"All on your own, nobody told you to purchase those shoes, and why in the hell do you need another man purse? They have their own damn closet?" Torin returns with a stronger argument.

"Because I wanted to, and for all of the questions, dinner is on you!" he responds.

"No dinner is on me. Now can we find my girl a ring, please?" I interrupt as we walk up to the case of rings. A tall slim white guy who clearly has a little sugar in his tank stands behind the case.

"Good afternoon; how may I assist you all on this fine day?"

"A fine day it is," Eric winks and smiles at him.

"Alright, man, chill out." I turn to Eric and laugh while he flirts with the salesman. This dude is a boatload of entertainment.

"No, you cannot." Torin grabbed me by my hand and pulled me out of the store. Eric winks at the salesman and follows.

"Torin, what are you doing?" I asked as she pulls me closer to the sidewalk.

"I looked at every ring in there before you hit the door. Tiffany's it is not... Not this time. Aubrey needs something that is just for her. Not a ring that flashes across the tv during a commercial break. We are going exclusive." Torin jesters with her hands for me to follow along in her vision.

"Listen to her. She knows her shit," says Eric while coating his lip with balm.

"There are a thousand jewelry stores in Manhattan alone," I say while she tries hard to convince me.

"Fine, you're leading." We walk for forty-five minutes, and finally, I take Eric up on that taxi.

"Next stop Soho," she says.

"Soho? Where do you buy jewelry in Soho?" I ask Torin.

"You don't know what I know." We get out of the taxi in front of a small jewelry store. Torin walks in first, and Eric and I follow.

Another tall slim white guy, this must be their industry.

"Good evening, how can I assist you?" he politely asks.

"Yes, I-" Torin interrupts and steps in front of me.

"We are looking for an engagement ring." Torin focuses on the case of rings as she walks down the aisle glancing at the gleaming diamonds. Torin interrupts and walks up face to face to the salesman.

"She would prefer a Radiant, Asscher, or Square Cushion cut," she says directly to him.

"Okay, is there a budget you would like to stay in?" he asked. Before I could respond with a yes, Torin responds for me.

"We will worry about that bridge when we get there. In the meantime, could you bring us those cuts from the back, have someone to lead us to a table with chairs and a few glasses of champagne, please? We may be here for a while," Torin orders the salesman, and he moves swiftly to her energy. I take notes and look over at Eric without saying a word.

"That's how we roll," he responds and winks as he moseys behind Torin. I don't know what just happened, but something tells me that my budget just went up.

A few minutes go by, and the salesman walks from the back of the store and leads us to another entrance.

"Please forgive me for not introducing myself. My name is Frances. I will be assisting you today. My sales associate is in the back, pulling the rings that you desire to see."

We enter into a small intimate space with sofas, love seats, and dark oak stained-glass cabinets that hold rare pieces in them. We all separate into different directions as we admire the jewels hanging in the glass displays.

"This is going to be fuuunnn!" says Eric.

Another salesman walks out with three champagne glasses on a tray and an ice bucket with the bottle. He walks up to Torin and Eric. They both take their glass. When he gets to me, I refuse.

"I need to be sober while I'm spending my money." I joke, but I'm as serious as a heart attack. Eric snatches the second glass off of the plate and takes a sip. They both look like they know how to spend money. Eric is definitely the "save mines, spend yours" type.

"Welp, I've spent enough on myself today, mind as well spend yours," he giggles and walks away.

Yeah, right, that was probably someone else's too. I know he's paid; Aubrey talks about her friends like they are God's gift to the world, so I know all of the positives. Frances and another associate enter from the back with black velvet cases stacked on top of each other. We take a seat on the sofa, and he places the cases on the coffee table in front of us. Torin opens the boxes, and I haven't seen so much bling in my life.

"Damn!" I say as she opens them up.

"Yes sir, damn is correct," jokes Frances.

I've never seen so many jewels in my life. Torin picks up a ring and takes a brief look at it.

"That's beautiful, right there. I think that's the one," I say, pointing at the ring as she picks it up.

"No, it's not." Eric sits back with his glass of champagne and legs crossed; he replies with all of his arrogance.

"Well, I think it's the one Aubrey would love it," I respond. I asked them to come with me, not take control of the whole experience.

"She picked up one ring, and already, it's the one." Eric rolls his eyes and sips his champagne. I choose to ignore him. There is no way I'm about to have a full-on argument with this dude. Meanwhile, with a bare eye, Torin is still analyzing the ring.

"It's flawed," she raves with a nonchalant tone. She raises the ring to France, and he takes out his mini microscope.

"There is no way," he replies as he strains to see where the damage may be.

"Sugar listen, I know diamonds, and diamonds know me. And that diamond is flawed," Torin sips her wine, sits back in her seat, and crosses her legs. She passes the ring to the salesman without taking another look at it.

"Well, ma'am, you are definitely a pro. You are correct," Frances replies.

"I told you," Eric snarls.

"We need an eye like yours at our establishment, ma'am, that is brilliant," Frances adds.

"No, no, I wear diamonds, not sell them," Torin smiles as if to say, "What in the hell makes you think I am looking for a job."

Two hours have gone by, and I don't want to look at another damn diamond ring. I know this is fun for them, but I thought we would've chosen a ring an hour and a half ago. Finally, Torin picks up a beautiful square cushion-shaped ring. I learned a little something while spending my day in diamond training.

"This is the one!" she screamed. She passed it off to Eric, and he takes a hard look at it.

"Yesss! Bitch! This is the one! This is it!" He rushes over to the chair, where I have separated myself from the ring charade. He puts the ring right in front of my face. The moment I saw it, I visualized it on her finger and the reaction I would get when she saw it. I got up out of my seat and felt like I was floating on cloud nine. This is absolutely the ring.

"This is it… This is the ring." My tone is very mild and appreciative of their effort. They came through.

"Frances, what is the cost of this ring?" I ask.

"Sir, that ring is actually on sale. For eighteen thousand…" My eyes grew out of my head. I was thinking more like three, maybe four, even seven or eight, but eighteen thousand?

"Eighteen thousand dollars? Oh, that's good… That's real good…" Torin gets up and walks over to me.

That's real good? What in the hell has she been smoking? I can fly to Africa and dig up the diamond, my damn self!

"Don't panic… She is the love of your life and will do anything for you. She has been through so much, and she deserves a ring of this stature plus some." She is trying her best to convince me. Frances was right; she would be perfect for this job. I feel for the man that falls victim to her because he is in for a ride. I meditate on my thoughts for a second. Aubrey does deserve to be on queen status. She deserves all of the great things coming her way. It's not like I can't afford it, besides the fact that I have been out of work for months and just returning. Shit! I have to close that big college basketball account. What would be messed up, though, is if she said no… But why would she do that? Would she do that? Fuck it… I mean, the worst thing that could happen is that she says no, embarrasses the hell out of me, and I have to bring the ring back. Wait, can I do that? I would probably be stuck with an eighteen-thousand-dollar credit that I would probably never use. I'm thinking too hard… Aubrey loves me. It's worth it.

"Frances, box it up. I will take it." Torin exhales and is relieved by my answer. They both jump up, screaming with excitement. I'm dancing on the inside, smiling on the outside, and throwing up in my mouth at the same time.

"Next stop, steak, and lobster!" yells Eric. I gotta get the hell away from these two.

Aubrey

I have been waiting for Carter to get back home all day. It's the perfect night for a little romance. Something about the rain makes me romantic and horny. Carter called and said that he is less than thirty minutes from the house. I know he's tired from that long drive from New York. I ran him a hot bubble bath and lit candles all around the house. I hooked up some lamb chops, lump crab cakes, sautéed spinach, and sweet potato soufflé. Torin's girlfriend from college had a pop-up shop. She started a lingerie line called Dirty Glamour, and the pieces were to die for. Tonight is the perfect night to premiere my new sexy. Torin just got back from a business trip too. She volunteered to babysit PJ. I'm happy we worked everything out. Torin is one of my best friends, and I know she wouldn't try to hurt me. She's always trying to protect me, and after we sat and talked, I realized that is all she was trying to do.

I sit down at my vanity and make my face up, curl my hair in big Dorothy Dandridge curls and spray on the Chanel perfume Carter just got for me. This canary yellow mesh laced bra and panty set goes perfect with my peacock blue satin robe. I hear Carter's car pull up in the driveway. I hurry down the stairs, skipping steps to get to the sofa before he enters the door.

He walks in, and I am lying across the sofa, posed like a pinup girl. He walks in with flowers in one hand, a toy truck, and his bags in the other. His smile spreads across his face. I can see him blushing through the candlelight.

"You look like the perfect painting," he smiles.

"Aw, that is so sweet. Now come over here and let me shower you with all of these kisses." He drops his bags and walks over to me with the flowers.

"Thank you, babe, these are beautiful." He kisses me like we haven't seen each other in months. I feel my panties getting wet as he kisses on my breast. Goodness, we are going to skip all the way to desert.

"Wait, wait, Carter... I made you a bath upstairs." He is uncontrollable when he gets started, and I love every minute of it.

"It can wait," he whispers.

"Ugh!" I moan as he makes his way to what he calls "paradise."

"But it's going to get cold, and so will your food." He flops down on the sofa like a kid who's not getting his way.

"How did you expect me to think about food and a bath with you sitting here like that?" he asks.

"I didn't. I expect you to want me so bad that you can't wait any longer, but first. I want to cater to you."

I grab him by his hand and lead him upstairs. The trails of candles guide us through the bedroom to our bathroom.

"Are you getting in with me?" he asks.

"No, you think you're slick. If I get in with you, we will never get to dinner, and I am hungry," I reply as I help him undress.

"Well, I'm hungry too..." Before I know it, I'm drenched in water, and dinner will just have to wait.

Trish

"Are your eyes closed?" Grant asks.

"Does it matter? I have on a blindfold," I laugh.

"What about you, Colby?" he asks.

"Yes, they're closed!" she giggles.

He gets out of the car and walks around to open the doors for both of us. Now that my stomach is hanging out of my jeans, I can barely stand up on my own. I got really big, really fast to be three months pregnant. That makes sense with twins. Yes, I said twins! It turns out they run in Grant's family.

"Alright, let's go." He walks us both across some grass and then pulls off the blindfolds.

"Wow!" screams Colby.

"A wood stick house!" she adds. Grant laughs.

"Well, kind of. I am actually having it built for us: six bedrooms, four in a half bath. Babe, I'm leaving all of the landscaping, interior design, and build out to you. I believe in your vision, and I know you will set us up nicely." He stands in front of me with a huge smile. I smile while tears run down my face.

"What's wrong?" he asks with concern.

"Absolutely nothing... You are a dream," I say.

"No, babe, you are the dream." He grabs my face and kisses me.

"Where do we start?" I ask.

"Well, you're the expert. I know it has always been your dream to remodel and do interior design, so I figure you could start with us. I've already looked into nannies and babysitters for us, and I think that after you meet a few of the prospects, you will be pleased. That way, you will have time for yourself and to go to school." He walks around the land and recites our plans. I never thought I would have acres of land, let alone someone loving me enough to buy it for me.

"Wait. What about California this summer?" I ask.

"Trish, there is no way in hell I'm going to California and leaving my pregnant fiancé home. Cali can wait. Besides, we are being blessed from every avenue. The way things are going, we may be able to buy us a house in California in the future." He looks like a young boy filled with hopes and dreams. Grant turns thirty-three this year. He has always wanted a family. I know he is on a high right now with all of these great things happening for him and us together. I just pray that my gray cloud doesn't bring a storm.

"So, what do you think?" he says as he rushes back to me.

"I think it's beautiful, I think it's a plan," I smile at him gently.

"But what about Porter's house?" I ask.

"Well, Porter left it to you, so I guess whatever you choose to do with it. I will not intervene with that, but if you want my opinion. I would keep it. Maybe you can rent it out until Colb is old enough to take it on for her own. I mean, every parent should desire the opportunity to give their children a piece of wealth. You can use this house to continue to build for her and educate her at the same time."

"Yeah, but she is still so young," I say.

"Yeah, but she will be so old in no time. And it's never too early to teach your children how money works," he replies.

"Yeah, you're right. That's what we will do. It will be all hers."

We all stand there looking up at the house, bursting with excitement. Good energy is in the air!

****

Grant decided to rent out a condo. Porter's house was way too much. There was no way I could stay there without getting emotional. My hormones are all over the place, and Grant can feel the tension and how hard it has been for me, so we rented out a condo in Canton. Colby loves it because it's so close to the dog park, and she loves dogs. She asks for one every other day.

"Baby, are you okay?" Grant asks. I feel bloated, sick, and guilty all at the same time. I have been throwing up every day since I told Grant. I don't know if it is the babies or my nerves.

"Yeah, I'm okay. It's just the babies. I think they are girls. I was sick with Colby all of the time," I smile to try to ease his worry.

"Or maybe they're boys, and they just want to give you a hard time," he smiles back as he grabs my waist.

"So, when are we going to tell Colby?" he whispers.

"Um, I don't know... When do you think we should tell her?" Shit, I am not ready to tell her yet. I have so much going on. So many changes are happening in her life.

"It's shocking that she hasn't noticed," he says.

I turn around and give him the side-eye.

"Wow, am I that big?"

"No, no, I didn't mean it like that. I'm just saying your appearance is starting to change. Like rapidly," he tries to explain.

"Actually, she has noticed. She told me the other day that I had a muffin top, and I should probably slow down on the large muffins." He burst out in laughs.

"Let's tell her in the morning." Grant sits down at the kitchen table and sits me on his lap.

"Tomorrow morning? Grant, babe... I don't know..."

"What don't you know?" he laughs.

"It's just a lot... She has been through so much, and every time she looks up, something new is happening in her life. Every time I look up, something new is happening. I just don't want to throw something else on her."

"But this is a good thing, Trish; it's a baby. Not one, but two!" he argues.

"Yes, I know... I just..." I hesitate.

"Okay, look, sleep on it... If you feel the same in the morning, then we will wait until you are ready."

"Okay, I will sleep on it" I smile and give him a kiss. Grant makes me feel safe and peaceful. His aura is covered in peace like nothing can shake him. He is like a mountain standing strong in a storm. Or maybe it's because he doesn't know he is in the midst of a storm.

Chapter 12
Truth or dare

Aubrey

It's been a week since I've spoken with Trish. Here she goes with her disappearing acts again. Life has gotten crazy for all of us, so I try not to be down her throat when she doesn't come around. I've taken on most of the responsibility in the lounge so that she can rest. She doesn't need any more added stress, plus I am keeping myself busy.

"Babe, you got some mail," Carter says as he walks in the room with PJ in his arms.

"It is eight o'clock in the morning. Why are both of you fully dressed?"

He sits PJ down on the bed, and with the biggest grin, PJ looks at me and rolls to the top of the bed.

"Hello, my sweet Prince." I grab him close and give him a kiss on the forehead as he hands me his plush Tyco Truck.

"So, I was wondering…" Carter looks like he is up to something.

"Oh goodness… That one statement sounds real suspect," I laugh.

"Shut up, I was trynna set myself up for this next plead," he shrugs with a smile. "You know I need to make a run-up to New York… I was wondering if you would let me take PJ." I felt the spirit of a lioness protecting her cub come over me.

"You said what now?" With damn near a growl in my voice, I ask him to repeat himself.

"Can I take him with me to New York?" he repeats himself in a less confident tone.

"New York? Carter, that is far away," I cry.

"I don't know about New York," I continue.

"Aubrey, you can't be serious? It's literally up the street. We will only be gone for two days. I already ordered toys and a little car bed for him to sleep in. I'm going to put it right next to my bed. We will be fine. I promise. It's nice and summery outside. He is going to be fine," he pleads his case.

"Carter, I swear to God if my baby comes back with as much as a scratch on him, I am going to fucking kill you!" I pick PJ up and squeeze him tight while he stuffs the wheel of his truck in his slobbering mouth.

"Damn, Killah," he replies. I laugh at him, but I am so serious.

"Okay, I'm serious; now take care of my baby." I stand up and hand PJ to Carter.

"I promise I will." He gives me a soft kiss on the lips. PJ watches and laughs.

"PJ, you take care of your dad, keep him out of trouble," I say.

"Dad?" Carter repeats as his cheeks turn rosy red. His face glows up like the sun has hit it.

"Well, you said you were all in, right? Porter will always be his dad, and so will you," I smile as he smiles back at me.

"Yeah, I'm all in. I just didn't realize how good those words would feel." He gazes at PJ as he walked out of the room.

"Be careful!" I yell as he walks down the stairs.

"Don't be using my baby to pick up women!"

"Girl, shut up!" he yells back.

"Yeah, aight!" I respond.

I sit back down on the bed and look at the mail. There is a piece of mail addressed to me, but no name. I can hear Carter walking towards the door.

"Babe, we're gone! See you in a few days. Love you!" he yells up the stairs before he shuts the door.

"Okay, I love you too." My eyes are focused on this letter.

Dear Aubrey,

I know I'm not supposed to write you, but I figured since you've been coming to visit me, there wouldn't be a problem. We have been friends for years. I made you suffer from the hurt that I was feeling from everyone else. And for that, I am deeply, deeply sorry. I'm sorry that it took for me to be in this hole to realize that you and everyone else that I've hurt were victims of my circumstances just as I was. These apologies also bare truth and forgiveness. The truth is Porter and I was together the summer you left for Virginia. We met that summer, and we were dating. He was my first. He left for basketball camp, and you returned home. I guess it was dumb for me to never give you his name, but I knew that if my father found out, I would get worse than what he gave to my mother. So, I made him my little secret. The day you two met in the cafeteria, I was there. I saw everything. I saw how he looked at you, and I saw how you looked at him. I was crushed… Sick to my stomach. That is why I stayed in my room for days. Then when he saw me, he acted as if WE never happened. He was the first boy I'd ever gotten that close to, and he acted like he didn't know me. My anger grew over the years. I felt violated not just from Porter, but from my father's abuse, my mom leaving me and your father… Your father… I wish I could fully blame him. He was wrong for what he pulled me into, but I was wrong to allow it to continue. I played mind games with him, just as he did with me. I have to get my fingerprints off of all of the people that have hurt me. As long as I am unforgiving towards them, I am going to suffer. I learned that in group therapy. I've really been working on myself in here. Talking to God and getting the help I need. I don't want to suffer anymore, and I don't want to hurt anyone else. I'm so sorry for what I've done to you. Everything Aubrey, and I hope that you find it in your heart to forgive me. If you ever run into Thomas, please tell him the same. I am sorry that I scarred him the way I did, and I hope that he lives a great life with Lisa. He deserves someone that is going to love him truly. I don't know where my life will go from here, but I needed you to know. Take care.

Lana

Detective Charles

Detective Charles walks onto the crime scene inside of Doc's motel room. The room reeks of a dead body. The smell is so bad he had to cover his mouth with a mask.

"Got damn! How long has he been in here?" he asks the examiner.

"I don't know as of yet, but by the looks of it, it has been a few weeks now, maybe a month, maybe two," the examiner replies.

"And no one came to check on him all of this time?" Detective Charles questions as he walks around the room, looking for evidence.

"The front office said that he paid to stay here for three months. That month ended a few days ago. The do not disturb sign was on the door. When the cleaning lady knocked on the door to get in, she didn't get an answer, so she went and got the manager, and he opened the door and found his body." A uniformed policeman walks up behind him and explains to Detective Charles what happened.

"So, he could've been in this room for a whole month or longer?" Detective Charles is disgusted by the thought and the vision.

"Yeah, it's a good chance," the officer replies.

"Are there any leads?" asks Detective Charles as he walks around the body and observe.

"Not as of yet, but we are retrieving the camera footage as we speak," the officer responds as he straddles behind Charles's every move.

"Get it to me as soon as you do… What is the guy's name?"

"The front desk gave us the name Dont'e Owens," the officer replies as he leaves the room. Detective Charles moves closer to Doc's face to get a good look at him. His skin is discolored and deteriorated, but Detective Charles recognizes his face. He takes a step back and takes his phone out of his pocket. He strolls through his pictures and looks at the close-up images from Porter's accident and the saved snapshots from the lounge footage.

"That's him," he whispers.

After hours of waiting for the footage, Detective Charles decides to go back to the precinct and wait on the footage while he tries to put Doc's death and Porter's accident together.

His phone rings as he paces the floor.

"Hello?"

"Hey, Chuck, it's Woods. I got that footage you were waiting for. I'm going to email it right over."

"Okay perfect, thanks, Woods." He takes a seat at his desk and opens up his email. After 10 minutes of downloading, the footage opens up.

"Oh, shit…" A chill of discomfort runs through his body.

Aubrey

Eric, Torin, and I meet up at Honey Bliss nail salon for some ratchet gossip, wine, and self-care.

"Girl, you have been extra busy," Eric says to me while we soak our feet in the warm water.

"Yes, it has been a lot going on lately, between PJ, the breakfast spot, and the lounge. I have been running racket. Not to mention Trish and this new baby."

"Sccuuuurrreed! What new baby?" Eric and all of his dramatics cuts me off.

"Aubrey, you are lying! Trish is pregnant?" ask Torin.

"Girl, yes, she and Grant are having a baby, and he is head over hills," I respond.

"Wow! This is great news! I'm happy to see that everyone is moving forward. This is beautiful. Hopefully, it's my turn to get married and settle down," says Eric.

"Maybe," I respond.

"Everyone is moving forward… but me…" Torin's face frowns up as she takes her last drop of wine. She signals one of the nail techs to bring her more wine.

"Girl, what are you talking about? You are on top of the world! Business is booming! Forbes is staring down your throat. Bitch you are opening a salon in London! Bitch LONDON!" I scream.

"Girl say it for the people in the back because she is trippin'," Eric cosigns with me. I elaborate on London because that is a big ass deal. How many black women do you know that has franchised their own salons from the ground up and has blossomed not only in the states but across the world. She is making major leaps in the beauty industry and is a great example of what success really looks like.

"Yeah, all of that is fine and dandy, but I am ready to start my own family. I know we are still young, but I feel like I've already accomplished so much, and I don't have anybody to share it with. Success, for me, isn't about the luxury and the monetary gain. For me, success is all of that plus happiness: a family and someone to celebrate with. I want my coins to be passed down. I want to build a legacy. I want a baby," she cries out.

"Girl lies!" Eric responds with his eyes rolling behind his head.

"No, I'm serious. After having PJ over, I realized that I want that… I want that kind of love. Even though he screamed and gave me the blues from time to time, it felt good to have another little human being in the house. I mean, I want to be married. I want all of that, but my heart is set on a little person. I just pray that I get the bundle package; you know, husband and children."

"Awww, you got bit by the baby bug! Torin, I never thought that you would have your eyes set on a baby. We've talked about it in the past, but you've never sounded like this," I say to her.

"Yeah, girl… This is a first for me too. Welp, I guess it's time for me to find some new hoes because you heffa's then went all 'House Wives' on a bitch," Eric cries out.

"Eric, please, you are probably going to settle down before I do," says Torin.

"Girl, please. I am the hit it and forget it type. And I'm doing the hitting and forgetting. These men are not serious, so why should I be? They stick around for a little bit and move on," he says.

"Well, what happened to that wedding planner guy?" I ask.

"Oh… Boy Toy? Because that is clearly all, he was with his cute little self. Cute as a button, but that was it. He had no money and no ambition. His momma got him that job!" he laughs.

"Look, maybe one day I will settle down, but right now, I am enjoying my career in this good old fashion industry, and I am having fun. I have the capabilities of being monogamists, just not right now. I travel the world and meet different types of men all the time…" Eric yaps on, and Torin interrupts.

"You're such a hoe," she laughs.

"I said, meet, not sleep!" He winks at us and sips his glass of wine.

"Oh really, what about our trip to Spain? I had to get a separate hotel suite," she adds.

"First of all! What happens in Spain STAYS in Spain! And unfortunately for you, it be like that sometimes. I told you I'm not the best roommate. Stella wanted to get a little groove, and everything about that man was screaming grooovvveee baby!" We all laugh.

"Bottom line is. I refuse to settle with just anyone. I want it to be real, and I want to be ready for him. That way, there is no confusion on the direction we are headed in," says Eric.

"Well, amen to that, Eric! I feel you," I add.

"Aye, girl! Don't dig into my big toe like that! What in the hell are you doing?" Eric yells at the manicurist as she cleans around his toes.

"Sorry, sir... Sorry," she replies, and then she starts speaking to her neighbor in Vietnamese. We knew they were talking trash about Eric, but he didn't say anything. He just doesn't tip and will write a review that will make you feel bad forever stepping foot in the place.

"I know this is a little off subject, but when was the last time you talked to your dad?" Torin asked.

"I don't know... It's been a while. Why?" I answer back without actually wanting to answer at all. I am not interested in talking about me and my father's relationship right now.

"I was just asking. I saw him the other day, Aubrey, and he looked pretty bad. You should go and see him," she continues.

"Honestly, Tor, this isn't a conversation that I am interested in having right now. My father has to lay in the bed that he made for himself, and that's that." They both get silent, and the rest of the day will carry on without a conversation about my father because I'm just not interested.

Trish

"Hello! One Second." I answer my phone and put it on speaker to walk away and help Colby.

"Colby, no, that is way too much icing." I rush over to Colby while she spreads boatloads of icing on tiny cupcakes.

"Sorry about that... Who is this?" Colby and I are in the middle of making cupcakes for her dance team. She was so excited to make new friends and decided to make cupcakes for everyone.

"Hey, Trish, this is Detective Charles. Are you available to speak?" My stomach balled up into a knot, and before I could answer, I had to find a seat and take it.

"Hey Detective, yeah, sure I'm available. What's up?"

"So, we just got back more evidence from Porter's case, and I need to sit down and discuss it with you."

"Okay, will Aubrey be there?"

"Actually, no. I just need to speak with you this time." I know this is about Doc. I have no idea how I am going to handle this. I have to call Aubrey.

"Ok, um... Sure. Would you like to meet tomorrow at La'Rose?" I ask.

"Yeah, sounds good. Is 9 am good for you?" he asks.

"Yeah, that's perfect. I will see you then." I quickly hang up the phone and call Aubrey. My heart is beating so fast, and my nerves are shot.

"Hello," she answers in a calm tone.

"Aubrey! Where are you?"

"Well, it's about damn time. Where have you been, Trish? This disappearing act will have to stop," she says firmly as if she is laying down the ground rules. I interrupt.

"Aubrey, shut up and listen. Detective Charles called me. He wants to meet with me and only me tomorrow. Aubrey, he knows! I know that he knows! What am I going to do?" My words fall all over each other.

"Trish, calm down. I'm leaving the nail salon now, meet me at the house. Carter is gone, so we have the house to ourselves," she says.

"Okay. I'm on my way." I hang up the phone and go into the bedroom where Grant is watching television.

"Babe, I have to make a run. I will be over at Aubrey's house if you need me. Colby is in the kitchen finishing up her cupcakes. Can you help her out, please? Before she destroys the kitchen."

"Yeah sure. Is everything okay?" he asks.

"Yeah, everything is good. I just want to get out for a little while and catch up with Aubrey. She doesn't even know about the twins. I will see you soon." I give him a kiss on the forehead and head out.

Aubrey

Knock, knock, knock, knock, knock!

"Who is it!" I yell while stumbling down the stairs.

"It's me." I open the door, and Trish barges in. Instead of taking a seat or even saying hello, she tramples my floor back and forth, and she is as big as a house.

"Trish, oh my God, you're huge. Like really huge!"

"Yeah, it's twins- look, what am I going to do? I cannot go to jail! Grant would leave me. What would happen to my children? He would surely take my babies, but what about Colby?" Her energy is on an excruciatingly high, and I cannot keep up.

"Twins! Oh, wow. This is... great... I guess... Look, calm down. Grant would never dishonor you in any way. He is a good loyal man. Colby and all of your babies would always be taken care of. If not him, me. But let's not think about all of that right now."

She tramples my floor so hard my mirrors are shaking on the wall.

"Trish, stop! We are not going to come up with a plan if you cannot calm down. You are going into this as a guilty person. You are not a guilty person; you are a victim."

She stopped moving and stood directly in front of me.

"Can I have some water? I think I'm over dehydrated."

I go into the kitchen and pour her a tall glass of water. She snatches it out of my hand and drinks it all the way down without breathing.

"Okay... We just have to come up with a plan. We don't know what evidence he has or if this is about you or not, but let's prepare ourselves for anything. So, this is what is going to happen..."

****

When I pull up to La'Rose, Detective Charles is standing outside waiting on me at the door. I garner my thoughts and prepare myself to have a conversation that holds my freedom in his hands. It feels like I am walking the green mile as I drag to the front door.

"Hey, Detective Charles! How are you?" I say with a fake bright smile.

"Wow, you've definitely grown since the last I saw you."

"Yes, I have. I'm having twins."

"Oh! Well, Congratulations!" he says as he follows me in. I can feel him glaring at me. There is definitely some tension in the room.

"Thank you!"

We walk into the half-decorated place. We have made so much progress.

"So, let's get down to it. I met Donte'. Not like I expected to meet him, but we met. He was in a body bag, and I was standing over top of him." At this point, I am complexed because I don't know a Donte'.

"I'm sorry, who?"

"Donte. That's the guy name that killed Porter."

"Donte?" I mutter.

"Well, maybe you may have had a different name for him, although you claimed to have not known him. So how do you want to play this out? Because quite frankly, the lies are getting old. The only reason you are not in cuffs right now is because I am giving you a chance to speak up before I have to turn this evidence in. Porter loved you and his daughter. I would hate for Colby to have to visit you in a jail cell. So, I need the truth."

I was prepared to make up a whole lie, but Aubrey thought it would be best just to tell Detective Charles the truth. She trusts that he would do the right thing.

"Detective Charles, to be honest with you. I was prepared to lie to you. I was prepared to make myself the victim in this situation, but it would have made me sick to hold this in any longer. I am prepared to face the consequences. I don't know that man as Donte'. His name is Nathaniel Docston, but I know him as Doc. I met him in Chicago while I was going through a very stressful time trying to survive and raise my daughter. He was the head of one of the most criminal activities that took place in Chicago. I used to clean money for him to make some extra cash to feed my daughter. He went away for a few years and asked me to hold onto his money. Over the years, I worked every job possible, but I struggled. So, I used some of the money that I held onto for Doc. Before I knew it, it was almost gone. I stopped answering his collect calls and tried to move on, thinking that he would be there long enough for me to start all over somewhere else. But before I knew it, I saw him out on the streets. I panicked and moved back to Baltimore. I had nothing or nobody in Chicago, and I haven't seen my family in Baltimore since I ran off to Chicago. So bottom line, Colby was all I had. I had to protect her.

Somehow, he found me a few days before Porter's accident. He told me that if I didn't pay him back his sixty-eight thousand, he would start killing people. I tried my best not to involve anybody. I really did! I tried to get money to him that Porter had saved up, but it wasn't there. Before I knew it. Porter was in the hospital with just a drop of life left in him! And it's all my fault!" I break down in tears and fall into a mental tangent as I reminisce on that day.

"Did you kill Doc?" he asks with a stern expression.

"He showed up at Porter's repast. At his fucking repast! After killing him? I told him I would get him the rest of his money, but he had to stay away from my family and me. I knew he was never going to stop. I knew he wouldn't! He is a bully, and that is what he does! So, I met him at his motel room to take him the money."

"I don't want to hear anymore," Detective Charles cuts me off.

"What?" I have no idea what's going on right now.

"I looked into his records. This dude has been on many cases for murder, robbery, and assault. All of this, and he suffers from seizures." I am so thrown back that I can barely speak.

"Look, you gave me enough. I just needed to know that you were not working with this man to kill my friend. Now that I know the truth, we are going to keep you out of jail. So, I need you to do exactly what I say, and it's going to keep your hands clean."

I sit down at the bar and take a deep breath.

"I am closing all cases. I have a video of you at the motel. No one will be able to identify you. You did a great job of disguising yourself. It doesn't show you leaving out of the room because the camera skips. Doc's death will be ruled out as natural causes because he has a history of illness. We will close the case with Porter and identify Doc as the murder suspect. We have no evidence or history to support why. We have no evidence of the money you were supposed to drop off, so bottom line... Case closed."

I feel so light that I can barely stand up. I thought I would be going to jail today.

"I hope that nothing like this ever happens again, but if you are ever in that type of danger and your life depends on it, please get the law involved. I'm not putting the blame on you, but this could've been avoided. If anyone asks you about this man again, YOU DON'T KNOW HIM."

Tears fall from my eyes. I am so relieved.

"Yes... Thank you so much, Detective," I mutter as I wipe the tears from my face.

"For the record. I knew you didn't have Porter set up. He talked so highly of you. I just needed to look you in the eyes and hear you say it. Take care of those babies. Don't ever let Colby lose the memory of her father. He may not have been the best, but he tried. He deserves for his name to live on."

I nod at him as he walks out of the door. I immediately jump on the phone to tell Aubrey what happened.

Chapter 13

I'm Suffocating

Aubrey

After a few glasses of wine and back to back movies, I fall asleep, fully dressed. The phone rings nonstop. It's 4 o'clock in the morning, who in the hell could be calling me?

"Hello," I barely open my eyes, and my voice cracks as I speak.

"Aubrey! It's Ms. Celia! Lana is in the ICU! She was attacked in the prison yard today!" Ms. Celia is, on the other end screaming to the top of her lungs. I jump up out of my sleep and put on the first pair of shoes I see.

"Aubrey, it's bad! It's really bad!" she cries.

"Okay! Okay! I'm on my way! Where is she?"

"They transported her to the hospital a mile from the prison."

"Okay, I am on my way there. I'll find it." I hang up the phone, grab my purse, and head out to the car.

When I arrive at the hospital, numerous prison patients are being transported into the hospital. It must've been a big fight. I get to the receptionist, and before I could give her Lana's full name, a woman calls my name. I turn around, and Celia was standing there.

"Aubrey!" She runs up to me and pulls me by the hand. "Could you give her a visitor pass please, she is Lana's sister?" I turn to look at her. She gazes back at me with bloodshot red eyes. Her lips tremble as she speaks. We quickly walk around to the Intensive Care Unit.

"I'm so happy that you are here. I didn't have anyone else to call. You are her only family." I kept walking without saying a word.

Finally, we got to the door. Upon entering, my spirit broke. Lana has done so many cruel things to so many people, but to see her lie in the hospital bed beaten and bruised that way dismantled my heart. Her face was cut up, and mountains of bruises covered her face. She didn't look like herself at all.

"The officer at the door said she was caught in a crossfire. Two groups of prisoners got into a big brawl, and before she could walk away, she was pulled in. Before they knew it, a dozen women were jumping on her. She was cut with some type of tool. I gotta get my baby out of here! I got to!"

I take Lana by the hand.

"Lana, it's me, Aubrey. We are going to get you out of here. You pull through. You have to fight. I know you can. We are going to get you out of here." I can feel myself getting worked up. It feels like I'm back in the hospital room, standing over Porter. It's too much. My heart can't take it.

"The doctor says that she was beaten badly. It will take her some time to recover," she whispers as she weeps.

"Ms. Celia, please forgive me, but I have to go. I can't take another traumatic moment. I just can't stand over another hospital bed like this. I'm going to do all I can to get Lana out of here, but I just can't do this."

Without waiting for a response, I walk out of the room. Before I exit, I hear Ms. Celia whisper to Lana.

"Don't worry, baby; mommy is here. I'm going to take care of all of it. I promise, and I'm so sorry!"

****

I slept for a good four hours. Before I knew it, my phone was ringing off the hook, and a thousand texts and voicemails came through from Trish. Before heading to the bathroom to brush my teeth, she calls again.

"Hello," I answer with a raspy voice and bad breath.

"Girl! I have been calling you nonstop!" she shouts.

"Yeah, I see. Could I at least use the bathroom first?" I respond.

"No, because I gotta let you know that it is all over. I can't get into details, but it's all over. Detective Charles has it all under control. You were right!" she shouts in my fragile ear.

"Thank God! I knew it would all work out. I knew it! Thank God! Now we can finally move on. I can plan this bomb ass baby shower and celebrate these babies and your engagement the right way!" My excitement overrides how tired I really am.

"Yessssss, I can't wait! Not to mention this big grand opening. Everything is going to be okay. I can admit, I didn't think it would. All I saw was myself in jail and my life falling completely apart."

"Girl, I-" Before I could speak, my line beeps.

"Hey, that's my line; let me give you a call back."

"Okay, sounds good."

"Hello."

"Aubrey? Hey sweetie." It's my mom, and from the sound of her voice, something is wrong.

"Hey, Ma, what's up?"

"Aubrey, please go and check on your father. He called me this morning, and he didn't sound like himself at all. I can't explain it, but he sounds like his soul was gone. He just kept saying he was sorry. Over and over again. I told him that it was okay, but he kept screaming that it was not okay, and he doesn't deserve us. Please go and check on him. I am so worried. I know that seeing you will make him feel so much better."

I sighed as I listened to her talk about my dad. I know it has been some time since I spoke with him, but I'm just not ready yet. He was my hero! My everything! Now I don't know who he is. I don't see the man I once knew when I look at him.

"Ma-" I drag.

"Aubrey, please! I am begging you!" she cries out.

"Okay, Ma... Where is he?"

"He has a condo downtown that we have owned for some time. He is there. There is a copy of the key here if you need it. It's in his office, on the desk. I have to get to my class, but please call me when you get with him. I will text you the address."

"Okay, Ma..."

"And Aubrey... Thank you," she replies softly.

I get up and throw on some sweats.

I pull up to the condos. I've been here before. This was Lana's place! This was the place that he got for Lana. I can't believe him! I can't believe he would stay here! Or that he would still have this place! I get to the door and knock like I am the police. I am pounding on the door.

"Daddy! Daddy, open the door!"

I knock some more.

"Daddy! Daddy, open the door!"

Still no answer. I take out the key from his office and unlock the door. The place is still decorated the same way it was when Lana lived here. He didn't even have the decency to change the decor in the place.

"Daddy! Daddy!" For some reason, the further I walked, the gloomier it felt. Finally, I entered the bedroom. My father was slumped over to the side with a gunshot in his chin. Blood is spread across the white comforter and pillows. I can't move. I can't speak. Before I know it, I've thrown up all over the marble floors.

"Daddy! Daddy noooooo! Daddy!" I cry out.

I run to him and try to lift his head.

"Daddy! Please, Daddy! Please! Daddy, I'm sorry! Daddy, I'm so sorry!"

As I kneel down, I feel something under my leg. A gun with a silencer on it. He had this planned out. He actually purchased a fucking silencer! Covered in his blood, I lay next to him in silence. I can't wrap my head around it. It's my fault. All he wanted was me to forgive him. I forgave everyone else for what they've done. He deserved the same, and now it's too late.

I finally got up, put his legs up on the bed, and covered his body with the comforter. I crawl to my phone because my legs are too weak to walk.

"Hello, please help me. I found my father dead. He shot himself in his condo," I can barely speak.

"Ma'am, what is the address? We will have authorities there immediately."

"2250 Bonds Street," I reply.

"Okay, ma'am. I will have someone there for you, and ma'am, I'm so sorry about your loss." Before I hung up, the phone line beeps.

"Hey, Brey, how did it go?" My mother's voice is filled with so much optimism.

"Ma? Mommy!" I cry.

"Aubrey! Aubrey, what's wrong?" she yells.

"Ma, he's dead! He's dead, Ma!" I heard the phone drop to the ground, and she screams at the top of her lungs.

"No! No! No! Why Lord! It was going to be okay!" she cries. I hang up the phone and go sit out in the hallway. I can't stand to sit in here any longer. My clothes are covered with blood. My phone vibrates; it's Carter. I just can't answer right now.

Finally, the police officers show up. My body is balled up in a fetal position on the hallway floor outside of the condo. My energy has drained completely from my body.

"Ma'am... I'm officer Blackstone. Are you able to talk to me?" I look up at him without saying a word.

"Ma'am, I know this is hard, but I really need you to talk to me," he continues.

"Can you call Detective Charles, please?" I pull up his number in my phone and hand it over to him. He dials the number, and Detective Charles answers.

"Hello," he answers in a raspy voice. It sounds like he is still asleep.

"Hi, Detective Charles, my name is Officer Blackstone. I am with..."

"Aubrey, my name is Aubrey," I interrupt.

"I am with Aubrey. She found her dad dead. She won't talk to me, but she asked me to call you," Officer Blackstone explains.

"What? I'm on my way! Please text me the address." He hangs up and texts him the address.

"Aubrey, I'm sorry this has happened to you. Please let me know if there is anything else I can do." Officer Blackstone gets up from kneeling to my level and walks into the condo.

In less than thirty minutes, Detective Charles was running down the hallway towards me. He picks me up slowly from the floor.

"Aubrey, I'm so sorry. I'm so sorry this keeps happening to you." He hugs me tight. I barely have the energy to wrap my arms around him. My sobs are silent. I have nothing left: no more air, no more breath. I feel like life is drifting from my body. I just want to be saved. Saved from this horror story called my life. I have nothing left. Nothing!

"He just wanted me to forgive him," I whisper.

"Oh, Aubrey..." Detective Charles picked me up and carried me all the way to his car. He put me in the front seat and drove me home. The drive is so silent. Not a word, no music, just the sound of hitting potholes as we drive through downtown Baltimore.

Finally, we pull up to my house, and Carter's car is in the driveway.

"I will be right back, Aubrey." Detective Charles gets out of the car and knocks on the door. Carter comes to the door with PJ in his hand. The moment I saw his angelic face, I broke down. Carter ran to the car with PJ in his hand.

"Man, please hold him for me." Carter passes PJ to Detective Charles and picks me up out of the car. I stand up, and without saying a word, he takes me by my hand and says, "I'm going to take care of you."

He holds me by my hand and guides me into the house. Detective Charles follows.

"I will be right back, Detective," Carter assures him.

"It's okay, man. Take your time." Detective Charles takes a seat on the sofa with PJ wrapped up in his arms.

Carter sits me down on the bed. I feel like I'm stuck in a trance. He goes into our bathroom and turns on the shower. My clothes are covered in blood. He pulls off my sweatshirt, then my shoes, and socks. My sweatpants, bra, and panties. He stands me up and walks me into the bathroom. I step into the shower and put my head under the water. Allowing the water to drench me from head to toe while I watch blood run down the drain and before I knew it.

"Aaaaaaaahhhhhhhhhhhhhhhhh!!!!! Daddy!!!" Carter stood there without moving. He let me get it all out. He steps in the shower, fully dressed, and squeezes me tight. I cry until I am hoarse and the water is cold. Carter washes my body and wraps me in a towel. I get in the bed under the covers without drying off.

Carter

This has to be it for her. There is only so much that a person can take.

"Aubrey," I whisper over her while she lays in the bed. She doesn't answer. I change my clothes and go down the stairs to get PJ.

"Detective, thank you for everything. All of this has been a whirlwind. Thank you for having her back."

"Listen, man. Aubrey has been through a lot. Eventually, she is going to break. I suggest that you find her some counseling."

"She was seeing a counselor once before, but I think she may have stopped. I'm going to look into it myself."

"I'm going to head back to the murder scene to get an update on everything. We need to make sure there was no foul play."

"Foul play? Aubrey would never do anything to hurt anyone."

"Yeah, you just never know. A lot of suicides aren't suicides," he responds.

"Aubrey can't be a suspect..."

"The truth of the matter is everyone is a suspect, but with all that Aubrey has been through, she doesn't have any more room for another horror story," he shrugs.

"Man, all of this is crazy." I shake my head as I walk him to the door.

"Like I said, man, just take care of her. With everything she has been through, she can snap at any point. So, keep a lookout on her."

****

Three days have gone by. Aubrey has slept through the days. I've served breakfast, lunch, and dinner for three days, and she will not get out of bed. She won't talk, she won't eat, and she won't open her eyes.

I make one of her favorite breakfast cereals. The house is so quiet and gloomy. PJ has been sleeping just as much as Aubrey has. I wonder if he can feel what's going on with her. Working remotely is the best thing for me right now because Aubrey and PJ need me. When I walk into the room, she has the blanket covering her from head to toe.

"Aubrey, babe, please, you have to eat something. I made you some cream of wheat." She shrugs her shoulders and turns over.

"Aubrey, please, I need you to eat. You haven't eaten in three days."

Finally, she turns over, still wrapped in the towel I dried her off with; she sits up and opens her baggy eyes. She looks completely drained. Her skin is pale and sunken in from crying so much.

"Everyone has been calling you. Your mother needs you, Aubrey. She can't go through this by herself. I want to check on her, but I can't leave you here alone. Trish, Torin, and Eric are with her right now. Your Aunt Elisa is on her way in town to be with her. Baby, please talk to me." She sips the spoon full of cream of wheat without speaking a word. Once the bowl is empty, she sits it on the nightstand and once again turns over without so much as breathing loudly. She covers her entire body with the covers and goes back to sleep. I sit on the edge of the bed. I have to do something to get her out of here. I haven't slept in days because I've been so worried about her. Mrs. Karen can't make these funeral arrangements alone.

"Trust in the LORD with all thine heart, and lean not unto thine own understanding. In all thy ways acknowledge him, and he shall direct thy paths. When I left for New York, you gave me a card with that scripture in it. Whenever I'm feeling lost or broken, I go back to that card, and I read it over and over again until it sinks in. I need you to do the same. I know that you are dealing with a lot. There are so many transitions and tragedies happening around you. I have no explanation for any of it—none, whatsoever. But I do know that you have stood tall. You have been through trial after trial, baby, and you are still here. You are what strength looks like. I could never tell you that it's not okay for you to feel what you feel because that would be wrong. I just don't want you to lose hope. The day I opened my eyes; coming up out of that coma; you were standing there. Even with tears in your eyes, you stood strong. I've watched you be strong and hide your pain throughout your entire life. So, I want you to know that you don't have to do that anymore. Feel free to be in pain. That is the only way that you are going to be able to heal. Just know that when you are ready, I will be standing here, ready to catch you. So, take all of the time you need."

I can hear her sniffles and weeps. My phone rings in the other room, so I leave out and shut the door.

"Hello."

"Hey man, this is Preston. I got your number from Torin. Look, man, I know that we don't know each other like that. Porter was our boy, but on behalf of Ryan and me, I want to just say thank you for being there for Aubrey and PJ. You are good for both of them. Aubrey's a good woman, and she deserves a good man in her life."

"Aye, man, thank you. I didn't expect this call. So, I appreciate it."

"No problem. Listen, please tell Aubrey that we called. I'm sorry to hear about her dad. If it's okay with ya'll, we would like to get PJ sometimes so that he can get to know us. We want to be in his life."

"Man, I'm sure Aubrey would love that. I sure appreciate it. It takes a village, you know."

"Yeah, man, definitely. Well, this is my number. Hit me up anytime we can link up, get some drinks, whatever."

"That sounds good. I will keep that in mind."

"Aight now. Ya'll be good. Talk to you soon."

Damn, the first time I saw Ryan and Preston, they eyeballed me for at least twenty seconds before they spoke. It's cool that he called.

Lana

"We are working on getting you transferred." Warden Brown stands over top of me while I am chained to a hospital bed. My body is in so much pain, and I dread to see how I look.

"Transferred? For what? I had nothing to do with any of that," I reply in despair.

"Lana, I understand, but we don't know what happened exactly or how you were put in the middle. All I know is that somehow you were either targeted or caught in a crossfire. The only options are to put you in a hole with the other inmates involved or move you to another facility. I've been watching your progress, and I don't want to have to put you in the hole, but maybe I can have you moved to a place that may be best for you."

"I want out altogether! I just want out! I don't know what I did to deserve this!" As I said those words, I thought about Aubrey and everyone else that I've hurt. What did they do to deserve what I did? Maybe this is my karma. Maybe I do deserve this.

"Warden, thank you for stopping by, but please leave. I need time to think." I give him a firm look.

"I get it. I will be back to see you. Hopefully, by then, we would have gotten to the bottom of all of this." I lean back and close my eyes without speaking another word. I know I've done some fucked up shit, but I never thought I would be laying in a hospital bed, chained down in pain. I really made my bed.

"Hey, can I make a phone call?" An officer is standing outside of my room. She has been pretty cool. She walks in and stands next to my bed.

"Look, I don't know if you are able to make phone calls or not, but I trust that you won't do anything crazy." She reaches into her pocket and gives me her phone.

"Hello." I didn't recognize the voice of the man on the line.

"Can I speak to Aubrey?" I ask.

"Who is this?" he asks.

"It's Lana. I'm an old friend."

"Lana, you were never a friend. This is Carter, remember me. The one you shot."

"Carter... Carter, I'm sorry for what I did to you..."

"Forgiven- now, what do you want?"

"Is Aubrey around?"

"Naw, that's negative, you can't speak to her. As far as I'm concerned, you will never speak to her again. So, don't call this phone. You're not welcome-"

"Wait, wait, please, Carter. I know you hate me, and you have every right to, but please, if you could, please ask Aubrey to call my mom. I am in the hospital. I was jumped in prison. I just need somebody."

"Don't we all. Look, Aubrey has her own stuff going on. She just lost her father, and she is not in a good place right now-"

"Wait, Colin is dead?"

"Yeah... he is. Now, if you would excuse me, I have to get back to caring for my woman." He hangs up the phone in my ear without a drop of remorse for me.

The officer sticks her hand out for the phone.

"Look, you have to hand me my phone."

Carter

Day five, and Aubrey is still in bed. Everyone has called and been past to see her, but she refuses to leave the room. But today is Colin's funeral. I can't let this day go by without her telling him goodbye. I take out her favorite black dress and a white one just in case.

"Aubrey, today is your dad's funeral. The limo will be here to pick us up soon."

"I put PJ down next to her. He crawls up on the bed and pulls the blanket down."

"Ma ma ma ma ma ma ma ma ma," he yells to her while tapping on her head.

"Oh, my God... Aubrey! PJ said Ma ma!" This kid is moving faster than his time.

But still, she doesn't move. I walk to the other side of the bed to look into her eyes. Tears are running down her face. She lays there without saying a word. She is broken. This one did it. I pick PJ up without saying another word and walk out of the room.

The limo shows up. I walk out with PJ in my arms and his diaper bag in the other. Her mom gets out of the car hoping for Aubrey to be there. She looks up at me with misery hovering over her.

"Where is Aubrey?" she asks.

"Mrs. Karen, I'm sorry. I've tried to get her out of bed. I think it's just time for me to give her some space," I shrug.

"Give me the keys." She snatches the keys out of my hand and marches into the house. I follow behind her but sit in the living room where I can still hear.

"Aubrey, that is enough!" cries Mrs. Karen.

"I know you have been through a lot, baby girl, and I know this has taken you over the edge, but imagine being in this situation and the only person that you can rely on is in the casket! You know how it feels to be out here alone. I need you right now. Life is funny this way. I am lost and confused, and I feel guilty. Please don't make me go through this alone." After waiting for a response that she never gets, Mrs. Karen marches back down the stairs and out of the door.

She gets back in the limo, and I follow.

"Hey, Carter! I haven't seen you in years! You are all grown up now!"

Mrs. Karen's sister Ms. Elise is sitting across from me dressed like a superstar in her all-black. I know she and Mrs. Karen were "hot shit" back in the day. They are both fine women.

"Hey, Ms. Elise. It's nice seeing you." Mrs. Karen grabs PJ out of my hands with a big smile on her face.

"You finally got the girl, huh?" We both pour out paper-thin laughs.

Mrs. Karen taps me gently on my wrist.

"Thank you, Carter... For everything," she says.

"Yes, ma'am," I nod at her with a gentle smile.

We walk into the church, and a sense of gloom came over me. I don't know how to explain it. We walk into the sanctuary in a single line towards the casket. Everyone is there, family, old and new friends. I look to the left of me, and Trish is trying to catch my attention.

"Where is Aubrey?" she whispers. Instead of replying, I just shake my head at her. I see Torin and Eric looking back to see if she is coming.

At least ten people have gotten up to speak on behalf of Colin, including me, and it seems like I am the only one who stuck to the three-minute rule that was put in place by the pastor in the beginning. Ms. Brown, Colin's assistant, is the last to speak, and as soon as she says thank you, Aubrey walks through the doors and to the front. She was dressed in the all-white dress I took out for her. She fixed her hair and made her face up perfectly to hide those heavy bags under her eyes.

"Hello, everyone. Sorry I am late... It took everything out of me to get out of my bed. I haven't seen daylight in five days. For five days, I laid in my bed. I was wrapped in the same towel that Carter wrapped me in after showering my father's blood off of me. I've been through a lot in the last few years. More than most people can bear. But this one... This one has broken my soul because I never had the chance to say I forgive you."

Tears run down her face.

"I'm sorry that I was too late... I'm sorry for realizing that you were not a saint, that you were human. And even though your actions and mistakes exceeded anything I would have ever expected from you. I'm sorry for taking so long to forgive you. You see, in my eyes, my daddy could do no wrong. He was my saving grace, and I was his Bean. He never let me fall too low before he caught me. He never judged me for the mistakes or decisions I made. He would let me go through things and learn from them and then teach me how to correct them. He was my daddy. The last time we were together, we sat at the kitchen table and shared a bucket of our favorite ice cream, butter pecan. Afterward, we sat on the sofa, turned on a movie, and he held me. He made me feel so safe. Like if a tornado came flying in right then and there, he would block me from it and succeed. Outside of his arms, I didn't feel safe. That day he told me there had not been a moment in his life that he has been prouder than the day he held me for the first time. We had an electrifying connection like soul mates. Like I was born just for him. My dad wasn't perfect, and yes, he has let me down, but I will never forget how he held me up. So, with my last goodbye... I want to say, Daddy, I forgive you. I need you. And my prayer is that God will open His gates to heaven and welcome you in with open arms. Thank you."

She steps down from the podium, and there is not a dry eye in the building. I stand up and greet her with my arms stretched wide. Her body collapses in my arms, and I can feel the weight lifting off of her as she exhales.

****

The repast is filled to capacity. Aubrey stands out on the balcony alone to get some air. Mrs. Karen greets everyone with a smile as they walk up to her. Preston and Ryan are feeding PJ and Colby while Trish, Torin, and Eric cut up in the corner with Aunt Elise. I walk outside to take a plate of food to Aubrey.

"What's up, Killah!" She looks at me and smiles for the first time in a long time.

"Carter... Thank you. God sent you to me. He really did. From the moment we met, you were meant for me, and I love you so much." She sits the plate of food down and hugs me tight.

When I look up, I see Torin coming towards me as if something is wrong. Before she gets to the outside, I let Aubrey go.

"Babe, give me one second. Stay here." I walk in the building towards Torin.

"Torin, what's wrong." She sighs with regret all over her face.

"Carter, I just got a call from a friend of mine who works in the prison where Lana is. She was attacked a few days ago, and she died sometime this morning in the hospital."

"What?" When I turn around, Aubrey is standing behind me.

"I just saw her. I was just at the hospital. She... She looked bad, but she... she wasn't dying..." Before I know it, Aubrey storms out of the repast. I tried to catch up to her, but I struggled as I tried to get through the crowd of people politely. When I got outside, she had already pulled off.

Aubrey

This cannot be my life! One thing after another! After another! After another! I storm into my bedroom door and grab my suitcases. I throw everything in there that's in my closet and drawers. I'm back to packing and running.

"Aubrey! Aubrey, what are you doing?" Carter runs up the stairs, out of breath.

"Carter, I am leaving! Please don't try and stop me. I just need some time away. I can't do this anymore. I don't want my baby to see me like this!" I pack my clothes as fast as I can. I let my tears flow like there is no tomorrow.

"Aubrey, please. I can't let you do this. I can't let you just go and be alone. You have to stop running! What about PJ?"

"Carter, you have to. I need to be alone. It won't be long, I promise. I promise you I won't. Just please take care of Porter. Please take care of my baby. I have to get right for him. I have to!" I glide past him with my bags in my hand.

"Well, where are you going?" he asks with tears welling up in his eyes.

"I don't know yet. I just know that I can no longer stay here. I can't..." I give him a kiss on the forehead.

"Take care of my baby... Please..." I look him in his eyes. He looks like his soul is shattered, but I can't think about him right now. I can't save anyone until I save myself.

"I will... I promise..." he replies as his voice cracks with sorrow.

I walk out of the front door and get in my car without looking back.

Chapter 14

Is this what freedom feels like?

Carter

It's been four days, and she hasn't called. I don't know where she is or if she is okay. I tried calling, but I didn't get an answer. Mrs. Karen wants to call the police. I know that she is okay... But it's hard to convince her mother.

"Why aren't you calling her?" Mrs. Karen yells as she paces the floor.

"Mrs. Karen, I know she is okay. I just want to give her the space that she has asked for."

"Space? She doesn't need space; she needs help! What is space going to do? Just make her crazy; that is all!" she yells at me for the thousandth time today.

I lay PJ down for his nap and walk out to the front lawn to get some air. My phone rings. I quickly pick it up, almost dropping it.

"Hello! Hello!" I answer.

"Hey, Carter, it's Ryan."

"Oh... Hey man... What's going on?" I just knew it was her this time.

"Just checking in on ya'll. Has she called yet?" he asks.

"No, man. She hasn't."

"Damn, okay, man. I know she is okay. Look, if you want, I can come over and take Lil' Porter off your hands for a little bit. My lady is cooking dinner tonight, so he will be fed good and everything."

"Okay, cool, man. I appreciate it."

"Aight, cool, be there around five."

"Sounds good."

I hang up the phone and proceed to walk back into the house, and the phone rings again.

"Aubrey! Hello!" I walk back into the house with the phone on speaker. Mrs. Karen is still pacing the floor with a glass of wine in her hand.

"Hello, Carter," she says in a mild tone.

"Aubrey! Aubrey, my baby, where are you?" Mrs. Karen yells.

"Is that my mother?" she asks with irritation in her tone.

"Yes, it is. Aubrey, where are you? We have been going crazy," I respond.

"I am okay. I am in Colorado."

"New Mexico? What in the hell are you doing there?" Mrs. Karen asks.

"I said, Colorado!" Aubrey yells.

"I've always wanted to drive to California, so that is what I am doing," she replies with a calm essence.

"Aubrey, baby, I know that you haven't been very spontaneous in a while, and life is out of control, but please don't do anything crazy. Just come home," Mrs. Karen cries.

"I will be home, Ma. I just need this time for me. I love you, and I will see you soon. Please don't worry. Now can I please talk back to Carter?" Mrs. Karen looks up at me, and I can tell that a weight has been lifted off her shoulders. I walk back outside with the phone.

"Aubrey for real. Are you okay?"

"Yes, I am fine. I really am. How is PJ?" she asks.

"He is doing good. He is definitely missing you. He is saying 'Ma' like crazy. And sorry to tell you this, but he said, 'Dada' for the first time yesterday," I smile.

"Awww, I missed it! I can hear you smiling through the phone!" she laughs.

"I am, I am really am," I chuckle.

"Aubrey, as long as you are good. I am good. Take as long as you need. Everybody misses you, but they are all doing fine. Trish called off the grand opening until you come back. Suga, Honey Iced Tea is running well. I went by yesterday just to check up on things for you. Ryan is on his way over to get PJ."

"Tell Ryan, don't take my baby to know strip clubs!"

"Okay, I will!" I laugh.

"Okay... Well, I am going to talk to you soon. Give PJ a kiss for me and tell him I love him. Please let everyone know that I am okay. Eric is blowing up my phone, so call him first. Thank you for having me, Carter."

"Yeah, I hear you. Just be home before PJ starts walking."

"I promise I will. I love you," she says softly.

"I love you too." The phone goes silent.

Aubrey

I've driven for days. I've stopped in Indiana, Minnesota, Illinois, and Colorado. Finally, I made it to Las Vegas. I've always wanted to come here. Porter planned for us to go a few years ago, but it never happened for one reason or another. It's one o'clock in the morning, and the strip is lit up like New York City. People are everywhere. I booked a room at the Cosmopolitan hotel and a full spa treatment for tomorrow. I figure if I am going to be in Vegas, I might as well live it up. I need a little retail therapy too. I know I have to deal with everything that has been happening around me eventually, but right now, I just want to be where I am.

I booked the terrace studio, and it is beautiful, fit for a queen. The room is so beautiful, with metallic gold wallpaper, bedding fit for a queen, and a view from the balcony that is to die for. I pour a glass of wine and let the view whisk me away.

****

The sun is beaming through my suite window. I stayed up all last night sitting on the balcony of the hotel drinking wine. I drifted into an unreal presence. I imagined myself being a powerful businesswoman away on a business trip. I cannot spend this time feeling down on myself. I'm too far away from home, and no one will be here to catch me if I fall. I slept so good in this bed. I wish I could take it back home with me.

I mosey out of bed and pull an outfit out of my bag; before I know it, I am putting clothes on the hanger in the closet. I haven't even been here for twenty-four hours, but Vegas feels like it's going to be home for a few days.

Bing. A text comes through to my phone.

"I know you said that you are fine, but I just wanted to say good morning, and I love you. Love Mom."

I know that she's not going to quit. I miss her too.

Bing! And another.

"Girl! Where in the hell are you? You can't drop off the face of the planet like that! We miss you, heffa!" Eric has his way of saying he misses me. I miss them too.

The breakfast was outstanding. That egg Benedict with smoked salmon did me right. Next, I make it to my spa appointment.

"Hi, you must be Ms. Bryant?" The receptionist greets me when I walk in.

"Yes, I am. Wow, this place is beautiful," I say as I admire the decor.

"Thank you, we hold ourselves at the highest expectations for our customers. Let me introduce you to your masseuse. Ms. Bryant, this is Lydia; she will be your masseuse this afternoon. Don't worry about anything; she will take care of you. We have your body scrub and facials scheduled right after. Please get comfortable and let us take care of you."

"Thank you so much." The young lady takes my purse, and Lydia leads me to the back.

****

"Somebody better come out here with some motherfucking answers! Right now, got damn it!" Celia has an uproar in the lounge area at the prison.

"Ma'am! I need you to calm down! We are doing our best to help you!" says the guard as he tries to calm Celia down.

"Calm down? Why in the fuck would I calm down? The last time I saw my daughter, she was lying in a hospital half dead! I had to hear from somebody on the street that my baby was actually dead! My one and only child is dead! I'm not the one who is going to need help! You are! Now instead of talking that bullshit to me, I advise you to find the motherfucking warden. Get him down here now!" she rages out as the guard stands there, and the guard at the desk calls the warden's office.

"Inmate Jackson, yes, Lana. Well, Cortez, Jackson, Smith, whoever the hell she is, her mother is down here about to start a damn riot. She wants to see the Warden about her daughter's death. Look, somebody needs to get down here, or I am calling the police!" the guard whispers.

"Bitch call'em. Please call'em! That's what I should've done because my baby was MURDERED!" she screams.

Twenty minutes goes by, and Warden Brown walks into the lobby with a stern look on his face. "Hi, ma'am, I'm sorry for the wait. I am Warden Brown. How can I help?"

"My daughter is dead, Mr. Brown. And your guards were supposed to be protecting her, so I want to know what kind of fucking operation are you running here?"

"Ma'am, I'm sorry for Lana's death. Listen, let's go up to my office so that we can talk."

Warden Brown and Celia walk into the office. Warden Brown takes a seat at his desk. Celia paces the floor.

"Can I offer you something to drink, Ms. Celia?" He hands her a bottle of water, but she declines.

"I'm good. Listen, Mr. Brown, something is going on. I need you to find out what's going on. Lana didn't have beef with anybody in here. She may have enemies on the outside, but not in here."

"How do you know that for sure?" he asks as he sips his bottle of water.

"Because she never mentioned it. Not once. She goes to therapy, right? Ask her therapist. I guarantee you that she is going to say the same thing."

"Ms. Celia, look. I went to see Lana the day before she died. To be honest, she was bruised and banged up, but she was very much so alive. I know that there was some foul play. I couldn't talk in front of the guards because I don't know who was involved, but I promise you we will get justice for Lana. We are getting an investigation started," the warden assures her.

"Settle it before I do," she replies.

****

"Girl, it's just way too much going on! I feel like I am living in an HBO special!" Eric says while he and Torin are going for a run in the park.

"How about that! I know I couldn't stand Lana, but I cannot believe she is actually dead. Shit, I can't believe Aubrey has skipped town! I've been telling her to do that for years. I guess she waited for the right time to do it," Torin says.

"Well, if this is the right time, I am good! That poor baby. She gets hit with a new tragedy every time she lays her head on a pillow. I wish there were something I could do for her. She is not answering any of my phone calls Torin."

"Eric, you know that when Aubrey needs her space, she doesn't answer the phone. This is a little more extreme than normal, but she will come back around. I know she will... But listen, word on the street is that Lana was set up."

"What! By who?" Eric stops in tracks.

"I don't know, but my girlfriend works for the warden. That's how I found out she was dead," Torin explains.

"Oh, my God! Poor Lana!" Eric exclaims.

"She said Lana's mother was at the jail yesterday. She must have caused an uproar because the warden went down to greet her personally. So, the shit is deeper than just a fight in the courtyard."

Aubrey

"Yup, I just packed my bags and hit the highway...." I've been sitting at the hotel bar for hours talking to this woman. I don't know her from a can of paint, but after my fourth drink, she knows my entire life.

"Damn Aubrey, I have never heard anything like that in my life." This woman is absolutely gorgeous. She reminds me of Lena Horne, so classy and regal.

"Yeah, I know. A friend of mine once told me that I would become my best writer when I experience the worst pain. I think I finally hit my plateau of pain. So as soon as I sit still, I am going to write my story."

She digs in her purse and pulls out a card.

"Well, as soon as you are ready, let me know. I am in public relations, and I represent a lot of big-time names in the entertainment industry."

"Wow, thanks. I will do that."

"One of my good friends is a book publisher, and I think you two would make a great fit. She is all about queens helping queens, and so am I. This is the year of the female, so we have to take advantage of it!" she shouts with her drink held in the air.

"Girl, yes! Cheers to that!" I shout.

"Look, I have to get back to my husband. I'm sure he has woken up from his hangover by now. Girl, he can't hang! But if you are ever in New York, please call me! We can hook up, and I will plug you with as many of my contacts as I can." I swear I think she's sent from heaven. No, I know she is!

"Oh my God, Lydia, thank you so much! You don't know how much that means to me!"

"Sis, you deserve everything that is about to come your way. You have been through enough; it is time for the page to turn. It's only blessings from here. And I will be sure to stop by your two spots when I come into Baltimore. Hit me up for the grand opening."

"Girl... I sure will, and thanks again." She walks away with her head held high, and her beautiful curly tresses were bouncing as she walks away.

"Wait, you are going to LA from here, right?" She turns back around to me.

"Yes, I am," I say with a bit of excitement.

"Okay, cool, text me as soon as you get the chance, and I will send you a few of my friends' numbers for you to have someone to hook up with. They are good people, and they are in the industry as well," she smiles.

"Okay, perfect. I'm about to head back to my hotel room, but I will text you now." I pick up my phone and send her the text. She looks at her phone.

"Okay, got it. Give me a few minutes."

"Alright, girl, you have a good night." I hug her, and she walks away.

I finish sipping my drink.

"All you need to do is write that story... It's going to be a hit." The bartender walks up to me and passes me another drink that I don't need.

"How do you know?" I ask.

"Because I was listening, and I would read it and watch it. It sounds like a movie. I've heard plenty of stories from people. Day after day... Once they've had a few drinks, the stories start flowing, but I've never heard one like yours. Your tragedy is going to become your blessing." I never thought of it like that. I take cash out of my purse to cover the bill, and I get up without saying another word, I slide the money to the bartender, but he slides it back.

"It's on the house. Just turn your pain into your prosperity, and that will be enough payment for me, Sistah." I nod my head in agreement, and he returns the gesture with a smile.

I woke up this morning with the headache of a lifetime. I had one too many Cosmos. Today is the day. My drive to LA is four hours long. I left my car in Las Vegas and rented a convertible Porsche for my drive. I've always wanted one. A chocolate convertible Porsche, to be exact, but this one is black. A 911 Turbo S Convertible! Such a beautiful automobile.

I blast my music way high and vibe to some Jay Z and trap music. Carter got me hooked, plus I feel like a gangsta while riding through the desert with the top down. The wind blows through my hair and slaps me across my face while getting stuck to my lip gloss. I reach in the glove compartment, grab one of the million napkins I took from the restaurant at breakfast, and wipe my lip gloss off. The backdrop of the desert is so beautiful. I cannot leave the scene and not get a picture. So, I pull over to the shoulder and take a few. It's so quiet. Literally deserted. Only three cars have passed me on the road since my drive begin.

I've been thinking a lot about what that bartender said to me last night. I once read an article about soulmates that said there is such thing as a complete stranger soulmate. A person that may be sent to you just to drop you a line or tell you something that God wants you to hear. Someone that doesn't know you at all, but they tell you things about yourself. I felt that last night. I felt like both Lydia and the bartender were both sent to me. Like I was supposed to be in Vegas at that bar at that specific time.

Five hours later and I've arrived! I sat in the desert a little longer than expected. It was the peace and quiet for me. I sit in my room alone all the time, but it never seems as quiet as it did in the desert. No matter where I am, my life always sounds so noisy.

Instead of getting a hotel, I've rented out a beach house in Malibu. Another dream of mine. Growing up, I loved Barbie, and from the looks of it, Malibu was the place to be. But first I had to see the Hollywood sign, just to find out that it's only a sign. Nothing special at all, but it's checked off of my list.

Once again, I park my car and pull over to catch the views of Malibu beach. It's the perfect day to take a swim. I get back in the car, put up the top, grab my new bathing suit that I bought in Vegas, and put it on in the car. I still have two hours before check-in, and I'm going to take advantage of it. I take off my flip flops and let the warm sand squish between my toes. I watch the surfers on the beach and a little kid with his surfboard trying to mimic the surfers. The waves rush in as the water sweeps across my feet. I focus on this one surfer who looks like he is a pro. I didn't know black guys surfed. He is a tall, dark chocolate man with washboard abs. He has a rosary around his neck that I notice he kisses every time he goes off into the water. It's like he controls the waves. Like they listen to him. I sit down in the sand and close my eyes. I just want to remember the sound of the water rushing towards me. It's the most peaceful sound I've heard in a long time. As I drift off into what seems like a deep meditation, I feel a tap on my shoulder. I look up, and it's the surfer guy with water dripping from his temple.

"Hi," he says with a deep tone and a smile.

"Hi, how are you?" I ask as I stare up at him and shade my eyes from the ray of light that is shining behind him.

"I am Casey," he reaches out his hand for me to shake it.

"Casey or KC?" I ask as I shake his hand back.

"Naw, just Casey." I stand up to stand face to face with him, although that was impossible because he is at least 6'3" and I am nothing more than 5'4". His entire package was staring me in my face, so it was only right to stand up and out of such an awkward position.

"Well, Casey, it's very nice to meet you," I reply. He is a beautiful man. This California sun has done his skin tone well.

"I've been watching you watch me," he says.

"Oh, you did, did you?" I laugh.

"No, I don't mean it like that. I mean, you look like you are interested in surfing," he smiles.

"Actually, yes. I am. I've always wanted to try."

"Well, let me give you a lesson. Free of charge." He hands me his surfboard.

"Uh, okay. Why not?" I reply with the jitters. We head out to the sea, and I lay flat on the board.

"Oh, my name is Aubrey, by the way." I look over at him as we are now face to face. He holds both ends of my board and glides me into the water. Here we go!

****

"I feel like most of the people that are here for Lana's funeral came for the food." Eric scans the room and sips on his lemon tea. Torin stands next to him with a placid demeanor.

"I hate to say it, but you're right. Did you see Thomas and Lisa? I did not expect for them to come!" Torin whispers.

"Girl, Thomas didn't drop a tear. I side-eyed him a thousand times. Not a sniffle, a watery eye- girl nothing. Not one. She made that man's heart so cold. I mean, even you dropped a tear, Torin. Got damn."

"Well, I guess she did enough for him to feel nothing about her death. Or maybe he was just putting on a front for Lisa, but the world will never know." She waved her hand detached from the subject.

"Oh, wait, here they come!" Eric gently taps on Torin's shoulder with exhilaration.

"Torin! Hey girl, how are you?" Lisa prances over to Torin with delight, and Thomas follows behind her with the baby in his arms. She grabs Torin and gives her a big hug.

"Hey, girl! It's so good to see you!" Torin exchanges the jester.

"Eric, Torin... What's going on?" Thomas greets Torin with a hug and Eric with a handshake.

"Hey ya'll, how is it going?" Eric says.

"Life is going great, man. Just out here living and enjoying life. That's all," Thomas replies.

"Well, we've heard that you are doing great things, and your little one is so beautiful! Hi, little baby!" Torin grabs the baby's finger and shakes it.

"Yeah, life is good. The firm is doing pretty well. Lisa helped me build it and get everything going," Thomas looks at Lisa and smiles.

"Now that's what I am talking about Power Couple status!" says Eric.

"Yes, when you have a vision of your family, that is what it's about. Working together to fulfill the mission and build the legacy, you know? Thomas and I are on the same page with that. And it makes it so much more fun when you're in it with your best friend and someone you like!" they all laugh.

"I'm serious! So many people get married and realize they love their mate, but they don't like them. I mean, for real. Like, hate their stinkin' guts! That's ridiculous. You will never be able to fulfill the overall purpose if you don't like the person you are on the journey with." Lisa goes on, and Torin channels into everything that she's saying.

"Wow, those are facts. Major facts! I never thought about marriage or relationships that way." Torin interjects and opens up for more conversation. She journeys off into her thoughts while the other three carry on with their conversation.

"You know I wasn't a big fan of Lana's. I didn't care for her at all. She has hurt a lot of people, but she's dead. Like gone forever. My heart is kind of hurting for her," says Lisa.

"Yeah, and just to know that she was trying to right all of her wrongs. Aubrey told me that Lana sent her a letter a few days before she passed away, saying that she apologizes for all of the pain and hurt that she bought on everyone. Even you, Thomas," Eric acknowledges Thomas, but instead of a reply, Thomas lowers his eyes.

"How is Aubrey doing. I didn't see her here," Thomas quickly changes the subject.

"We don't know. Her dad passed away, and she found out about Lana's death at her dad's repass. We haven't seen her since. Carter said that she is okay, though. He said that she packed up her bags, got in her car, and left. Her mom said she drove clear across the country. The last time they spoke, she was in Colorado." Torin gives Thomas and Lana the spill.

"What!" they both respond.

"Her dad died? Wow! This has got to be the worst time for Aubrey right now. She's losing people left and right. Damn. Well, when you talk to her please tell her that I said hello and she can give us a call anytime. I hate to say it now that she is gone, but Lana didn't deserve a friend like Aubrey," says Thomas.

"Wait a minute now... Lana wasn't the best person Thomas, but she was still human, and she had a lot of pain and hurt that exceeded our understanding. Yeah, she did a lot of messed up things, but hurt people, hurt people. I know she hurt you. We all know that, but-" Eric interjects.

"But what! She paid someone to run me off the road, man! She tried to kill me! She made life with her a living hell! She never loved me. She loved what I could do for her, and that's it. A pair of shoes opened her heart for me. As far as I am concerned, Lana can rot in hell!" Thomas storms off.

"Guys, I'm sorry. He is really dealing with this differently. It's time for Chance's nap anyway, so we're going to go. Tell Aubrey we are praying for her."

"Lisa, let's go!" Thomas yells back at Lisa, and she scurries off behind him.

"He seemed pretty upset, but I don't blame him," Demari walks up behind Torin and Eric.

"Where in the hell did you come from?" Eric is shocked to see Demari because she has been missing in action for so long.

"Oh, I've been around. Here and there, you know," Demari responds as she tries to stay inconspicuous.

"Yeah, well, you've done a great job of being on the low because I haven't seen or heard from you since... I don't know how long," Eric says with a side-eye and suspicion.

"Well, sometimes it's better that way. To not be seen or heard. But I had to be here for this. Just to make sure she was dead." A cold expression comes across Demari's face. Torin and Eric stand there in silence while they stare into each other's eyes and communicate without saying a word.

"You know... one way or another, people always get what they deserve. She had it coming, and so did Porter. Life is coming full circle. And those, as you would say, Torin... Are major facts." Demari walks off in a super confident stride with her head held high with pride.

"That was some gloomy ass 1976 Carrie type shit right there. What in the fuck is up with Demari? She minds as well had said, 'Revenge is best served cold.' That bitch is on some other, other shit!" Eric rambles on while Torin pierces her eyes on Demari as she walks away.

"Yeah, she is... Isn't she?" Torin replies.

****

The sun has gone down, and after my lesson with Casey, I drove up to my home for the week and fell asleep under the canopy in the garden overlooking the ocean. You haven't had a good sleep until you've slept outside. Voluntarily, of course. Casey invited me to a kickback on the beach tonight. I was going to stay in and just enjoy this time alone, but I've decided to go. After my lesson with Casey, which went better than I expected, I'm something like a pro now; we talked for at least two hours. He is ex-military and spends most of his time traveling the world with his fiancé. That sounds like the life to me. They live here in Los Angeles together. She is originally from Brixton, England, and he is from upstate New York. I would've never guessed, though. Everything about his demeanor screams born and raised in Los Angeles on the beach. He's very cool and laid back—the "No Worries" type of guy. After telling him about my life and what got me here, he said that he and his fiancé are traveling to Thailand in a few days with some friends. They are going to a new life retreat. Sounds interesting, like somewhere I need to be.

As I walk down the path towards the beach, I realize how dark it is. As if there is nothing there. I can hear the tides coming in, but it's like I am staring into space when I look out onto the ocean. I can see the bonfire that Casey told me to look for. It's pretty much in the same location where we met.

When I walk up, there's a group of people sitting around the bomb fire talking with music playing loudly. Casey is clearly sitting next to his fiancé because he's giving her googly eyes. He pops up and walks my way when he sees me coming.

"Hey, Aubrey! You made it! Let me introduce you to everyone." I follow him back to the fire where everyone is congregating. People of all different shades, wow, I think I may need to diversify my friend list a little.

"Aubrey, this is Mecca, Lena, Lee, Dina, Nasir, Chase, Kasi, and my beautiful lady Chassidy, but we call her Chaz for short." Everyone greets me with a friendly hello, but Chassidy gets up and greets me with a warm hug. Honestly, I expected the total opposite because I would have been looking at her like, "Bitch, why is my man inviting you to bonfires and shit?" But that's the Eric in me.

"Hey Aubrey, it's so nice to meet you. Come sit." I follow her to the log where she and Casey were sitting. Chassidy gives me Elle Varner's vibes with a dash of Ella Mai. Big curly hair, real cool, calm, and collective with an accent that I want to snatch out of her voice box in exchange for mines.

"So, Aubrey, we were just discussing some of the things that are going on in the world right now. Did you hear about the guy that was killed by the cops in Chicago recently?" Kais ask.

Okay, so this is something that I am definitely not used to. My friends and I talk about fashion and gossip and whatever the hell else is in the forefront of our lives in the present moment. I don't think that my mind, body, or soul can take on the thought of another death.

"To be honest, no. I haven't. I have been so wrapped up in my own life and the craziness going on around me that I have not taken any time to step outside of it all until now." They all get silent to hear me speak.

"Well, that's understood. Life has its way of swallowing us whole sometimes," says Mecca.

"Yeah, Aubrey's story is like nothing I've never heard before. It's amazing that she is still standing," says Casey.

Before I knew it, I was back telling my story again. The more I tell it, the easier it is. I don't know, maybe telling my story is like therapy. Or maybe this is all a block from me having to deal with it all.

Three hours have gone by, and this group of people is sitting around me listening to my life as if I am a preacher on the pulpit or a teacher giving a lecture.

"Wow, Aubrey, you are a soldier," says Lena as she swings her long braids around her back.

"Girl, yes! You have been through the fire, the storm, and cross the damn ocean!" says Chassidy.

"Have you ever thought about making this a story?" says Dina.

"Actually, yes. I am a writer," I reply in a modest tone.

"Really? So am I!" Nasir's deep voice travels across the group filled with enthusiasm.

"Lee is a screenwriter as well. We are working on a project as we speak," Nasir continues.

"Yeah, Aubrey. We have a class coming up in a few days; it teaches you how to build characters and explore the art of storytelling. You should come," Lee adds.

"Damn, thank you. You really think my story could be a movie?" I ask.

"Hell yeah!" they all reply like a harmonizing choir.

"Okay, bet! I'm in," I acknowledge their enthusiasm and agree to go to the class.

The night goes on, and after a few conversations on police brutality and racism in America, I am tapped out emotionally and physically. I realized that the conversations that I have on a regular basis need to change a little. My life is up in shambles, but there is so much going on in this world that I have yet to give any energy to. I don't know if that is a good thing or a bad thing.

"Well, guys, it's been real, but it's four in the morning, and I can barely keep my eyes open." They all give me puppy dog eyes and spit phrases my way like "You can't hang." and "We just got started." I am surely not about this life.

"Well, we will probably be here to watch the sun come up, but we understand if you are tired," says Dina.

"Yeah, I'm definitely gonna miss that sun," I laugh.

"Okay, well, let me walk you to the car," says Casey.

"Okay, cool," I respond.

"Babe, you wanna walk?" he asks Chassidy.

"Naw, go ahead," she waves him off. I've never seen some open, trustworthy shit like this in my life.

"Oh, so you're going to just let me walk back to the fire in the dark by myself? What if the boogeyman gets me?" he jokes.

"Oh goodness, Casey, stop your whining! Okay!" He looks back at me and grins as she gets up and walks over.

"She knows I'm going to loiter her to the car for some action," he smiles.

"TMI brother, TMI," I laugh.

"Aubrey, I was thinking a lot about your story, and I am not a therapist or anything, but it seems like you may be going through the stages of grief right now. A lot has happened to you, and it doesn't sound like you've had a moment to yourself just to let go," says Chassidy. I walk aside them without acknowledging Chassidy's statement.

"Look, I know it may be hard to talk about how you feel right now, but I do want to invite you to Thailand with us. I know it's very last minute, and I have no idea how much the flight will be, but Lee had to step out, so I know there is space at the retreat. Give me your phone." I pass her my phone.

"Here is the information for the retreat. If you decide to come, we will see you there." She leans in and hugs me.

"Thank you. I will keep it in mind," I reply.

"Well, you have our info. Don't make this the last time we see you, Aubrey Bryant. We are friends for life now, and keep your head up." Casey comes in and embraces me with a big hug.

"Thanks, Casey. It's been a pleasure." He opens the car door for me, and I get in and close the door. I watch them walk away with his arm wrapped around Chassidy's shoulders. I miss that.

I sit out on the terrace and watch the sun come up; it's the most beautiful thing I've ever seen. Chassidy was right. I've never been to Thailand. I've never been out of the country. I take out my phone and look at the information that Chassidy gave to me.

"Chiang Mai?" They leave in four days. The trip is ten days long. I've already been away from Carter and PJ for almost ten days, and I'm missing them like crazy. But this is an opportunity of a lifetime. Who knows, this might be just what I needed?

I wake up to a text from Lydia.

"Hey, Aubrey! I hope you are enjoying the sunshine and palm trees. Forgive me for sending this so late, but here are a few people that you should get to know while you are there. They are good friends of mine and will be expecting your call. Call Bea first."

I take a shower and get my hair together. I go through my messages to get Bea's number.

"Hello," a woman with a sultry voice answer.

"Hi, my name is Aubrey. I am looking for Bea." I can hear her boost of energy change in the tone of her voice.

"Oh, hi, Aubrey! Lyd told me you would be calling. I can fit you in today at noon. I am located at 1955 Melrose Avenue. Is that time good for you?" I have no idea what's going on.

"Fit me in? For what?" I ask.

"Oh! Lydia said that you were talking about getting a new look."

"Oh! Yes! She is right. I did say that! I forgot that I mentioned it to her. You know what's funny when I looked in the mirror this morning, I was thinking to myself that I really want a haircut."

"Well, I would be delighted to be a part of your new look," she says cheerfully.

"Then noon it is, and thank you," I reply.

****

While sitting in the salon chair, I go through all of my pictures to see my baby's face. I keep going and end up at a picture of Porter, drawing a face on my stomach during my pregnancy. I can feel the tears welling up in my eyes the further I go back in my photos.

"One second, please." I jump up out of my seat and run to the bathroom with hair dye running down the side of my face. I need a moment to gather myself before I go back to the chair. I walk back to the chair like nothing happened.

"Is everything okay?" Bea asks.

"Yes, everything is good. Sorry for running off like that." I sit back in my seat, and she does the finishing touches on my color.

I am looking like a Halle Berry, Rhianna, with the short haircut bombshell three hours later!

"Oh my God, I love it!" I admire my new razor-sharp hair cut in the mirror.

"This is exactly what I wanted." Bea stands behind me with her arms folded and her comb in her hand.

"Your auburn hair was beautiful, but this deep jet black and this short cut is the new you! Now all you need is a pair of aviator shades, and the new Aubrey will be in full effect!" I hear everything that she is saying, but I cannot stay out of the mirror. I feel so free! I feel sassy, sexy, edgy, bossy, and fearless, all wrapped up in one. She is right; this is the new me.

"Well, new hair calls for a new wardrobe!" I text Lydia and thank her for the new recommendation. She told me to give her friend Brian Wellington a call. He is a talent manager, and he may be able to point me in the right direction for my story. Every girl should shop on Rodeo Drive at least once. The goal is not to blow all of the money Porter gave to me on clothes.

Chapter 15
I SPY...

Torin

I don't know what's going on, but something is up. Demari has something to do with something, and I am going to get to the bottom of it.

"Hey, Trish! How is everything going?" Trish sounds like she just woke up from a nap.

"Girl, I am fat, hot, tired, emotional, hungry, and FAT. These twins are wearing my ass out! What's up?" Damn, she sounds like she has had it!

"Okay... Well... I was wondering if you could give me the number to that Detective Charles guy."

"Detective Charles? Why what's up?"

"Well, between me and you, I think Demari had something to do with Lana's death and maybe even Porter's."

"Porter's how so? And Lana was in jail. How could she possibly have had something to do with that?" She seems very intrigued by my theory.

"I'm not quite sure yet, but the way she was acting at Lana's funeral and some of the things she said makes me wonder. My thing is, what if she does? Who's to say she wouldn't be after Aubrey next? I just don't trust her. Something is not right."

"I wouldn't be surprised. I've ran into Demari at some very random moments, and Porter told me to stay away from her because she can't be trusted."

"And he was right. She can't. I've kept her close enough to watch her, but somewhere down the line, Lana fucked her head up some kind of way."

"Well, keep me in the loop and let me know how it all goes. I need to get back to sleep before Colby's dance class starts."

"Tell my little dancing diva I said hello! I will be sure to come to get her for some retail therapy soon," I giggle.

"I sure will."

"Okay, get some rest. Talk to you later." Trish hangs up the phone and sends me Detective Charles's information through text.

****

It's a cool night tonight, and I've been sitting down by the pier waiting for Detective Charles to show up. The wind is rushing in off of the water, and it's getting late. Twenty more minutes go by, and I've decided to call it quits.

Then I see this tall, handsome guy walking towards me in a leather jacket and jeans. I remember his face from Porter's repast.

"You must be Detective Charles." This leather motorcycle jacket is a whole vibe.

"And you must be Torin. It's very nice to meet you," he smiles at me with charm and reaches out to shake my hand.

"Yes, I am. It's nice to meet you as well," I smile back.

I feel a vibration between the two of us. I don't know what it is, but the moment he touched my hand, I felt it. I know he felt it too. He gazes at me with so much intensity. We let each other go after a long embrace. He breaks the ice and snaps out of it.

"So... How... How can I help you?" he asks.

"Aubrey and Trish are good friends of mine, and they told me that you were on Porter's case. I know that the case is closed, and that's great. I want my girls to be able to move on with their lives, but I think that there is more to it." We walk along the pier that overlooks downtown Baltimore. He stops and looks at me once again with intensity.

"What do you mean?" he asks.

"There is a woman named Demari. We all went to school together. She and Lana were really close at some point, but word on the street is that Lana set her up to be gang-raped when we were in college. Lana did a lot of vicious things to people that quite frankly made no sense at all. A picture of her was supposed to be circulating around the campus. They say that Lana was blackmailing her. Look, I don't know the whole story, but to make a long story short... I think she got Lana killed, and I think she may have had something to do with Porter's death as well."

"Where are you getting all of this?"

"She was at Lana's repast. Her energy felt so cold. She said something like, 'Lana and Porter both got what they deserved, and she was only there to make sure Lana was actually dead.' I feel it. I know she had something to do with it."

"Was she at Porter's funeral?"

"Yes, she was there briefly. She is the missing in action type."

"Okay, I'm going to look into it. But how would she get Lana killed in jail? She would have to have major clout or money."

"Look, Detective, I don't know. But what I've learned in the past two years is all of these bitches are capable of doing whatever in the hell they put their minds to. I don't put anything past anybody. You never know... She may have someone that works on the inside. I know I do. My girlfriend from high school is the warden's secretary."

"How do I know that you didn't set her up?" I stop dead in my tracks.

"Because I don't have time for extra drama and bullshit, Detective. I am running businesses from here to London, and the last thing I need to be worrying about is if I am the main suspect or not. Besides, Lana has messed up almost everyone's life around me, but she knew better not to come my way. We had our words, but that was it. She knew that my bite was a lot bigger than my bark. She prayed on the weak. That was her M.O."

"Well... I guess that settles that," he says.

"Yes, it does..." I walk away without saying another word. I can't believe that he just accused me of setting Lana up when I am the one who called his ass out here! It's chilly as hell tonight. I could've been wrapped up in my faux fur blanket and satin sheets with my a/c set on blast.

"You're just going to walk away from me like that? I didn't even get the chance to sweep you off your feet," he says in the coolest, mildest tone. I turn around and slowly walk back towards him.

"There will be no sweeping me off my feet, detective," I reply.

"Well, at least let me take you out for dinner."

"Dinners are too close to a nightcap... How about brunch?"

"Then brunch it is," he smiles. "Tomorrow?" he offers.

"Thursday," I counter offer. "You have work to do," I continue.

"Mhm..." He latches on to his jaw bone and gives me bedroom eyes.

"I like you," he says softly.

"Do you now?" I reply. Then I turn around and walk away. I can feel his eyes undressing me as I walk off.

Aubrey

This hair cut has me feeling like I rule the world. Freedom! They say that hair has feelings too. It feels stress, and it holds energy. Cutting off that bad energy is the best thing that I could have done. I felt rejuvenated with every clip.

Lee's writing class was amazing! I learned so much about the writing process that I've never known. I spent all of those years in college, focusing on Porter and barely graduating to realize that I barely learned anything about writing. I don't know how I ended up with that job at Glow.

I spent way too much money shopping, but it felt good. PJ may not need anything for months. I shipped everything that I bought with me, including some of the things I purchased; back home. I left a note in there for Carter so that he didn't think something was wrong.

I thought that I would be driving back home across the country, but instead, I'm about to board a plane to Chiang Mai, Thailand. I drove back to Vegas and booked a shipment for my car to be sent back home to BWI airport. I am nervous as fuck! I am leaving the country, and no one knows, but the people that invited me. This is crazy!

I received a text from Chassidy saying that they are in Beijing, China waiting for the next flight. Seventeen hours long, I've never flown that long in my life. I'm going to pop a sleepy pill and go out like a light.

As soon as I board the plane, my phone rings.

"Hello."

"Ma ma ma ma ma ma." My heart shattered in pieces.

"Hi, baby! Hi, my baby! I love you!" PJ's voice builds me up with anxiety.

I was two seconds from jumping off of the plane.

"Hey baby," Carter gets on the phone. His deep sexy voice makes me fall hard.

"Hi, baby! I miss you so much!" I say.

"We miss you too. Where are you?" he asks.

Highly strung by his question, I answer with a stutter in my voice.

"I... I am on the plane," I say reluctantly.

"You're on your way home? Thank God!" He is full of excitement, but he is about to be let down.

"No, baby. I'm not... I'm on my way to Thailand..."

"Thailand! Aubrey, what in the hell are you talking about? Thailand! Aubrey, please get off of the plane! Get off! Whatever we need to do to make things better, we will! I promise!" He goes into a tantrum abruptly.

"Carter, I am okay. I am doing this for me. I promise you I need this and it's for me. I'm sorry that I didn't tell you, but I didn't want you to talk me out of it. That is why I have not been answering any of your face time calls."

"What are you going out to Thailand for Aubrey?" he asks with sorrow in his voice.

"I met a group of people on the beach a few days ago, and they are going to a retreat in Thailand. It's a meditation retreat, but when I looked it up, I learned that it's a healing retreat, and I will learn more about who I am and tap into my purpose. I don't have any stamps in my passport, so... What the hell... Carter, I just want to be free from these shackles. You may not see them, but I know that they are there."

"Okay, Aubrey. I hope that you find what you are looking for because we need you to come back to us. But bottom line, this is some crazy shit. Thailand? You do realize how far that is?"

"Carter, I'm coming back..."

"How is everybody? How is Trish?" I ask.

"She is doing good. I went over to help Grant put the nursery together. Colby has been asking about you. Everyone's trying to keep her busy. Trish is huge. She will have to deliver the babies early. She has great plans for the grand opening. She is just waiting for you to return."

"Tell them all that I love them so much. I will be back home soon."

A young petite Asian woman walks up to my chair and says, "Ma'am, we are preparing for takeoff. Please put your phone on airplane mode."

"Yes, ma'am. Thank you. Hey Carter, the flight attendant said we are about to take off. I will call you when I land in Beijing. The times are way off. I'm sure you will be asleep, but keep your phone on."

"I will. Aubrey, please be careful. I love you."

"I love you too. Give PJ a kiss for me."

I hang up the phone, say a prayer, and pop a melatonin gummy. Out like a light.

****

"Ma'am, ma'am, what would you like to eat? We are serving duck and chicken." I open my eyes, and the same flight attendant is standing over me.

"Duck and Chicken? How long have I been asleep?"

"We have been in the air for eight hours now. You slept through the first meal. I didn't want you to miss another," the flight attendant says politely.

"Thank you. And I guess I will try the duck," I reply.

"Okay, ma'am." This plane is huge, but the seats aren't that comfortable. I am flying first class for my flight back home. They have beds and everything. I look through the catalog of movies on the screen in front of me and choose a movie to watch.

"Here, you are, ma'am." The flight attendant passes me my food.

"What is this?" I say.

"It's duck," she answers. My face curls up like a kid who hates broccoli.

"It's actually pretty good. You should try it," says my neighbor. I take a piece off and put it in my mouth, and to my surprise, it was pretty good. They could do a little better with the presentation because I was scared.

Torin

Well, he wasn't late this time and a sharp dresser. He's dressed very summertime casual in a pair of loafers, a jean button-up shirt, and mustard yellow fitted pants. My shoes match his pants perfectly.

"I guess we had the same style idea today, huh?" I say as I walk up to the table and sit my clutch down. He stands up to greet me.

"I guess so," he says as he wraps his arms tightly around me for a hug. Goodness, I haven't felt an embrace like this in way too long.

"You look beautiful," he says as he pulls my chair out for me to sit.

"Thank you. You don't look too bad yourself," I reply with sass.

"Now that we are on a date," he smiles at me, but I interrupt.

"Did you find out anything?"

"Yes, I did."

"Why are you smiling?" I say.

"You know... Most women that I've dated would have hated for me to talk about work," he says.

"Well, first of all, I am most definitely not most women. Secondly, I pulled you into this, and third... I am intrigued by the job of a detective. I would love to know more about your experience in that world." Our eyes stay connected like we pause in time. Then he reaches down in a bag that he had on the floor next to him.

"So, I've found out a few things that may actually put Demari in the suspect department. Did you know that she has a half-brother that works at the prison?"

"No, we all thought she was the only child."

"Well, here he is." He pulled out a picture of him.

"How did you find that out," I ask, filled with curiosity.

"It just so happened that Demari used to date one of the officers at the prison, and he got him the job. Her brother is ex-military. He moved here two years ago. The officer from the prison doesn't work there anymore. I pulled up Demari's Maryland State ID photo. My new partner recognized her, he is a rookie, and I am showing him the ropes, but he used to work at the prison entrance during his C/O days. She used to bring her ex-boyfriend and her brother lunch all of the time."

While he puts everything together, I follow along and sip my glass of water. "What? I never knew any of this." My mind is boggled right now.

"I spoke to the warden of the jail, and he's doing his own investigation. He will have the recordings over to me in a few days. If her brother was in that yard when Lana's jumping happened, we will have a lead. That will be a major link to Demari if she did had something to do with it. Lana's autopsy reports haven't gotten back yet."

"I think we should've had this conversation at the conclusion of the date. I think it killed the vibe."

"No, no, no, it doesn't have to. Let's just start over." He puts the pictures of Demari and her brother back.

"How are you doing today?" He pushes my hair out of my eye and runs his finger down the lob of my ear.

"I am doing just fine," I blush.

"That you are... Thank you for meeting me," he smiles.

God, his smile is going to make my panties melt! Focus Tor! Focus! We are not looking for a quick hit. Our husband is looking for us! So, focus, girl! He might be it, so control the vagina, bitch. Put your game face on! That smile, though!

"It was my pleasure," I say as I collect myself.

"So, tell me more about yourself." I move closer to the table to give him my undivided attention.

****

I usually try to keep my dates down to a ninety-minute time frame before I make my exit, but this one feels different. We have been together for at least four hours now. He has already decided that we will have a second date and we are going to keep certain questions about each other for the next date.

"Torin, I've enjoyed your company," he smiles as we walk through Fell's Point.

"Same here. I enjoyed yours as well. I think I expected you to be different."

"Oh yeah? How so?" he asks.

"I don't know. I guess I thought you would be sterner and more unattractive. Not in a physical sense, but in an intellectual sense, I guess," I explain.

"Okay, well, you are exactly what I thought you would be. Intelligent, assertive, beautiful, deep, outgoing, secure, funny. In one date, I feel like I've known you forever. This has been a pleasure," he says with a smile. He has a cool breeze vibe about him. Like work is just that, but he knows how to separate that side of who he is.

"Most people think that I am all about my work. That I carry it around everywhere I go. It is my work, and I do take it seriously, but it is a job. I made a vow to myself a long time ago that I would never take my job so seriously that it slept next to me at night. My coworkers love me, but they only see the hard side of me, but in my type of work, you have to be that way."

"I understand. I struggle with new friendships and relationships. Most people shy away from me, or they are intimidated by my success. Of course, I have to hold up an image and be the boss, but that's not all I am. I want love, friendship, all of those things. I have a great group of friends that support me, but I travel a lot, and I meet a lot of people. I get tired of women rolling their eyes at me because they think that 'I'm all that' it's so exhausting. My career and my success doesn't totally define me. I have feelings, and I have needs."

"Speak, Sistah!" he jokes. We both laugh as we walk back towards my car.

"Well, like I said before, I enjoyed my time with you, and I can't wait for the next. I won't rush you. You just call me when you are ready, and I will be there," he says with a strong embrace.

"Enjoy the rest of your day, Torin."

"You too..." I smile. I watch him watch me as I pull off. I pick up the phone and call him.

"Hello," he answers.

"Do you like crabs?" I question.

"I love crabs," he answers. I can feel his smile through the phone.

"Do you like baseball?" I ask again.

"Yes, Torin. I love baseball," he replies.

"How about Crabs and the Orioles Saturday night?" I inquire.

"That sounds great. I'm looking forward to it." I hang up the phone and do a little wiggle celebration dance in my two-seater! I've got a date!

Celia

"Warden Brown, this is Celia! Again! I've called and left a thousand messages, but I haven't heard back from you. Please call me." I pace the floor awaiting a call back from the warden, and finally, the phone rings.

"Hi, Ms. Celia; this is Warden Brown."

"Well, it's about time, Mr. Brown. What's going on?"

"Well, it looks like we are getting a little lead way on Lana's case. There is a detective on the case right now, and he has gotten a tip from someone. He told me not to discuss the case with anyone because it's so sensitive. We don't know who is who yet, but it does look like it's coming together."

"You know, warden... I am putting my trust in you because I would hate to have to put this situation in my own hands. It might get ugly for everybody."

"Ms. Celia, I am not interested in your threats. As I stated before, we are on the job. I understand that you are mourning your daughter, and I would never try to understand how you feel, but let us do our job." I hung up the phone without speaking another word. If Warden Brown knows what's good for him, he will get to the bottom of this.

Torin

I'm so excited about my new date that I have to tell somebody, and since Aubrey has gone M. I. A on her own "Eat, Pray, Love" moment, Eric will have to do. We meet at Suga, Honey, Iced, Tea for a late lunch. The only place where we will get discounts for life since it's owned by our girl now.

"Girl, I called to check on PJ and Carter today, and guess what he told me?" says Eric while he swallows a honey biscuit whole.

"What? And can you eat like you got some got damn home training!" I say, disgusted by his eating.

"Girl, I am sorry, but this new trainer I got has been putting me on a strict eating schedule, and I don't know why. I know my hips are spreading a little, but if I've got to juice one more damn beet, I am going to murder somebody! Shit, I need calories! Carbohydrates! But he's cute girl, so I'm trynna stick around a little bit to see."

"To see what?" I question. You never know where Eric is going.

"To see what cup, he dips his stick into, because I think it's the sugar pot, but I'm not quite sure yet. I'm going to play this little game with him, but eventually, it will come out." He sips his tea like always after a shady phrase.

"So anyway, what happened, Eric? What did Carter say?"

"Biitttttchhhh! Aubrey's ass then went to Thailand! Thailand bitch! Did ya hear me?"

"You are lying! Thailand? Why Thailand?"

"Girl, she done went off into some 'Eat, Pray, Love' adventure for real girl! Carter said when he spoke to her, she was already on the damn plane about to take off!"

"What? He didn't even know she was going?"

"Nope! I think she has lost it this time for real. Driving to New York was one thing. Driving to Los Angeles is another, but flying to Thailand! That is halfway around the world! A day behind or ahead, I don't even know! I wouldn't be surprised if she came back bald-headed wearing slippers made out of bamboo!"

"Eric, she is going to be fine. Maybe Aubrey needed this. Her life has been harder than I could imagine, and we've had front row seats. She has never been alone, and she's always had someone to talk her in or out of something. She needs to experience some parts of life on her own. Before she gets old and never gets the chance to know herself, all she has ever known was Porter, then Lana, then PJ, then Carter, then all of these new businesses. Not to mention Trish and Colby and all of the bullshit that she has encountered. When will she have the chance to deal with her shit? Everything that's in her. She never really had the chance to mourn Porter. She had to take care of the baby and help Carter get back on his feet. From there, it was one hit after another. Now her dad... She is dealing with his death, forgiving him, feeling guilty. That's a lot of shit. So, I hope she stays away as long as possible to get her life in order."

"Damn, you're right. I just hope my girl is okay because she is literally out there by herself."

"I'm sure she will be fine."

Carter

Every day without Aubrey has been hard, but I can say it has given me a chance to be a dad to PJ. Watching him play with his toys in the tub has become my new norm, and I love it. It's slowed me down from the constant ripping and running.

"Come on, lil man. Let's get you dressed. We have a house to go look at. Are you ready to go to New York? Can you say, New York?" He looks up at me with those big innocent eyes. I know that I'm doing the right thing.

My phone rings.

"Hey man, it's Charles."

"Hey Detective, what's going on, man?"

"Nothing much. Look, I've been trying to call Aubrey, but she is not answering."

"Yeah, man... Aubrey went a little off of the deep end after her father died. Lana's murder was the icing on the cake. She's in Thailand right now."

"Thailand? Why Thailand?" he asks.

"That's the question of the century... I don't know, man. She's just trying to find herself, I guess."

"Well, with everything that she has been through, bro, what do you expect? She has got to figure some things out. Look, I don't want to hold you. I just want to know if you know a woman named Demari?"

"I don't know her personally, but I know Aubrey knows her. She was a part of her circle at one point, I believe. You should probably ask her girl Torin or Eric."

"Okay, man, well, thank you. Tell Aubrey I asked about her. If you find out anything about this Demari person, please let me know."

"Okay, will do." I don't even want to know what that was about. I can't wait until all of this shit is over.

"Aight, lil man. Let's get on the road."

Aubrey

"I can't do this shit!"

"Aubrey, please. No foul language in meditation. This is a moment for you to breathe and release." Everybody else around me is in tune with themselves. They got this down packed, but I can't stop thinking about the dress I'm going to wear for the opening night.

"I hate to break it to you, love, but this isn't working. I can't do this." I get up and pack my things. The meditation instructor follows me out into the humid hallway.

"Aubrey, it is not working because you won't let go. You are holding on to so much. You have been coming to this class for the last five days, and you have yet to tap in. Let me help you. I do not want you to return to this class. We are going to have a private session on the beach tonight at sunset. Just you and I."

"What makes you think that will work?" I ask.

"I know it will because I can see behind that beautiful face, the sunglasses, and that smile. You are like a volcano about to erupt. You have so much pain and insecurities built-in you, and if you don't free yourself while you have the opportunity, you are going to explode." I grit my teeth and hold my position in front of her without letting her see that what she is saying is true. I walk away without saying another word.

"I will meet you on the beach at seven-thirty! You know where!" she shouts.

After pacing the floor a thousand times, I take a shot of smooth Thai rum. I gather myself and walk down to the beach. Before I announce myself, I watch her sit on the beach without any movement staring out into the water.

"Mrs. Maleese," I say. Mrs. Maleese is a beautiful woman. She's from the states, but she moved to Thailand twenty years ago with her husband. Her family is Japanese, and her husband is African American. Her family didn't accept them as a couple, so they packed up and moved to Thailand after one visit. Their children were born and raised here.

"Aubrey, I knew you would come…well, actually, I didn't, but my husband reassured me that your spirit is asking for help." She walked me over to the water and set me close to where the waves were rushing towards us.

"I want you to close your eyes, Aubrey. I want you to let go of what you are feeling right now—any thoughts from the past, from the present, or about the future. Just focus on the rush of the water. I want you to strip yourself of everything you know about yourself. Now imagine yourself walking down the beach, and a person appears. Who is it?" she says in a whisper.

"It's Porter..." I can feel the tears running down my face.

"How does he look?" she whispers in my ear.

"I can't see his face yet. He is walking towards me, but he is wearing a white linen shirt with linen pants and no shoes. He has something in his hand," I cry.

"What is it?"

"I don't know... Oh... It's... Mr. P!" I smile.

"Who is Mr. P?"

"Mr. P is the teddy bear that he won for me at the state fair years ago."

"Is he closer to you yet?"

"Yes," I quiver.

"He is standing right in front of me," my cries get stronger.

"He looks so beautiful and peaceful," I add.

"Tell him whatever you need him to know," she says.

"Porter... I'm sorry..." Mrs. Maleese interrupts.

"Ugh, uh, we are not going to start this off with an apology because you did nothing wrong. Tell him the truth, Aubrey. Tell him how you really feel." A chill comes across my skin. All of a sudden, I feel invigorated.

"You hurt me... YOU HURT ME! You left me here to carry all of your weight! I don't know what love feels like because of you, Porter! You broke me, Porter! I don't know who I am! WHAT ABOUT ME? You told me you would always have me! And you dragged me through the dirt with a BIG FAT FUCK YOU in the air! You lied to me! You left me, Porter! You really left me!" I drop to the sand and fall into a fetal position.

"I can't do this! I can't do this, Mrs. Maleese," I cry out.

"Yes, you can, Aubrey. You have to. You have to do this. You have to forgive Porter and your father and Lana and yourself. They need your forgiveness. You need your forgiveness. Carter will never have you, and neither will your baby until you fix yourself." She gets on her knees and pulls me up into her arms, and cuddle me like a baby.

"Aubrey, I am going to help you through this. I promise." Mrs. Maleese holds on to me as a mother would their child while we lay in the sand.

The next morning, I go out into the marketplace and race back to the villa. I sit out under this tree that reminds me of my favorite tree on Federal Hill. I write until my hands cramp. When I finally put the pen down, I realized I've written to the last page of the journal, and I can't recall what I wrote. I hadn't seen Casey and everyone since meditation yesterday. I spent my time in prayer this morning and staying as quiet as I can. Night has finally fallen, and I am back at the beach, waiting for Mrs. Maleese. After ten minutes of waiting, I go into a meditation on my own.

****

Wait a minute! What time is it? I wake up on the beach to the sun beaming down on my skin and the water rushing up on my feet. A monkey is standing in front of me, picking away at the bug he swept up out of the sand. First of all, I'm tripping because how in the actual fuck did I fall asleep out here? I grew up in Baltimore, and that shit is just not okay. Secondly, where is Mrs. Maleese, and how could she just stand me up like that? I put on my shoes that had somehow become my pillow at some point, and I rush back to the villa to see Mrs. Maleese.

When I get to her door, I see that she is in prayer, so I let her finish. When she gets up, I tap on the door.

"Mrs. Maleese, how could you let me-" she interrupts.

"Did you sleep well on the beach?" she asks.

"Wait, you saw me?"

"Yes," she answers with assurance.

"Did he come back?" she asks. I ponder on that thought for a second. I was remembering my encounter with Porter last night.

"Yes, yes, he did come back... He asked for my forgiveness," I added.

"Well... Did you forgive him?" she asks as she focuses on burning her sage.

"Yes. Yes, I did, Mrs. Maleese. I forgave him," I gracefully lower my head.

"He looked peaceful. It's like, I know that he is okay," I say.

"He is okay; the teddy bear was a peace offering. He wanted you to know he was sorry for everything. He wants you to move on with your life. He didn't have any scratches or bruises because he has been healed. He asked for forgiveness and received it. He just needed you to forgive him too, and now he can be free," she explains.

"Wow. I don't know what to say..."

"Just say that you will continue to do the work. You have a lot of it left to do, but I know we can do it. Just trust me and trust yourself." She passes me a cup of tea, and we sit down for what I can tell will be a nice long lecture.

Chapter 16
I've Arrived

Carter

It's been two months now. Aubrey decided to stay in Thailand longer than expected. I have been calling her nonstop. She hasn't answered the phone in almost a week. Just texts to say she's okay, but I need to hear her voice. The time difference is so off, and I can't keep up.

"Aubrey, please call me back. You haven't answered the phone, and everybody is worried. I checked the tracker on your phone like you told me to, but it's not showing me anything at all. Please call me. I'm getting worried."

I pick PJ up and take him for a walk to the park near the house. He's trying to walk now, but these shoes that he has on are not helping. I guess sneakers aren't for everybody—my phone rings.

"Hey, have you talked to her?" Torin and Trish have been calling me nonstop.

"No, she hasn't called. I don't know what's going on. Ya'll didn't tell Mrs. Karen, did you?" I ask. She will kill me if I told her I haven't talked to Aubrey.

"No, I haven't, but I spoke with Mrs. Garrett earlier. She and Trish were out taking Colby shopping. She said she spoke with Aubrey a few days ago."

"What did she say?" I ask urgently. I put the phone down on speaker so that I could change PJ.

"She didn't say much. She just said she would be coming home soon."

"I knew Mrs. Garrett couldn't keep a damn secret." I turn around, and Aubrey is standing over top of me.

"Oh, my God! Oh, my God! Is that her! Aubrey! Girl, I've missed you!"

Torin sings through the phone. Without any thought, I jump up and grab her so tight. For the first time in a long time, I felt tears well up in my eyes. She wipes my tears and gives me the kiss I've been missing.

"I've missed you, Carter. I've missed you so much," she cries. PJ pulled himself up on my legs. Aubrey bent down to pick him up.

"Awww, my baby! Hi, my baby, you are so beautiful. I love you so much." She goes off into a world with her and PJ while I stand and watch. She looks so different. She looks brand new. Her skin is glowing as if the sun-kissed her personally.

"Everything about you seems... new," I say to her as she cuddles PJ in her arms.

"I am... I have been renewed Carter," she smiles like there is not a care in the world. I have never seen that on her before. A smile that didn't have something behind it. I walk up to her in flick her sharp fringes that fall in front of her face.

"I love your new hairdo," I smile while I hold them both.

"Well, thank you," she smiles.

****

A week has gone by, and we are all adapting to the new Aubrey, but it has been good. Every morning, she wakes up to pray, meditate, and work out a little bit before starting her day. She has not given her attention to anyone outside of the house. It's just us for now. The grand opening is tomorrow night, so I guess that will be the day that all of our lives change.

"So, you're going to do it?" Preston asks. He and Ryan bought the bar, where they all hung out. We all meet up there sometimes when I get a second away from PJ. Aubrey is trying to get used to Porter's friends being my friends now, but shit, there is a lot of things we are all getting used to.

"Yeah, man, I'm going to do it tomorrow at the grand opening."

"You think she's going to say yes?" Ask Ryan while he sips on his beer.

"I hope so," I respond.

"Don't get discouraged, man; however, the chips fall; just know that Aubrey knows what's best for her right now," says Preston.

"Yeah, man. From what you say, she is on a whole 'nother level right now so, just roll with it," Ryan states.

"Yeah, you're right about that man. We will see," I say.

Detective Charles

"Thanks for getting back to me, Baker. Did you collect that footage from the hospital?... Okay, what about the additional photos from Porter's accident that night?"

"Okay, cool, can you have the photos printed and delivered to me by tonight? Oh, okay, well, email them over, and I will print them out here. Sounds good. Thanks."

I have been spending every waken moment on this case and with Torin. I definitely prefer one over the other. Torin does it for me. I want her to know how serious I am. I know it's early, but I sold the bar I owned to Porter's friends, and I got a little money saved up, so I'm going to take a break from work after I crack this case and go over to London with her while she gets her salon up and running. Maybe I will see something over there that catches my eye. I've always wanted to own a gym. Our conversations go beyond the normal. She inspires me to want to do more. I used to question why I didn't have a woman or children. Now I know that I was waiting on her.

"Babe, we are almost there," I call Torin to give her the news.

"Almost where?" she asks.

"The case, Torin..." Clearly, she's busy.

"Oh. Shit! I'm sorry, Suga. I was looking over inventory. I think one of these heffas are stealing products," she says.

"You may need to put cameras in their babe. I know you think you should be able to trust everybody, but sometimes you just gotta look truth in the eye," I say.

"Yeah, you're right. I can't watch everything. Do you think you can put them up for me?" she asks.

"Sure, I can, and whenever you are ready to go back to Miami, I will book our flight and hotel. I can put those in too."

"That would be great! Let's go after the grand opening. Maybe a little before I leave for London."

"I wanted to talk to you about that..."

"Okay, what's up?"

"I know we just got started in this thing, but this is a connection that I've never felt before. I want to be with you, Torin. I want to be with you all of the time. I see a future with you. I even appreciate that we haven't had sex yet. You want us to explore each other on a different level; that shit is different for me. You make it easy. I don't even want sex- well, that's a lie... I do. I definitely do, but what I'm saying is I don't want it right now. I just want to learn you and learn from you. It may seem like a lot since it has only been a little over a month, but if you would have me- I would like to go to London with you." Man, I feel like I held my breath through all of that.

"For real! You really wanna go?" she said with so much innocence and excitement in her voice.

"Yes, I do. And I'm not asking you to pay for anything. I will pay for both of our flights. If you want me to stay in my own place, I will do that too. I just want to be there with you, Torin." The line is silent, but I can hear her sniffles through the phone.

"Babe? Are you crying?" I ask.

"No, no, it's my allergies... Charles, of course, I want you to go; that would make me so happy," she says.

"Okay, then it's settled. Just tell me when..."

"Okay, I will... Charles?" she says.

"Yes."

"I've been waiting for you..."

"I've been waiting for you too."

Carter

She comes down the stairs dressed like the leading lady, ready to accept her Oscar. The most beautiful human being I've ever seen. Covered in red from head to toe, her shoulders peek out from her dress just right, and so does that left thigh that peaks out of her split. She carries herself with more grace and poise than ever before. This is her night.

"Aubrey, you look beautiful," I say, mesmerized by her beauty.

"Thank you, Carter. How is PJ doing?" she asks.

"He is good. Mrs. Garrett said Mr. Garrett took him and Colby fishing."

"Fishing? He's not even one yet, and he's teaching him how to fish?" she questions.

"Hey, don't get in the middle of a man and his grandson," I say. We both laugh at the joke. I quickly straighten up and gather myself while she put the last touches of her lipstick on.

Aubrey

"Aubrey..." When I turn around, he is on one knee with the most beautiful ring I've ever seen in the palm of his hand.

"I know we haven't been at this thing for a long time... But you have been the one for me since we were kids. I've spent most of my life watching you with another man when I knew that you belonged to me. I just want you to see that I am serious about us. You are everything that I've ever wanted, and I promise to protect you, love you, and provide for you. I promise to kiss your scars and help heal your heart. I just want the chance to have my dreams come true. Because that is what you've been for me, Aubrey... A dream... A dream that I never thought would come true until now. I love you, Aubrey, and I will never let you forget what that feels like." I can barely stand up straight, and the room is spinning, but I refuse to mess up this make-up that I paid seventy-five dollars to get done. I put my head back to catch my tears.

"Carter, I love you so much. You have been my protection, and I love you more than I can explain. The moment you jumped in front of that bullet for me, I knew that your love for me was real... I just..."

"You just what? What, Aubrey?" Anxiety falls over his face.

"I just can't accept your proposal right now."

I watched his soul rush out of his body. His skin turned pale, and his eyes went blank. He got up off of his knees and sat on the sofa. He put his head in his lap and covered his face. I pulled my gown up and leaned down to his level.

"Carter, please understand me. For the first time in my life, I am learning about who I am. I am more in tune with who I am and what I want more than ever before. I am healing Carter. I am exploring parts of myself that I've never taken time to explore because I was so caught up in the world around me and moving at everyone else pace but my own. For the first time ever in my life, I am putting myself first, and it feels good. I love you, Carter. I am head over hills in love with you, but I need to fall in love with me. I need to get to know me. I came out of a relationship that ended in tragedy. Jumped head first into another without coming up for air. I didn't give myself enough time to mourn Porter's death, my father's, or Lana's. I focused on everything and everybody around me without thinking about what I really needed. So, to answer your question. Not today, baby, I love you, but not today. Today I am marrying myself, but if you will have me, I would like to revisit this proposal in another year or so. Just don't let me go because I would hate to realize that I let my knight and shining armor slip through my fingers."

He looks up at me and stares into my eyes.

"You're messing up your makeup," he says.

"Well, can you kiss my tears?" I ask.

He leans in and kisses my lips as a knight and shining armor should.

****

Finally, we make it to the grand opening after some really, really good sex and new makeup. La'Rose looks absolutely beautiful, and the place is packed. We tried to change the name to Porter's, but it just didn't sit right when the sign went up. Porter named it La'Rose, and if he wanted it different, he would've changed it. So, at the last minute, we changed the name back to La'Rose. We added a cigar lounge and named it Porters Cigar Lounge. The room is covered with paintings of Porter smoking his favorite cigars.

"Ahhhhh, she is back! My girl is back!" Eric says. He, Torin, and Trish all run up to me with open arms.

"Aubrey, we've missed you so much!" says Torin.

"Yes, girl! I thought you were leaving me with all of this headache. You knew I could not handle all of this and carry these babies," Trish cries out.

"But you did it, though, like the strong woman you are! And look at the belly you are about to pop!" I say while rubbing her belly.

"Yes, I am. Literally! I am actually on bed rest, but I told my doctor that he would have to wait until the day after the grand opening because this is a big fucking deal. Okay!" she says and throws her hand back, and all three of us follow.

"Okay!"

"Babe, I'm going to go and kick it with Grant. I will be right back."

"Okay, babe." Carter kisses me on the cheek and walks over to Grant.

"Wait the hell a minute. I spent two damn days in New York, spending all of my little funds and shopping for a beautiful engagement ring for you. Now where the hell is it? Eric gets up close to me and grits his teeth together.

"Okay, ya'll. Listen. I want to marry Carter, but not right now," I reply.

"What!" exclaims Torin.

"Look, I took a lot of time to get to know me and work on some things. I still have a lot of work to do, and I don't want to complicate things right now. I like where I am. I am getting my shit together, but I need my shit to be all the way together before I say yes to that man. He is way too good to me, and I do not need to damage him with all of my shit. So, I told him to give me a year to get myself together, and I will be ready for him then. He agreed and made a different type of love to me afterward. I mean, he made sure I knew what I had in store!"

"Well, you know what, Aubrey; I am damn proud of you. You are finally thinking for yourself and taking control of your own life, so cheers to that," says Torin. We all lift our champagne glasses.

"Ugh, ugh bitch, that better be water!" Eric says to Trish.

"Shut up, Eric, it's apple cider," we all burst out in laughs.

"Wait a minute Torin. Where is this man that you have been ducking me out for?" says Eric.

"Oh... Don't worry. He will be here," she smiles mischievously.

"Congratulations, Aubrey. I guess you are finally getting what you deserve," Demari walks up next to me, looking as sinful and sneaky as always.

"Thank you," I say with nothing more than a dry look on my face.

"Who in the fuck invited her?" Trish questions.

"Oh, I did. Don't worry. She won't be here long," says Torin.

"Everyone, can we gather around! Let's give a round of applause for Trish and Aubrey! Haven't they done a great job with the place," Mrs. Garrett stands at the front of the stage.

"What is Mrs. Garrett doing here?" I whisper to Trish.

"Mr. and Mrs. Garrett couldn't bare to miss this Aubrey," says Torin.

"Ladies, I just want to say that my son could not have chosen more beautiful, intelligent women to carry on his legacy. I am so proud of both of you. Thank you for our grandbabies, and thank you for carrying on my son's name," she weeps and steps down. PJ and Colby are both dressed in their best. Mr. Garrett is holding PJ, and Colby stands right next to him with her hands wrapped around his waist.

"Would you ladies, please come up and say a word?" Mrs. Garrett adds.

We both walk up to the stage, and she greets both of us with a warm kiss. She hands Trish the mic, and Trish passes it to me. She doesn't care to do a lot of talking.

"Hello, everyone. Thank you so much for blessing us with your presence tonight. I see a lot of new and old friends. My friends from LA and Vegas flew all the way here to support me."

"And New York Aubrey!" Yells Julissa from the crowd.

"Oh, and New York. Well, where ever you came from, I am grateful for you. This has been a long journey. Life has taken us all through so many ups and downs. And I stand here today realizing one thing... That we are all still standing. I am grateful for that. Mom, I see you standing there looking as beautiful as can be. I want to thank you for showing me what strength looks like. Eric and Torin, thank you guys for always being there for me when I needed you. Ya'll are true friends. Carter, I love you so much, and I am looking forward to our journey together. Trish... Trish... You were brought into my life in some very unconventional circumstances, but I am so thankful for you. You have become a sister amongst all, and I wouldn't want to travel this journey with anyone else. So many people looked down on us. I'm sure we looked like idiots to them. But who's laughing now!" We both look at each other and laugh with the rest of the room.

"And Porter... Porter may not have done everything right in his life, but who has. He was human. He fought with his identity, and he fought with his demons, but more than anything, he fought for his family. No matter how unconventional it may have seemed, he made sure that we were taken care of. He was a good man-"

"A good man? A good man? What the fuck about Porter was good? He was a liar, a cheat, a conniving, backstabbing, sex addict. And you stupid bitches fell for it!" Demari blurts out.

"You stupid, skank, bitches, I should've killed the both of you when I had the chance!" she yells.

Before I knew it, cops were rushing through the entrance following Detective Charles. "Aubrey, I'm so sorry I had to rush in like this..." says Detective Charles while the police officer behind him puts Demari in handcuffs.

Then he walks over to Torin.

"Sorry, I'm late, babe, but I wore my suit." He kisses her and then walks back up to Demari. My mouth dropped to the ground, and so did Eric's.

"Demari Simmons, you have the right to remain silent. Anything you say will be used against you. You have the right to an attorney," he recites.

"Get me out of these got damn handcuffs! Jail for what? Call my lawyer!" she shouts.

"For the murder of Lana Jackson and accessory to the murder of Porter Garrett." The whole room gasps.

"You bitch!" Ms. Celia walked right up to Demari and slapped her in the face.

****

"Whether you admit it or not, we have you for both."

Detective Jackson pulled out the pictures and video of Demari entering the hospital dressed in an oversized correctional officer uniform. She enters on the post where Lana's room was, posing as an officer on duty. Demari enters the room for a little over ten minutes and then returns to her post and replaces herself with another guard.

Detective Charles

"So, before you speak, I know your brother Allen works at the same prison where Lana was. As a matter of fact, he was in the courtyard when Lana got jumped. He wasn't even slick enough to hand the prisoner the weapon that was used to try and kill her but back to Allen. He already confessed that you put him up to everything. You even paid him twenty- thousand dollars to have it done and give a percentage to the inmates. I guess you thought he was a loyal one, huh?" She sits there with a grim look on her face.

"Demari, I got all day, sweetheart, so we can play this however you want. Should I go into the traffic image we have of you pointing a gun at Porter while he was waiting for the light to change?" I sit on the edge of the table, waiting for her to answer.

"That bitch deserved to die... And so did he. All of a sudden, she got to jail, and all bets were off. Fuck that. She said that we were going to take Porter out. That's what she said! She had me planting letters and shit, following him around for her to call it off. 'Cause all of a sudden, she wanted to be a better person. Fuck that! You're either in, or you're out. So, I took her ass all the way out too. I had Porter's ass. The only reason Porter didn't catch that bullet was because my gun jammed, and before I knew it, a big ass truck was running into him," she admits.

"So, you were there to kill him... Why did you kill Lana, Demari?" I sit down to get as much out of her as I can.

"Lana had put me through so much shit. First, she told me to kill Porter. Then she told me we were going to be together when all of this was done. People would finally know about us. I've been there through it all, and I had to keep playing this unknown motherfucker that she hated. When she knew it wasn't true. Porter had her heart. Thomas was the husband. Aubrey's disgusting ass father had some kind of hold on her at one point. Where in the fuck was there room for me! I was just a fantasy she wanted to explore every once in a while... I knew my brother was weak, though. I had him in there watching her every move. I even know about the guard that slipped into her cell. He was fucking her and the roommate. I kept my head down. But when that bitch told me it was over and she wanted to be free. I decided to free that bitch. Fentanyl does the job every time. I watched her eyes roll back in her head while she laid in that hospital bed. And I told her she was finally free," she smiles with a look of pleasure.

Oh, this crazy bitch is going under the jail. She wanted this. It's clear that she has nothing else to live for because she didn't deny any of it. It's like she couldn't wait to tell her story.

"People always pay attention to the loud one. The one that is perceived to be the strongest, but Lana was weak. I sat in the corner for years with my head down, watching her fuck up everybody's life, even mine. But she hated herself behind closed doors. She cried like the pathetic piece of shit she was."

"Okay, I don't need to hear anymore. We have enough. Throw her ass in a cell," I order my partner through the intercom.

Well, now we know. You can watch the boss, but you may wanna keep your eyes on the flunky.

Chapter 17

Five Years Later

Aubrey

"Hey, babe. As soon as I leave this interview, I will be on my way home... I am not catching a taxi home. This New York traffic will eat me alive. Carter, I will catch the subway. Just meet me at my stop, we will be fine. Okay, I will call you soon. I love you."

"Hey, Aubrey! How are the children?" The doorman at my building opens the door for me and welcomes me in.

"They are doing great, Ray, thanks for asking."

"24th floor, please." I step onto the elevator with my trench coat barely covering my body. Spring in New York is beautiful, but a bit windy for me. I exit the elevator and enter my office.

"Turning Point Publishing!... Yes, she just walked in, but she has a meeting right now. Yes, I can take a message," my secretary Alexis, signals me that my interviewer is in my office.

She jumps up out of her seat, almost spilling her tea all over her clothes.

"Oh, my goodness Mrs. Chambers! It's so nice to finally meet you," she greets me with a handshake while her other hand is occupied with her computer and phone.

"It's very nice to meet you as well. Erykah, isn't it?" I ask as I hang up my jacket and take a seat at my desk. I walk over to my window and stare down at central park for a few seconds. The leaves are growing, and the flowers are finally blossoming.

"Yes, it's Erykah. First of all, I just want to say thank you for taking the time to do this interview. I have been following your story and reading your books for years. You are an inspiration, and it is surely a pleasure. So, on behalf of Eloquent Magazine, thank you," she says with as much jitter in her voice as she can dig up. I can tell she is nervous, so I try to break the ice.

"Girl, thank you! It's nothing like having a mirror sit right in front of me while I tell my story. You remind me so much of myself. Like I feel like I am looking at myself," we both laugh.

"So, let's get started," I say.

After two long hours, I realize I am running late for PJ's fifth birthday party, and if I don't get home, he will be blowing my phone up for sure. Trish, Grant, Colby, and the twins are already there. Those little boys are off the chain. All three of them together are inseparable.

My mom, Mr. and Mrs. Garrett, and Carter's mom, are there helping with decoration. Torin and Charles are on the way. I can finally meet my new nephew that she has been raving about and Eric is out shopping for all of the children. Ryan and Preston are also on their way. With the wives and kids. So, I don't have much time.

"So, after the grand opening, Carter and I went back home. I rolled over and told him that I want to take PJ and travel the world. That I would bring PJ back whenever he wanted. So, for months at a time, I would be gone with PJ, and for the holidays, I would come back to the states, and PJ would stay with Carter for a few months and with his grandparents. While I was gone, my mom and Trish ran the restaurant and lounge. I received a fat check every month. I took that time away to write my book and discover more about myself. It was like a sabbatical. My girlfriend Lydia kept her word, and she got me my first publishing deal. After writing my last page, I returned home from Africa and decided that the next time I traveled, it would be with my husband. When I got to New York, Carter met me in front of this beautiful brownstone in Harlem. It was old but newly renovated, and he said it was ours. He got on his knees, and so did PJ, and asked for my hand in marriage. But this time, he got a yes out of me.

It took a little time, but eventually, I gave in and sold my house in Baltimore. I packed up the entire house by myself. It was like therapy for me. I got down to the last box that was stored in the coat closet by the door. I picked it up, handed it to the mover guy, and noticed an 'X' on the floor. I used my hammer to peel up the floor. I stuck my hand down in there and pulled out a picture of Porter and me. Our first day of college. We look so happy. So green. I remembered that feeling. It all felt so new and scary. I sat there for a moment and stared at the picture. I was just reminiscing on the memories. I stuck my hand back down in there, and I felt papers peeling. I got the hammer and pulled back more wood. I stuck my hand in the hole and grabbed out bricks of money. Too many to count. Until this day, I don't know how much it actually was. I counted twenty-four bricks. Who else could I call to split it with? Trish and I sat on that floor with a bottle of wine, and we laughed our asses off. Porter may have been a lot of things, but he made sure his family was straight. We both took two out and made a few donations. I paid off my mother's house and Porter's parent's house. Trish even reconnected with her parents. She paid their home off, and until this day, they still don't know how their house was paid off. I even sent money to Mrs. Maleese, but she sent me a letter back with a check saying all she wanted was for me to be free, and no money could buy that. After our third year of marriage, we were surprised with London, who is our two-year-old daughter."

"Mrs. Chambers," she interrupts.

"Girl, please call me Aubrey," I smile.

"Okay... Aubrey. Whatever happened to your friend Lana's mother?" she asks.

"You know what... I have no idea... the last I saw her was at the grand opening." I look at the time and realize I am running way behind.

"Sweetie, I hate to cut this all short, but I really have to get home for my son's birthday party. My daughter won't stop crying, and according to this text, I'm sure my husband is about to lose his mind."

I get up and grab my jacket.

"Okay, okay, I understand! Well, it was a pleasure and congrats on the new baby. It looks like you're going to burst any day now!" she says, staring down at my belly.

"Yeah, he is definitely running out of room in there," I laugh.

"Lexi will see you out, Erykah, and thanks again. I can't wait to read it," I say, rushing out.

"Oh... I'm sorry, Aubrey. One more thing. The new film that's about your book... What's the name of it?"

"Oh... Easily Enticed..."

What Really happened to Colin?

Celia

He got exactly what he deserved. It's funny how a person can get into someone's mind so well that it causes them to take their own life. That piece of shit was easy. All I had to tell him was that Aubrey would never forgive him for what he did to my baby Lana. He might as well blow his fucking brains out. After a few shots of whiskey. I laid that gun right next to him, and before I made it down the hallway of that apartment building, I here, the slither of the bang that came from the silencer on the gun. See... One way or another, we all get what we deserve. It's just a matter of time.

The End

CPSIA information can be obtained
at www.ICGtesting.com
Printed in the USA
LVHW031612130521
687356LV00002B/277